NEW WAVES, OLD HANDS, AND UNKNOWN PLEASURES

New Waves, Old Hands, and Unknown Pleasures

The Music of 1979

Sean Egan

Backbeat
Books

Guilford, Connecticut

Backbeat Books
An imprint of The Rowman & Littlefield Publishing Group, Inc.
4501 Forbes Blvd., Ste. 200
Lanham, MD 20706
www.rowman.com

Distributed by NATIONAL BOOK NETWORK

Library of Congress Cataloging-in-Publication Data available

ISBN 978-1-61713-732-7 (paperback)
ISBN 978-1-4930-5068-0 (e-book)

♾™ The paper used in this publication meets the minimum requirements of American National Standard for Information Sciences—Permanence of Paper for Printed Library Materials, ANSI/NISO Z39.48-1992

CONTENTS

INTRODUCTION   vii

1. JANUARY   1
Armed and Hostile Forces: Elvis Costello   1

2. FEBRUARY   9
The Northern Irish Question: Stiff Little Fingers and the Undertones   9
Swindles and Metal Boxes: Life After the Sex Pistols   29
Scared to Live: The Tragedy of the Skids   39

3. MARCH   49
Squeezing Out a Career: Graham Parker   53
I'm the Man (Well, Sometimes): Joe Jackson   58

4. APRIL   61
45 rpm to the Rescue: The Year in Singles   62
The Wide-Boy Demi-Monde: Squeeze   69
The Dancing Queen Finally Goes to the Disco: ABBA   74
The Unsmiling Face of the Future: Gary Numan   77

5. MAY   83
Independence Day: The Specials and the 2 Tone Revolution   84
Spasticus, Mr. Funky, and Second-Album Blues: Ian Dury   92
Two Out of Three Ain't Bad: David Bowie   101

6. JUNE   107
Fame Is a Fickle Food: The Knack and Sham 69   112
Unknown Pleasures and Death Wishes: Joy Division   130
Forgotten Icons: The Boomtown Rats   137

7. JULY   145
The Fall of the Glitterball   146

8. AUGUST   153
Judas Finds God: Bob Dylan   154
Dinosaurs to the Rescue: Led Zeppelin   159

9. SEPTEMBER   **171**
Triumph Through Turmoil: The Eagles   175
From DIY to EMI: The Buzzcocks   182

10. OCTOBER   **189**
Indulgence and Experimentation: Fleetwood Mac   190
A New Sound: The Police   199
One Step Beyond Ska: Madness   207
The CBGBs Runts Come Good: Blondie   218

11. NOVEMBER   **229**
The Advantages of Self-Education: The Jam   230

12. DECEMBER   **237**
The Clash and a Belatedly Acknowledged Classic   237
Spitting in the Face of Success: Pink Floyd   245

ACKNOWLEDGMENTS   253

SELECTED BIBLIOGRAPHY   255

INDEX   257

INTRODUCTION

Nineteen seventy-nine marked the end of a tumultuous decade in popular music.

It was a decade that started with the trauma of the breakup of the Beatles and a feeling of anticlimax that was the sixties overhang. It sagged in the middle as the rock aristocracy took their audiences for granted and issued increasingly somnambulant product. It was jolted back into life in 1976–1977 by the emergence of punk. The seventies' best year, though, is one that has never been recognized as such. Nineteen seventy-nine had an automatically enhanced resonance in that, as the year denoting the end of a decade, it was looked to as a possible pointer to the future, the quality of its releases assessed not just for aesthetic merit but for proof of continuing vitality and cultural relevance. It more than lived up to that scrutiny. Only 1965 can match the popular music of 1979 for variety, quality, and sociopolitical import.

Nineteen seventy-six and 1977 might have been the years of UK punk and new wave, but it was actually '79 when it all came to fruition, in terms of the maturation of those overlapping genres' acts. The year also saw the emergence of a new angular, slightly dispassionate form that, despite not being punk, was so inconceivable without it that it could only be given the term "post-punk." British acts of this generation, already prone to writing songs addressing the state of the nation, were given further compositional impetus in May: the election of Margaret Thatcher's hard-right Conservative administration in the UK made previous grievances about the James Callaghan Labour government seem trivial. The same applied to the artists on 2 Tone, a new artist-friendly record label musically influenced by ska but infused with punk's social conscience, especially in its overt striving for racial harmony. The fact that 1995—the year of Britpop—was hailed as a great one for British music seems laughable when looking at a list of some of the albums released by UK artists in 1979: *Armed Forces* by Elvis Costello and the Attractions, *Cool for Cats* by Squeeze, *A Different Kind of Tension* by the Buzzcocks, *The Fine Art of Surfacing* by the Boomtown Rats, *Inflammable Material* by Stiff Little Fingers, *Labour of Lust* by Nick Lowe, *London Calling* by the Clash, *Look Sharp!* and *I'm the Man* by Joe Jackson, *Metal Box* by Public Image Ltd., *One Step Beyond . . .* by Madness, *Reggatta de Blanc* by the Police, *Scared to Dance* and *Days in Europa* by the Skids, *Setting Sons* by the Jam, *Specials* by the Specials, *Squeezing Out Sparks* by Graham Parker and the Rumour, *Replicas* and *The Pleasure Principle* by Tubeway Army/Gary Numan, *The Undertones* by the Undertones, and *Unknown Pleasures* by Joy Division. Many were great records, and even those that weren't contained much that was socially and musically remarkable.

In complete contrast to the political agitation of punk and new wave was disco, whose glitter-strewn hedonism was, for many, the correct response to depressing times. The Bee Gees, Gloria Gaynor, Donna Summer, and the Village People virtually owned the US singles chart for big chunks of the year. Established acts like ABBA, Blondie, and even Pink Floyd jumped on the disco bandwagon in a way that might have been considered despicable, were it not for the fact that it resulted in some cracking records. Moreover, that disco was oriented around singles was a highly fortunate fact, for without the genre's contribution to the vitality of the singles market, the music industry would have seen almost no glimmer of financial hope in a year that saw the recent slump in album purchases continue unabated.

Even so, disco's success was repugnant to many. Such people hoped that the phenomenal rise of the Knack was a sign that disco was a flash in the pan and that rock would soon reign triumphant once more.

They welcomed the return after long absences of several titans of guitar-based music: the Eagles, Fleetwood Mac, Led Zeppelin, Pink Floyd, and Roxy Music. For those "dinosaurs" who had sat out the punk wars, '79 was an interesting test as to whether they would still be wanted in a transformed musical landscape. Other established artists were subjecting their fans to tests of their own. Bob Dylan's *Slow Train Coming* purveyed a fundamentalist Christianity that was the very type of thing he had always been considered to oppose, David Bowie was concluding his mainstream-spurning "Berlin Trilogy," and Joni Mitchell was confounding her demographic with the puristly jazz *Mingus*.

It would be impossible to explore or even mention in this book all the significant releases of 1979, and inevitably some readers will be angered by omissions. However, with the help of new and exclusive interviews with artists, producers, and record-company executives, *New Waves, Old Hands, and Unknown Pleasures* seeks to reveal the stories behind the year's key recordings, trace the trajectories of significant commercial and artistic successes, and explain the musical and sociopolitical context to the sounds of a varied, vibrant, but often unexamined year.

1
JANUARY

Armed and Hostile Forces: Elvis Costello

At the beginning of 1979, Elvis Costello was pretty much on top of the world. His third album, *Armed Forces*, was released in January to critical acclaim and commercial success. His intricate, literate lyrics had people talking of him in the same breath as Bob Dylan. Perhaps most importantly, of all the figures to emerge from the new wave, he was proving to be the one to whom America was the most receptive. Notes Costello's bandmate Bruce Thomas, "We had a gig booked at Shea Stadium and 250,000 ticket applications." However, following an altercation that March in a bar in Columbus, Ohio, which left Costello facing accusations of racism, said gig never materialized, nor did the riches that were at that point his for the taking.

Costello was born Declan MacManus in London in 1954. He became Elvis Costello upon signing to Stiff Records in 1977. Juxtaposing the name of the most glamorous figure in music history with Costello's bespectacled and studiedly gauche appearance was the type of irreverence-cum-provocation at which the independent label excelled. The joke soured unfortunately quickly when, five months after the release of Costello's debut record, "Less Than Zero," Elvis Presley was found dead. In fact, in today's terms the image Costello started cultivating around the same time as the name change might be considered more offensive: Costello ramped up the geekiness to something more resembling a "retard" image (to use the non-PC term of the era) by doing such things as standing in promotional films with his feet pointing toward each other.

On his 1977 debut album *My Aim Is True*, Costello's acidic, simile-suffused songs were incongruously backed by American country-rock outfit Clover. He then recruited the Attractions, consisting of Thomas on bass, (the unrelated) Pete Thomas on drums, and Steve Nieve on keyboards. Although his musical style was unimaginable without the back-to-basics approach of punk, Costello's new colleagues were undeniably musos, which probably explains why it was that he attracted an inordinate amount of interest from the US, traditionally not so indulgent of lack of technique as Britain. A trio of his songs were even covered by MOR chanteuse Linda Ronstadt. However, if Costello was the ideal artist for people who wanted to imagine they were embracing the zeitgeist but were actually a bit dubious about it, it was hardly Costello's fault, nor was it an indictment of his music.

This Year's Model (1978), which included the jagged, glittering singles "(I Don't Want to Go to) Chelsea" and "Pump It Up," was the first release to feature the Attractions, but the record was credited to Costello alone. Bruce Thomas successfully petitioned for the backing group to get a billing from the follow-up onward. "The music was all arranged by the band," he states of Elvis Costello and the Attractions' recording process. "He would come to us with things in a fairly rough state: guitar and chords." He adds, "I've given him the odd line, so has Pete, but there was never any question of collaborating on songwriting, simply because he churned out so much. He was hardly stuck."

Like the previous two albums—and the next two—*Armed Forces* was produced by Nick Lowe, a key figure in the music of '79, whether as producer, performer, or writer. Musically, *Armed Forces* was bright, poppy, and layered, but Thomas says this wasn't a deliberate decision. However, he does concede, "*Armed Forces* was an attempt to be a bit more sophisticated. We didn't want to make the same record twice. The songs are more stately, they're less urgent, they're more orchestral, probably more white, less R&B." In terms of lyrics, Thomas says the "overriding resonance" of *Armed Forces* was the melding of the military and the romantic. "He had quite a complicated emotional landscape. You know what the original title was for *Armed Forces*? *Emotional Fascism*." Invoking a line from "Chemistry Class," Thomas notes, "'Are you ready for the final solution?'—another sexual metaphor." Costello himself has denied that the LP's songs were informed by his relationship with the model Bebe Buell, for whom he around this point temporarily abandoned his wife and young son. As for Costello's writing *modus operandi*, Thomas recalls, "He used to write down every possible lyric idea in a book. Any appealing image or phrase. They wouldn't appear in a song in the same order that they went in." Sometimes, this would result in sublime turns of phrase. Other times, it engendered meaningless wordplay. Thomas: "There's one awful one in 'Busy Bodies' about a wave of somebody's hand being tidal. That don't mean anything. Sometimes it got a bit contrived."

The record's key song was "Oliver's Army." Despite its Cromwell-referencing title, it was a more recent conflagration than the English Civil War to which the track alluded. Costello visited Belfast in 1978, at the height of Northern Ireland's "Troubles." There he saw, he later wrote, "Mere boys walking around in battle dress with automatic weapons." Costello's lyric, largely finished by the time his flight home had landed, effectively accused UK governments of solving the problem of high unemployment by dispatching troops to strife-torn parts of its dwindling empire. Musically, Thomas reveals, "'Oliver's Army' was modeled on 'Don't Worry Baby' by the Beach Boys." In his dramatic keyboard flourishes, Nieve took inspiration from ABBA, at a time when it wasn't in any way hip to express admiration for the Swedish quartet.

"We weren't arch or camp about it," says Thomas. "They're good. Even the bloody Sex Pistols copied ABBA."

"Oliver's Army" occupies that unfortunate wasteland inhabited by the likes of the Beatles' "Strawberry Fields Forever" / "Penny Lane," the Sex Pistols' "God Save the Queen," Squeeze's "Up the Junction," Ultravox's "Vienna," and Pulp's "Common People": great records that never quite made No. 1 in the British charts. The Bee Gees' "Tragedy" and Gloria Gaynor's "I Will Survive" successively kept Costello and co. off the UK top spot over the course of three weeks. However, the unlikeliness of "Oliver's Army" even becoming a hit at all was its own triumph. It was remarkably hard-hitting and often lapel-grabbing (one of its lines was, "One more widow, one less white nigger"). The secret to its unlikely success was candy-coating. Costello's twisting and almost jaunty melody conformed as much to Tin Pan Alley traditions as new-wave archetypes. Drunken pub revelers could mindlessly chant the chorus even as studious young people in bedsits were pondering its verses. Costello told Simon Goddard of *Q* in 2008, "I always liked the idea of a bright pop tune that you could be singing along to for ages before you realize what it is·you're actually singing." "Oliver's Army" will consequently forever be Costello's signature song. "If I walked out of here now and got knocked down by a tram, the BBC would play 'Oliver's Army,'" Costello said to journalist Graeme Thomson in 2002. To Goddard, though, he noted another downside: "Some people only hear the tune and never listen to the words."

Released with a sleeve that featured—apparently apropos of nothing—a painting of stampeding elephants, *Armed Forces* was a UK No. 2. Fairly astonishingly, across the Atlantic it made No. 10 on the then rather conservative *Billboard* album chart. The only concession Costello made to help achieve that was to drop "Sunday's Best"—overly predicated on Britishisms—for an old Nick Lowe song, "(What's So Funny 'Bout) Peace, Love, and Understanding."

Costello actually gave away what was arguably his best song that year, "Girls Talk." It featured a quintessential Costello line, the type his admirers find ingenious and his detractors groan-makingly artificial: "Though you may not be an old-fashioned girl, you're still going to get dated." Dave Edmunds's propulsive recording of "Girls Talk" was a UK No. 4. Moreover, it was a rendition informed by the artist's rather innocent personality: Edmunds was certainly not dogged by the accusations of misogyny that Costello was.

The success of *Armed Forces* and "Oliver's Army" made Elvis Costello and the Attractions unlikely pinups. Their sour, un-chiseled faces were soon staring out from the glossy pages of the likes of *Smash Hits*. "We were a hot band for a while," recalls Thomas. "We were going and buying stuff in thrift stores, and then designers were referencing it for their new clothes lines and things. We all have our fifteen minutes."

The Armed Funk American tour of February to April 1978 was the band's fourth trip to the States in a year. Thomas notes, "We were just absolutely fried." That fact helps explain what went down in Columbus. Another explanation is that, while Costello and the Attractions may not actually have been punks, like many UK musicians of their generation they had a contempt for the softness to which rock had succumbed in the first half of the 1970s, and which—in their eyes—still afflicted much of the music scene in the US, where punk and new wave hadn't been such a purging presence. When Costello and Thomas encountered in a bar the mellow recording artist Stephen Stills, also currently touring, a certain amount of banter was perhaps inevitable. Also in attendance was Bonnie Bramlett, well known as half of Delaney and Bonnie, but currently working as Stills's backing singer. "It got more pointed," says Thomas of the repartee. "Then it just got a bit darker, and then it just went off the rails."

He adds, "I basically told Stephen Stills's band [they] were shit and all that. 'What have you come to our country for?' 'For your women and your money.' He said, 'What about American music?' We said, 'Well, it's all shit, like your fucking band.' So then he said, 'Well, the one thing you can't really touch is American roots music. What about James Brown, then? What about Ray Charles?' 'Ah, fucking bollocks. It's all crap.'" At some point in the proceedings, Thomas aimed the insult "Tin-nose" at Stills. "He had to have his cartilage in his nose replaced, 'cause he had lost it all by snorting coke," Thomas explains. This may have been gratuitous and childish—not to mention, Thomas concedes, hypocritical—but Costello stepped up the vitriol several levels when he assured Stills and Bramlett that Ray Charles was "nothing but a blind, ignorant nigger" and James Brown "a jive-ass nigger." A furious Bramlett knocked Costello off his stool, necessitating that his arm later be put in a sling. "You have to put things in context," reasons Thomas. "Forty years ago, the word wasn't loaded with all the PC connotations that it is now. John Lennon had just recorded 'Woman Is the Nigger of the World.' 'Oliver's Army' has the word in its lyric. It was offensive rather than taboo-meltdown . . . it was a bigger deal in America because of the advancement of black culture. Honest to God, it was not an attack on either of the two individuals cited, or a racist remark. It was simply done to be as offensive as possible to Stephen Stills and Delaney Bremmer [*sic*]. But being fucking septic wimps that they are, they had to go and capitalize on it . . . they leaked it to *Rolling Stone*."

Thomas avers that the Bramlett–Stills camp told the premier American music magazine about the contretemps because its publisher, Jann Wenner, was known to be a fan of Bruce Springsteen. "We were really seriously rivaling him for being the top band in the world at the time." He further adds of "The Boss," "The way was cleared for him by the demise of the Attractions."

That demise started with their records being taken off playlists, the campaign group Rock Against Racism—of which Costello had been a patron—picketing their gigs, and even threats on Costello's life. "We had to have plainclothes guys and bulletproof vests," Thomas says. Costello sort of apologized for the incident, but the consensus was that his belated *mea-culpa* press conference was as half-hearted as that of the Beatles in 1966, after John Lennon's we're-more-popular-than-Jesus comment. "As I'm not a racist, why do I have to apologize?" Costello snapped. He was more articulate and temperate when speaking about the incident to *Rolling Stone*'s Greil Marcus in 1982: "I said the most outrageous thing I could possibly say to them—that I knew, in my drunken logic, would anger them more than anything else . . . if I hadn't been drunk I would never have said those things."

Back in '79, contacted by the media for comment, James Brown simply observed it wasn't the first time he'd been called that word, while Ray Charles merely shrugged, "Drunken talk isn't meant to be printed in the paper." The wider American public was less forgiving. The Shea Stadium gig was now out of the question. Meanwhile, while it can't be proven that *Armed Forces'* drop down the *Billboard* chart was directly related to the bad publicity, that drop was notably vertiginous. The album had reached its peak position of No. 10 on March 10, and was still there two days after the Columbus incident happened. The week after his half-hearted apology, it dropped from 11 to 19. Two weeks later, it was out of the Top 50.

"We stayed out of America for fifteen months after that," says Thomas. "We had to start almost from scratch again. It knocked us out of our curve." However, he also says, "To be fair, if that incident hadn't happened, we'd probably all have been dead by 1980, anyway." That dramatic statement echoes one by Costello in his memoir, *Unfaithful Music and Disappearing Ink*, published in 2015, a point by which he was estranged from Thomas: "That Ohio evening may very well have saved my sorry life." If this sounds perplexingly vague, Thomas offers no objection when it's suggested to him that their lives were saved because Costello and the Attractions' grueling touring schedule, and more importantly the drug consumption necessary to sustain it, was forcibly alleviated by the Ohio incident.

Costello continues to be a successful recording artist to this day, albeit at a significantly lower level than the sales achievements of *Armed Forces* indicated he would forever occupy. It's not something by which he appears to be traumatized. In 2004, speaking to another *Rolling Stone* writer, David Fricke, Costello said, "I didn't want to be bigger and bigger. And it's worked out. Once in a while I'll have a hit . . . that pays the rent and frees me to do stuff that I want to do."

This may smack of rationalization, but again it chimes with his ex-colleague's perspective. "In retrospect, I've thought whether Elvis did something subconsciously to sabotage himself 'cause he didn't want to be a pop star," Thomas says of Ohio. "It was going to get big, and I think he just didn't want it."

2
FEBRUARY

The Northern Irish Question: Stiff Little Fingers and the Undertones

Nineteen seventy-nine saw the release of powerful debut albums by two bands from Northern Ireland. The songs of one of the bands, Belfast's Stiff Little Fingers, were pocked with the sort of imagery then endemic to their nation: Armalite rifles, Molotov cocktails, and bomb scares. The wares of Derry's no-less-loved Undertones, however, were concerned with girls, chocolate bars, and mail-order shopping. What made so striking SLF's decision to engage with the Troubles was the fact that half their membership was from the Protestant community. The exclusively Catholic backgrounds of the members of the Undertones would theoretically make them more inclined to sociopolitical commentary, it being the consensus that the minority Catholic population was disadvantaged in comparison to the Protestants. As the respective stories of the two bands' development and debuts demonstrate, however, life is more nuanced and complicated than assumptions allow for.

The origins of Stiff Little Fingers lie in a band called Highway Star, comprising Jake Burns on vocals and lead guitar, Ali McMordie on bass, Henry Cluney on rhythm guitar, and Gordon Blair on drums (the latter shortly replaced by Brian Faloon). As was the norm for the time, their style was pseudo-American. "Singing songs about bowling down the Californian highway when I'd never been further west than Galway," Burns now scoffs. Two things occurred to change their approach. One was DJ John Peel, whose name will crop up frequently in this text. As someone whose employer, BBC Radio 1, was then the only national broadcaster of popular music in the UK, Peel had an inordinate amount of power. Unlike with some of his colleagues, there was no question that he used that power benignly and adventurously. His late-evening show was a rare showcase for cutting-edge sounds, and an artist's appearance on it would spread interest far and wide.

Peel played punk records at a time when those jockeys who were aware of it either couldn't play it because of formatting, time-slot, or playlist restrictions, or disdained to do so because they personally didn't consider it "real" music. Burns himself wasn't initially overwhelmed by the punk strains the DJ championed: "I found the Damned funny, and I thought what was going on 'round the Pistols was incredibly exciting, if not them themselves." (He does at least add, of the Sex Pistols, "The first three singles were fabulous.") However, when exposure to the genre guided Burns to the Clash's 1977 eponymous debut album, it engendered a Damascene conversion. "To suddenly realize that these guys were writing about growing up in west London made me think, 'Fuck me, I can write about *here.*'"

The other impetus for change was meeting Gordon Ogilvie, Northern Ireland correspondent for British newspaper the *Daily Express*. Burns explained to Peter Silverton of *Sounds*, "We'd thought that if we sang about Northern Ireland . . . kids would say, 'You're only cashing in on what you've been through.' It just took somebody like Gordon, who was basically an outsider, to say to us, 'Fuck it. You're not exploiting anybody. You've been through it as well. Write about it if you believe in it.'" Burns set about turning his band into the Northern Irish wing of the punk movement, transforming their set of cover versions into all-original material that tackled the terrain outside his front window.

That terrain was grim. The dilemma described by many punk anthems—the unemployment queues or dead-end jobs—seemed a profound grievance up until such time as Stiff Little Fingers came along. As Burns noted in 1978, "Punks in England complain about hassles in the street . . . but they've never seen hooded men at a barricade. Their cops don't carry sub-machine guns." The scenario he described had its roots in the "Partition" of 1921, when Great Britain became the United Kingdom of Great Britain and Northern Ireland. The new adjunct was created as a concession to, and safe haven for, the Protestant population of the "Island of Ireland." Decolonization had seen the vast majority of Ireland ceded to its inhabitants (and ultimately rechristened the Republic of Ireland), but a section of it—Northern Ireland—remained under British rule, and would (the assumption was) do so forever, due to it being predominantly populated by Protestants loyal to Britain. Unfortunately, the Roman Catholic minority in this newly partitioned section of the Emerald Isle soon found themselves in an iniquitous, even impossible, position: discriminated against in housing and employment due to their religion, but unable to do anything about it because they were designedly outnumbered at the ballot box by those who were discriminating against them. Meanwhile, the country's police force—the Royal Ulster Constabulary—was comprised almost exclusively of Protestants, thus compounding the day-by-day bias felt by the minority. When in the early seventies a section of the Catholic population—the Provisional Irish Republican Army—began a bombing campaign intended to force the British government to withdraw from the country and thereby pave the way for "reunification," the Loyalists responded with their own violence. Perennial low-level civil war was the outcome.

SLF's entrée was "Suspect Device." The debut appeared on Rigid Digits, a label set up by Ogilvie, who became the band's co-manager. Its lyric was Ogilvie's handiwork, albeit considerably cut down in length by Burns. The composition took a common term for a package that it was feared might contain a bomb and turned it into a symbol of rebellion, telling the audience that they should become suspect devices and rise up against those who would take away their freedom in the name of liberty. The terminology, including a repeated denunciation of an undefined "they," was cleverly ambiguous. Burns noted to Silverton, "When 'Suspect Device' came out we had a full-page spread in the Irish edition of the *Daily Mirror* where they just about said we were Republicans. The *NME* described us as Loyalists . . . If people can't put a label on us that's great." He could have added that SLF's attempts to prevent people putting a label on them—they batted away interview questions about their religious backgrounds with formulae of words like, "We're just sick of the whole thing"—was predicated on something more profound than a desire to not be ghettoized: identification could literally be a life-or-death issue for them or their families.

Nonetheless, the specifics of the makeup of the band did leak out here and there. In March 1979, Phil Sutcliffe of *Sounds* reported that two of the quartet were Catholic, two Protestant. This rather served to demonstrate that the province's political situation wasn't black and white. Protestants/Loyalists, no less than Catholics/Republicans, had to grow up in a country where premature death was a daily possibility. Moreover, that Protestants were not a homogenous mass was indicated by a line in the band's song "Alternative Ulster": "The RUC dog of oppression is barking at your feet." The province's police were clearly no more tolerant than any other seventies constabulary of leather-jacketed youth, especially that part of it identifiable as punk, regardless of their religious background. Sutcliffe also reported that all of the band members were blue-collar, which of course came with its own universal problems.

"Suspect Device" was given exposure by Peel, and naturally his enthusiasm provided a rocket booster to SLF's progress. The excellence of their follow-up only accelerated that momentum. "Alternative Ulster" was a song with an unusual origin. The title came from the name of one of the countless mimeographed punk fanzines of the time, this one edited by Gavin Martin, who would go on to become a major music journalist. Martin approached the band after coming up with a plan to give away a flexi disc with the magazine. "He asked us to do 'Suspect Device' for it," says Burns. "We couldn't, because we'd just recorded it as our first single, but, 'I tell you what, I'll write you a song.' So we wrote 'Alternative Ulster'—and he didn't like it. So we went, 'Oh fuck it, we'll keep it.'" In contrast to Martin's disdain, others instantly recognized the Fingers/Ogilvie composition as a classic fit to stand alongside "New Rose," "Pretty Vacant," and "White Riot" in the pantheon of punk anthems. A rousing call to carve out an acceptable reality within a society that offered nothing, it was particularly notable for the way its blazing fury didn't prohibit a certain majesty. Interestingly, its unforgettable riff was played on twin guitars—something highly reminiscent of another group from the Emerald Isle. "Thin Lizzy were a big influence," Burns admits.

The single was ultimately released across the whole of the UK on Rough Trade, which might oxymoronically be described as a major independent. The band then set about preparing their debut album for that label. What followed across the course of two weeks in Spaceward Studios in Cambridge was the archetypal quick and simple punk recording process. "There were only about two guitar overdubs on the whole record," Burns later told journalist Francis Jones. *Inflammable Material* included a re-recorded version of "Suspect Device" and a remixed "Alternative Ulster." It concluded with a curio called "Closed Groove" in which puns and juxtapositions like "Punctuality's a waste of time" were set against slow, circular, post-punk instrumentation. The rest of the disc was wall-to-wall rebel anthems, all pocked with intriguing local color, an attribute underlined by the vocals. The public had already been acclimatized by UK punk musicians to songs not being performed in the pseudo-American accents *de rigueur* until '76, but SLF went one better by rendering their lyrics in a Northern Irish accent largely unknown in popular music.

With the exception of one cut, the material on *Inflammable Material* was written by either SLF or the Fingers/Ogilvie partnership. The sole cover was an epic, eight-minute version of Bob Marley's "Johnny Was," wherein the band managed to create a nexus between senseless death in Jamaica and slaughter in Northern Ireland. Initiated by bullet-hail drumming and Kalashnikov guitar, its musical centerpiece was a guitar solo by Burns whose lengthiness managed to sidestep punk's prohibition on self-indulgent virtuosity via the obvious fact that it was executed by someone with more enthusiasm than technique. "Here We Are Nowhere" was an exhilarating example of the sort of deliberately self-parodic punk proliferating in the era, cramming its statement into an absurdly short timespan (in this case, fifty-six seconds). "No More of That" (sung by Cluney) was a raggedy marching song for an army of the disaffected, juxtaposing soaring verses with brutally syncopated choruses.

"State of Emergency" and "Wasted Life" were fairly one-dimensional roars of defiance. They were nonetheless exciting, their fury in no way prohibiting above-par instrumental flourishes, such as the blurred, spiraling guitar figure that closed "State of Emergency." "Breakout" was a valedictory to the culture that had created the band but which their talent had secured them an escape route from. It was replete with a gee-up for those they were leaving behind ("If I can do it, you can do it too").

Other material provided a more lateral view of the Troubles. "Barbed Wire Love," the closest thing to a love song on the record, found a protagonist trying to pursue romance against a backdrop of war. Its bridge saw the group lurch from abrasive punk tones into perfectly executed, suave doo-wop. The penchant for lyrical smart-aleckry (of which "Closed Groove" was the *reductio ad absurdum*) was present in lines like, "You set my Armalite," a pun on the "Widowmaker" brand of rifles favored by the IRA. "White Noise" was a song seen through the eyes of a racist ("Rastus is a nigger, thug, mugger, junkie") delivered with such passion that it unsettlingly felt like an endorsement of the sentiments it expressed—right up until a final verse in which British stereotypes about the Irish were articulated in similar fashion.

The two weakest tracks were not flawed musically—both were galvanizing—but by what might be termed the group's mealy mouths. "Law and Order" was a vignette of police harassment that might have possessed power were it not for a bridge in which Burns whined, "I'm not saying we're always right." Said sentiment could be posited as an admirably non-didactic approach unusual for young people and especially punks. However, it—fairly or unfairly—couldn't help but seem like the words of a Goody Two-shoes. Less ambiguously risible was the following track, "Rough Trade." In what seemed like an audacious case of biting the hand that fed them, SLF snarled that they had been "betrayed by rough trade lies." Except that the song wasn't about the record company Rough Trade (the use of the name was—what else?—a pun) but about Island Records, which had wooed the band and then—once they had quit their day jobs and relocated to London—backed off. SLF publicly admitted that they had declined to identify Island in song in case the label took legal action. What self-respecting no-future punk gave a shit about the prospect of being sued?

Not only was Rough Trade blameless, but the album's production, by the label's founder Geoff Travis, in association with Mayo Thompson, was unusually good for a punk record, the pair not afraid to lend a certain slickness to the fiery soundscapes. Rough Trade's reward was for SLF to decamp to major label Chrysalis for their next album.

The LP's slightly boring cover—the inflammable warning symbol laid out nine times like a Tic-Tac-Toe grid—couldn't detract from the fact that its title was perfectly apposite. Released in February 1979, it secured a rave from the notoriously hard-to-please *New Musical Express*: "It was perhaps always inevitable that Belfast would throw up the vital punk record," enthused Paul Morley. "There are parts of *Inflammable Material* that are not just exciting or stimulating but quite humbling." The record proceeded to achieve a commercial success that was, for a punk band without any hits to their name, extraordinary. The album reached No. 14 and stayed in the UK Top 100 for nineteen weeks. "It was the first independent album ever to break the Top 20," points out Burns.

SLF were suddenly contenders for the mantle of Britain's foremost punk group. "We went from being an unknown support band to being almost the name on the back of every leather jacket in three months flat," Burns muses. Yet the praise wasn't universal. Fellow Ulstermen the Undertones derided them. Undertones guitarist and chief song-writer John O'Neill explains of his feelings at the time, "For one thing, before punk they were a heavy-metal band. They played Deep Purple songs. Punk was anti-rock and all those rock bands that came from the early seventies, like Deep Purple, Led Zeppelin, Pink Floyd. Then the fact that a journalist from the *Daily Mail* or somewhere wrote the lyrics. For us, they were just the antithesis of what punk was about."

For some, SLF continued to be, as one critic put it, "Airfix punks" (a reference to a well-known manufacturer of plastic scale-model kits). Ogilvie's former Fourth Estate employer was a rather conservative and exclamatory newspaper that like most such publications took a sneer-ing attitude toward not just punk but rock and youth culture *per se*.

Moreover, requiring an outside collaborator couldn't help but make the band seem less organic and valid than their self-reliant peers. On top of that, Ogilvie's involvement raised suspicion of the group being manipulated. The aura of a punk Monkees wasn't helped by the fact that their name was inspired by a song by the Vibrators, widely considered the archetypal fake, opportunist punk group. Even the fact that Burns wore glasses offstage played into this phony aura, like he was really Clark Kent rather than Superman.

It also couldn't be denied that there was a rather secondhand air hanging over SLF. In the case of their debt to the Clash, the situation verged on the ridiculous. *Inflammable Material* seemed to have been deliberately assembled to a grid laid out by the first Clash album. "Barbed Wire Love" was the equivalent of "Deny" in being an antimatter romance number, "White Noise" owed a linguistic, spiritual, and sonic debt to "White Riot," "Breakout" had something of the class-conscious, new-horizons melancholy of "Garageland," and "Johnny Was" didn't just ape the fact of being a punkified reggae cover but was even placed in the middle of side two, just like "Police and Thieves" had been on *The Clash*. Moreover, "Rough Trade" was (ostensibly, at least) in the same record-company-baiting vein as the Clash's anti-CBS single "Complete Control."

SLF's second album, *Nobody's Heroes*, appeared in 1980. The LP featured "Wait and See," a moving but bittersweet fare-thee-well to Faloon, who had quit the band, replaced by Jim Reilly. The album found SLF broadening their sound, nimbly executing reggae rhythms without losing punk's roaring sonic impact. However, it also marked the point where they began refusing to write about their home country. Their grounds—that it would be hypocritical to do so when they no longer lived there—might have been admirable, but they had lost their unique selling point. Consequently, there was now a suspicion of casting around for things about which to get enraged. Album closer "Tin Soldiers" was apocalyptical in its fury, but in essence concerned nothing more than a young soldier misunderstanding how many years he had signed up to serve for.

After a split and reformation and comings and goings in the personnel department—including a fifteen-year stint by ex-Jam bassist Bruce Foxton—the latest version of SLF features from the classic lineup Burns and McMordie. Songs from their first album continue to be lapped up by their live audiences, even though the situation they describe no longer exists.

The burning issues addressed by *Inflammable Material* have been shunted into history by the 1998 Good Friday agreement that brought peace to Northern Ireland, and by the demographic time bomb that is projected—after exactly a century—to give Catholics population parity in the province. Once a work whose vistas and vocabulary were ripped from the headlines of newspapers, *Inflammable Material* is now a document of a bygone age. It remains, however, a supremely listenable record, a thrilling and moving soundtrack to a particular time and place.

The Undertones were formed in 1974—sort of. "We used to hang about in our sitting room, just talking about the band even before the band," recalls John O'Neill. Other members were the rhythm guitarist's brother Damian (lead guitar), bassist Michael ("Mickey") Bradley, and drummer Billy Doherty. They would be profoundly influenced by punk—although, unusually, not so much by its British variant. "We were always far more influenced from American punk," says O'Neill. The Undertones were also infused with a love of the glam rock that had been the soundtrack to their boyhoods. O'Neill says that it is probably this that made the sound of the Undertones an unusual pop-punk hybrid.

In 1975, the quartet finally found someone with the confidence to be a vocalist. However, O'Neill avers that Feargal Sharkey played no part in the development of the Undertones' style, either then or in the future. "Feargal wasn't really that much into music. He was just there because he was happy to sing. He never even bought records." Most lead singers who don't play an instrument gravitate toward providing the song words—partly to keep themselves occupied, partly as a way of asserting that they are not expendable—but, O'Neill says, "Feargal would never come to us and say, 'I've got some lyrics.'" He adds, "It was never really an issue." Despite his creative role being restricted to interpreting song words (and not always in a way of which O'Neill approved), Sharkey was a magnetic presence. Visually, he was sharp-cheeked, piercing-eyed, emphatic of body language, and perennially parka-draped. He was distinctive aurally for more than his asthmatic voice, like SLF delivering the lyrics in his natural "Norn Iron" tones. Less inspired were the names Sharkey chose for the previously anonymous band, undeterred by the fact that the Hot Rods and Little Feat were both already taken. In early 1976, Doherty saw the word "undertones" in a school history book, and the others adopted it largely because it sounded like "Ramones."

Even with the influence of punk—an intrinsically gritty music—the lyrics Sharkey sang betrayed no hint of the problems afflicting the group members' home country. Those problems ranged from regular sectarian murder to more mundane disputes, such as the insistence by Protestant inhabitants of the band's hometown that its proper name was Londonderry. "We obviously were aware, especially when Stiff Little Fingers were getting played, that people might be expecting us to write about the situation in the North of Ireland," explains O'Neill. "I did try, but it always did seem too forced. The natural thing for me and for all of us as a band seemed to be to write songs about relationships.

We were just learning how to write songs and we were quite young and rather than trying to do something that may end up sounding crass or pretentious, it just seemed to be more honest. In that sense we reinterpreted what punk was."

Graduating from performances at youth clubs, scout halls, and schools, the Undertones secured a berth at a rough Derry pub called the Casbah, where they proceeded to hone their chops over the course of a year or so. The next step was a record deal of some sort. "We wanted to make it an EP, as a tribute to what the Buzzcocks had done with *Spiral Scratch*," O'Neill says, in reference to the famously self-financed four-song Buzzcocks entrée that helped establish UK punk values back in '77. "The Buzzcocks were the British band we would probably associate with most in the sense that they were trying to go down that pop sentiment and sensibility." The Undertones' own four-song EP was *Teenage Kicks*, released by Terri Hooley's Belfast label Good Vibrations in September 1978.

Although Davy Shannon was the record's engineer, the Undertones acted as their own producers. Not that there was much to do. "We chose the four songs that were the least difficult," O'Neill says of "Teenage Kicks," "Smarter Than U," "True Confessions," and "Emergency Cases." "They weren't really particularly hard to play." O'Neill recalls that the group were not too impressed by their own handiwork, initially feeling the EP "really weak and twee." At least one person disagreed. John Peel's love for the record's John O'Neill–written title track—a roaring but melodic celebration of adolescent romance—was instant and absolute. He rhapsodized about it on air, even playing it twice in a row. Naturally, his encomium carried no little weight, and *Teenage Kicks* and the Undertones were suddenly a talking point far beyond the borders of their hometown. Not that it turned the Undertones' level heads too much. O'Neill: "He used to say it was the greatest record ever made or something, and it's obviously not that. The record itself does sound great, but the song isn't particularly a great song. It's full of clichés, and it's quite a predictable chord sequence." Others could see Peel's orgasmic point. "Teenage Kicks" was the first song to marry punk's aural assault to an endearing property perhaps best described as innocence.

Eyebrow-raisingly, O'Neill asserts that the Undertones would have been as happy as not if the *Teenage Kicks* EP had been the sum total of their career. "We were about ready to break up at that stage. The difference between ourselves and Feargal was becoming more and more apparent. We didn't particularly think we were all that great anyway. The idea of making another record never really occurred to us." However, within days of Peel playing "Teenage Kicks" back-to-back, the band were getting interest from major record companies. O'Neill was the only band member whose family had a telephone. "Our home phone never stopped ringing from A&R people from most labels." The Undertones weren't so lacking in ambition or guile that it occurred to them to spurn such offers for day jobs, or even just another Good Vibrations release ("You didn't know whether they were going to be able to afford to put out another record, never mind make an LP"). Then there was the fact that one of their major-label suitors was Seymour Stein, co-founder of Sire Records, home of no less a band than their adored Ramones. As soon as the Undertones signed on the dotted line, Sire issued "Teenage Kicks" on single, and it climbed to No. 31 in the UK chart.

There is an argument for saying that from this point, the Undertones were never as good again. Despite the fact that over the next few years they would issue more than several worthy-to-great songs, for some nothing they did ever bettered the concentrated artistic excellence and sonic punch of the *Teenage Kicks* EP. Some of this may be down to the compromises and mistranslations involved in handing over power to outside sources. Recording follow-up single "Get Over You" under the auspices of Roger Bechirian was a very different experience to laying down the Good Vibrations EP. Although O'Neill says it was very exciting to be working in top-notch London studio Eden with a man known for his work on Elvis Costello records, Bechirian was naturally not there to be told what to do, like Shannon had been. "We kind of trusted him, just let him do what he thought was good. Afterwards, we were going we probably trusted him too much."

"Get Over You" was another snarling-riffed O'Neill song about adolescent adoration, and was actually the number that went down the best with their audience. Yet it was noticeable how tame it sounded compared to the debut EP, particularly the brittle, bland drum track. "We still didn't take ourselves that seriously," says O'Neill. "We thought, 'Make one record and it'll do all right, and we'll probably [be] dropped after that anyway.' And the same after doing the second record, and the same after doing the third record."

After all the hoopla surrounding the triumphant story of the Undertones' emergence from the boondocks of Northern Ireland to nationwide acclaim, the mediocre chart progress of "Get Over You"— which stalled outside the Top 50 after its February 1979 release—was a dash of cold water. Come April, "Jimmy Jimmy" put the band back on track, making No. 16. Because of its scathing references to a little mummy's boy who did what he was told, and its picture sleeve depicting a school-uniformed Sharkey beamingly holding up a trophy, some have assumed it to be in the same vein as a future Undertones single, "My Perfect Cousin," and have jumped to a further conclusion that the group possessed an antipathy to nice boys. However, O'Neill reveals a literary impetus. "I was influenced from a short story by E. M. Forster,

'The Celestial Omnibus,' about this guy, the omnibus taking him away
to live in his imagination, having a better place to live."

In any case, a hostile party line on goody-goodies would hardly
have made sense considering the group's own ingénue aura, one that
"Mars Bars"—the heartfelt paean to confectionary on the B-side of
"Jimmy Jimmy"—seemed to work, rest, and play up to. All the band
were at this point living at home with their parents—something that
wouldn't begin to change until 1980, when O'Neill became the first of
them to get married. He concedes, "We probably were the boys next
door." However, he also says of the band-of-innocents image, "I always
felt we were a bit tougher than that anyway. We came from a horrible
place in Ireland and we were aware of the real world, even though we
may not have written songs about it."

The Undertones' eponymous debut album was released in May
1979. All members got writing credits except Sharkey. John O'Neill
wrote half of the fourteen tracks alone, and chipped in on most of the
others. He admits, "That whole first LP, most of maybe the second LP,
all of those songs were totally about my wife and my relationships with
her friends. We used to go away on tour for three weeks, four weeks,
and we were literally crying in each other's arms every time going out
the door. It was young love. It was that intense." He adds, "There was
two sides in the Undertones. There was Mickey's: 'More Songs About
Chocolate and Girls,' 'My Perfect Cousin' . . . I never really liked any of
those songs that much. And then my songs were a bit more that homage to sixties R&B—not so parochial, if you like." He further admits,
"Mickey's words are always better than my words, anyway . . . 'My
Perfect Cousin' are great words."

Although the tenor of the album was uniquely Undertones,
O'Neill's comment that "we were trying to replicate our influences on

the LP" is backed up by the way he points to an outside derivation for at least part of every cut. For instance, he describes his "Girls Don't Like It" as "me trying to copy the Shangri-Las." For the spoken-word intro, Bechirian's work on another 1979 hit—"Lucky Number" by Lene Lovich—came in handy: it was her voice that could be heard at the beginning. "Male Model" was written by the triumvirate of the two O'Neill brothers and Michael Bradley that contributed most of those songs not written by John O'Neill alone. Its subject was the weekly-installment mail-order catalogues that multiple families would share at Christmas. "That's how you'd get your clothes and all that sort of stuff [in] working-class Derry." O'Neill's Velvet Underground–inspired "I Gotta Getta" featured organ from Damian O'Neill. It being the case that the Undertones were famously Derry's only punks, it might be assumed that they would be worried that the sweetening might seem "un-punk," but O'Neill reasons, "Punk for us wasn't about sticking to formulas," and points out of the American proto-punk compilation *Nuggets*, "There's Farfisa organs all over that." O'Neill's "Jump Boys" was inspired musically by the Who's "I Can't Explain" and lyrically by a biker element in the Undertones' live following that conferred a certain coolness on the band. It was the most sophisticated track, arrangement-wise, featuring punchy, cooing harmonies, a tingling guitar solo, and a pulsating respite.

One familiar Undertones song—"Jimmy Jimmy"—was followed by another in the shape of the Bradley/O'Neill brothers collabora-tion "True Confessions," a re-recording of a song on the *Teenage Kicks* EP whose inclusion was necessitated by the fact that the Undertones' disinclination to include many singles meant they were fast running out of material. The album version was deliberately redolent of Donna Summer. O'Neill explains, "Disco was getting slagged off a lot, but we liked disco." He also concedes, "It was a bit of a mistake in retrospect."

The music of "I Know a Girl" (by the O'Neills and Bradley) is a sort of tribute to "I Can Only Give You Everything," a creation of Derry songwriter Phil Coulter covered by Them and the Troggs. The lyric, meanwhile, stemmed from a real-life incident reminiscent of an episode of the British sitcom *Father Ted* wherein the red-faced priests are stranded in a lingerie department: O'Neill's girlfriend asked him to take an unwanted clothing purchase back to the shop.

The album closed with a brief and musty tribute to the band's origins called "Casbah Rock" which was credited to John O'Neill, but which he readily admits is "an obvious rip-off of 'Louie Louie.'" He elaborates, "There was another verse written. It was a full two-and-a-half-minute song, but we thought it was just too much of a rip-off to actually record it properly, so it was just like a demo version that was recorded live in the Casbah [and] put on the end of the LP."

Side one's closer was the joyous John O'Neill composition "Here Comes the Summer," a re-recording of which was released as single a couple of months after the album and made No. 34 in the UK. One of its two B-side tracks, "Top Twenty," included a snatch of T. Rex's "Solid Gold, Easy Action." O'Neill: "Back to our glam-rock influences. We were always [keen] to show that." So keen that they dismissed any thoughts of legal action from the publishers. "I think they were totally oblivious to any B-side of an Undertones record. You can't get much more obscure than that."

The album was critically well received, acknowledged as fulfilling much of the promise of "Teenage Kicks." If none of the tracks matched the quality of that already-celebrated recording, meanwhile, that could pretty much be said for any release by any artist that year.

Promoting the album was, as ever, a surreal experience. "As far as everybody was concerned, Feargal was the main songwriter," says O'Neill. This misapprehension even prevailed among people who it might be expected would know better, i.e., music journalists. There was a reason for this, other than them receiving white-label review copies lacking credits: "He never contradicted anybody when they said that to him." O'Neill adds, "We didn't mind. It kept the spotlight off us."

The original edition of the album was soon history. The Undertones decided that they wished to renegotiate a recording contract they had signed in haste. Sire was gracious enough to agree to this but, in the bargaining process, band manager Andy Ferguson felt that the Undertones had to give ground to the label in one of the few ways that wouldn't adversely affect their finances—namely, acquiescing to an augmented reissue of the album. "I don't think the LP sold all that well," explains O'Neill. "We were told it was because you should have included the singles on it." In a day and age of reissues with bonus tracks such as contemporaneous standalone singles, the public has got used to the idea of augmented albums. *The Undertones* could be said to be a precursor to that concept. Within five months of its release, the LP was reissued with a fresh cover (the new design paying homage to the aerial group shot on the front of the Who's *My Generation*) and a beefed-up tracklisting. "Teenage Kicks" and "Get Over You" were included, and "Here Comes the Summer" was replaced with its single iteration. The Undertones were at least able to wrest the concession from Sire that the rejigged LP would be sold at a budget price until the end of '79. The original album had peaked at No. 13 in the UK albums chart four months before the release of the revised version, and the latter version now hoisted *The Undertones* back into the Top 40. The rejigged album also made No. 154 on the *Billboard* 200, the band's only US album-chart placing.

Asked if he considers the first release of the LP the definitive version, O'Neill shrugs, "I wouldn't be that purist, really. I don't mind either version of the first LP." Perhaps the explanation for this is the fact that the exigencies of a recording career soon put the band's idealism into context. "By the time the second LP came out . . . we were struggling just writing enough songs to make a full LP. We didn't even have the luxury of keeping singles off, even though we did leave 'You've Got My Number' off *Hypnotised*."

Released in October 1979, "You've Got My Number (Why Don't You Use It?)"—which climbed to No. 32—was no less than the fourth Undertones single of the year. "It was the punk thing," O'Neill says of their prolific-work-rate-cum-largesse. Despite following so quickly on the heels of their last product, the single had a noticeably more sophisticated timbre. "We never really captured the whole live thing properly, but we were definitely getting a bit more comfortable in the studio by that stage."

The Undertones' biggest success was ahead of them. "My Perfect Cousin" (1980) made the UK Top 10, "Wednesday Week" (also 1980) brushed it, and "It's Going to Happen!" went Top 20. Moreover, critical consensus has it that their albums *Hypnotised* (1980), *Positive Touch* (1981), and *The Sin of Pride* (1983) broadly speaking mark a trajectory of increasing lyrical, musical, and production sophistication. However, the seeds of the Undertones' destruction were present in their modesty and down-to-earth characters.

When they were back at base, the band made the most of it. O'Neill: "We still stayed pretty close to all the friends that came to see us in the Casbah. We always came back to Derry. We stayed in Derry. We rehearsed right up until the last LP in Damian's bedroom— we never had practice studios. We tried to stay as true to our roots as we possibly could." While such an attitude may have cemented their punk credentials, O'Neill admits, "It was definitely detrimental to our careers. That was what was causing the difference between ourselves and Feargal at the end." Sharkey may have evinced zero artistic objectives, but his other ambitions were far bigger than those of the rest of the band. "That naive punk ideology that I felt I had to stick true to, he didn't have that. As far as he was concerned, the music industry was about a career, making money."

When Sharkey announced to the Undertones in 1983 that he was leaving to pursue other career options, he was theoretically replace-able in five minutes. However, O'Neill points out that the band's assumption that "there's no point us staying together, because nobody's gonna be interested in the Undertones without Feargal," seems to have been borne out by the lack of radio play given to their releases since they resumed their recording career in 2003 with new vocalist Paul McLoone. "As far as they're concerned, it's not the Undertones."

Moreover, Sharkey's departure seems to have been a blessing in disguise for O'Neill. Certainly, it sounds as though that juncture found him disillusioned with both the band and a music scene whose excellence from 1977 onward he had assumed would "last forever." He recalls, "You couldn't wait to turn on the radio to hear John Peel and hear what is going to come out. That's my memory of '79." For O'Neill, a decline started in the early eighties with the advent of the New Romantic movement, which reflected the fact that the "idealism that I felt that punk seemed to be about had totally gone." He says, "It was all about selling records, about making money, and not about just doing it for the fun of it."

He continues, "I was definitely running out of ideas as well, if I'm honest. I needed a break from it. That's why, when Feargal said he was leaving the band, it was a relief." There was also the fact that O'Neill had changed his mind about the Undertones' approach to songwriting. That Petrol Emotion, the pointedly titled band he proceeded to form with Damian, would address across their six albums the very type of political subject matter his previous group avoided.

Feargal Sharkey graduated from a successful solo career (in which he finally began showing an interest in composing) to A&R man ("We used to think, 'Feargal knows nothin'!'" O'Neill scoffs) to music-industry executive. His ex-colleagues now hold down day jobs, their occasional recording and performing amounting to "just a hobby." As to that first, fondly remembered Undertones album, O'Neill says, "It's probably still the best one, in the sense that it's us at our most spontaneous. It was us at our purest."

Today, after the delicate series of compromises involved in Northern Ireland's Peace Process, the Undertones' hometown is rendered as "Derry/Londonderry" on signage and some official forms. O'Neill, though, feels vindicated in ignoring the Troubles. "We did know it was important not to show we were taking sides in the war. We knew that it was important for our own creative development that the imagination should be allowed to keep its integrity. I think that honesty is what has somehow given our songs their longevity." .

Swindles and Metal Boxes: Life After the Sex Pistols

In their brief lifetime, the Sex Pistols exhilaratingly redefined notions of stardom, career, image, and even music. They also quickly besmirched their singular legacy, a process that largely occurred and concluded in 1979.

Some felt that the London quartet ceased to exist in any meaningful form in February 1977, when bassist Glen Matlock departed the ranks. Without him, the Pistols' songwriting became instantly less subtle, as well as less productive. However, their cache of unreleased songs from the Matlock days enabled them to carry on releasing records that were both classics and genuinely insurrectionary. The latter was epitomized by the roaringly republican "God Save the Queen," released into a culture in which it was still taboo to criticize the British Royal Family. Proof of such is provided by the fact that all the evidence suggests that the record was denied by political imperatives rather than sales statistics the formal status of the nation's top-selling single in the week of June 5, 1977, which happened to coincide with the monarch's Silver Jubilee.

With the January 1978 departure of lyricist and lead vocalist Johnny Rotten—walking out of the group after the end of their chaotic American tour—few doubted that the curtain had been drawn on the Pistols' days as a meaningful band. Of course, being a meaningful band is not the same thing as being a moneymaking operation. That latter project persisted in the shape of a mock-biopic called *The Great Rock 'n' Roll Swindle*. Pistols manager Malcolm McLaren continued to shoot the movie and compile its soundtrack even as the Pistols disintegrated yet further around him. Jon Savage, who would write what is regarded as the definitive history of punk, *England's Dreaming*, spent in 1979 a lot of time with Jamie Reid, the Pistols' art director, and some time with McLaren. He recalls, "What Malcolm was doing was a last, desperate rear-guard action."

This moneymaking operation wasn't even terminated by the martyrdom/squalid death of Sid Vicious, a.k.a. John Beverley. Vicious had replaced Matlock on bass. He couldn't play the instrument very well and had no songwriting ability, but he possessed height, sharp cheekbones, a brooding brow, impeccably spikey hair, and a patent death wish. Such iconography was arguably more important than any music now that—in the glare of fame—the Pistols' onetime edgy image and style had tipped over into cartoon nihilism. Vicious's last act as a Sex Pistol was to record and film his profane deconstruction—or punkification—of Paul Anka's "My Way." The price Vicious exacted for that act was McLaren relinquishing his management rights over him. This was something Savage feels Vicious was pressured into doing by his equally disturbed girlfriend, Nancy Spungen: "Relations between him and Malcolm had completely broken down, and part of it was that Malcolm and [McLaren's company] Glitterbest had tried to kidnap Nancy and send her back to America in late '77." Vicious and Spungen relocated to the US in August 1978. Within six months, both were dead. Spungen was fatally stabbed in an incident at New York's Chelsea Hotel in October '78; Vicious was charged with her murder. Evidence subsequently emerged that, in fact, the real culprit was more likely a drug dealer named Rockets Redglare, but by then Vicious was long gone, suffering a fatal heroin overdose in February '79. Less than a week after Vicious's demise, McLaren was fighting over the Pistols' assets with John Lydon—the former Johnny Rotten—in London's High Court.

Lydon vs. Glitterbest was a seven-day hearing. At the end of it, a receiver was appointed to look after Pistols-related capital and exploit the band's artistic assets. Mr. Justice Browne-Wilkinson had decided that monies due to the band had been misappropriated to fund *The Great Rock 'n' Roll Swindle*. Paul Cook and Steve Jones—Pistols drummer and guitarist respectively—started the case as witnesses for McLaren before switching sides. The case, though, was not fully resolved until 1986, when McLaren abandoned his claim to a slice of the pie and agreed to hand over control of his companies to the ex-Pistols in exchange for not having to pay their costs.

So far, February '79 had seen a Sex Pistols–related death and a court case. The 26th saw yet further Pistols activity in the form of the release of the *Swindle* soundtrack. Notwithstanding that its contents were impossible to fully understand without the benefit of having seen the as yet unreleased film, it was immediately clear that it served as a tombstone for the band's principles. Across the course of its two discs could be found—in addition to Vicious's unforgettable version of "My

Way"—Pistols anthems in orchestral, disco, and folk-street-performer versions; musty rehearsal tapes (of both Pistols songs and oldies); an unreleased, post-Matlock original ("Belsen Was a Gas"); some infernally catchy but risibly conventional Cook and Jones newies ("Silly Thing," "Lonely Boy," "No One Is Innocent," "The Great Rock 'n' Roll Swindle"); a couple of gutsy but random, Vicious-sung Eddie Cochran tunes ("Something Else" and "C'mon Everybody"); a McLaren rendering of an old hit by MOR entertainer Max Bygraves ("You Need Hands"); a brace of contributions by bug-eyed Rotten wannabe Edward Tudor-Pole ("Who Killed Bambi?," co-written by him with McLaren's wife Vivienne Westwood, and a cover of "Rock Around the Clock"); and a grandiose, strings-festooned version of public-domain sea shanty "Friggin' in the Riggin'."

All of this was, on one level, an entertaining listen. That reaction involved, though, tucking away any knowledge of what the Sex Pistols had stood for until only just over a year ago. The Pistols' famous year-zero dismissal of every artist that preceded them was hardly consistent with the cover versions with which the set was peppered. The studied vulgarity suffusing many of the tracks seemed to suggest that the Pistols camp now thought rude words were the same thing as insurrection. The exploitative ragbag nature of the anthology made a nonsense of the anti-careerism that had been the band's *raison d'être*. Most importantly, though, the music was almost completely devoid of the menace that had made the Sex Pistols so thrillingly special.

Not that this prevented that music being successful. The soundtrack made No. 7 in the UK. (The music was given further shelf life the following year in the form of a single-disc version that jettisoned the tracks with Rotten vocals.) The album itself was relentlessly mined for singles and yielded six UK chart entries, four of them Top 10s. "It's funny that that rearguard action should have produced the two best-selling

Pistols singles of all of them in the seventies," notes Savage. "'C'mon Everybody' and 'Something Else' both sold more than 'God Save the Queen.' There was a huge [audience] after the first wave of punk for this." He also says something that will surprise those cognizant of his knowledge of the genre's history: "I liked the *Great Rock 'n' Roll Swindle* album." Although he does admit it was "a mish-mash," Savage opines, "The Black Arabs track was terrific. It was good to have 'Belsen Was a Gas,' which was so frightening, on record. It was nice to hear the Pistols running through 'Substitute.' There was still a bit of magic there." But surely retro covers and naked profiteering traduced the original point of the Pistols? "By this time, it was morphing into something else. I liked the ideas, actually. There are a lot of situationist ideas in *The Great Rock 'n' Roll Swindle*. I thought it was interesting, and Malcolm was really doing his best, bearing in mind he'd lost the charismatic lead singer. I didn't think the whole thing was over and done with."

For Savage, that point came in February 1980, when Virgin Records issued *Flogging a Dead Horse*, an absurdly straightforward compilation of A- and B-sides, and one that was hardly called for, considering that the band's back catalogue was so small. Critical reaction to the release was colored by the fact that it followed similarly exploitative Pistols-related releases from the previous year. August 1979's *Some Product* was a collection of profane Pistols media interviews, while *Sid Sings* scraped together Vicious's few non-Pistols recordings just in time to fill punks' (ripped fishnet) Christmas stockings.

The Julien Temple–directed *Swindle* film appeared at the belated stage of May 1980. "The way the film begins with the Gordon Riots is very interesting," says Savage. "There's always lots of ideas [with] Malcolm, and little bits of history. He was able to take forgotten events from the past that were in themselves extremely interesting and dramatize them and bring them into [the] context of a very successful punk-rock group." However, Savage also says, "Unfortunately, *Great Rock 'n' Roll Swindle* is one of these films that have not aged well. I watched it again fairly recently and just thought it was pretty shit, actually . . . there's all sorts of faffing around, and it's too bitty. It's also very cynical, which is not a quality I like."

McLaren had the starring role in a picture that depicted Steve Jones as a private detective trying to unravel the Pistols' "swindle" and encountering along the way a voice coach, a porn star, a train robber, and a miscellanea of famous British character actors. Throughout, McLaren posited the Pistols as a cold-blooded device to make money, explicitly claiming they couldn't play. This notion was somewhat undermined by the inclusion of promotional films of their early singles, which sizzled with musical class. Animated sequences were also interspersed, primarily as a way of representing a noncompliant Rotten.

McLaren's role in the movie was "The Embezzler." Perhaps a more appropriate title for him would have been "Provocateur." "It wasn't even shock tactics with Malcolm," says Savage. "He was quite detached. He just wanted to provoke just to see what people's reaction was and what that said about British society, and if you look at what he did, it was incredibly successful. We're still talking about the Sex Pistols forty years later." Despite his admiration for McLaren, Savage notes, "I wouldn't want to do business with him . . . I don't think he was very good in human terms. He was very fond of Steve, he was very fond of Sid—genuinely—and tried to do more for him than people realize, but with Malcolm it was always the next idea, it was always the event."

For his part, John Lydon avers that McLaren was a frustrated artist, claiming that the manager got "very annoyed" when he himself turned out to have a gift for lyrics. Says Lydon, "He even took singing lessons privately. And we found out and went, 'Well, we're not paying for that.'

He thought he could have a go at it: 'Oh, if he can write things like that then so can I.'"

The fact that the court case started just days after Vicious's death raises the possibility that, had Vicious held on just a few days longer, the Sex Pistols might have reunited. After all, with Lydon and Vicious's resented former Svengali out of the picture, the main obstacle to them and the Cook/Jones axis working together again had been removed. Savage doesn't dispute this possibility but is skeptical about the worth of the post-Matlock iteration of the Sex Pistols. "They didn't work together that well, really. There are a few tunes after Glen, but they're pretty much a barrage. Glen was the arranger of the group as well as the bassist and the songwriter. Steve was a brilliant guitarist, and he could write a riff, but he wasn't necessarily an arranger."

In any case, Savage says that Lydon had probably already outgrown the Pistols. His new band, Public Image Ltd., had released their first album the previous December, and would in November '79 issue a follow-up, *Metal Box*, which Savage adjudges to be "a brilliant record." Summarizes Savage, "The Pistols became this national drama. It's not conducive to making music, being in the center of that particular storm."

Of all the records released in 1979, none divided opinion more sharply than *Metal Box*. While some, like Savage, found it exciting, many was the party at which it was played where the air resounded with cries of, "God, what a drone!" or, "Get that fackin' thing off!"

As the group formed by the Sex Pistols' former lead singer, PiL—as the band stylized their acronym—were always destined to attract attention. "It was a period of great confusion," Lydon recalls of the band's origins in the wake of the US tour that splintered the Pistols. "I didn't know what I would do next. I was left stranded in America, without a plane ticket." Returning to the UK, he found that the legal battle he was now obliged to enter into left him penniless and even nameless. "It was horrible," he says. "Everything was held. The management had claimed they owned everything, including my name. That's why I had to revert to John Lydon. I would have carried on as Mr. Rotten. That created problems, too, in a fan-base kind of way, because they presumed I was changing my personality."

Yet, for Lydon, that he would start a new band regardless was fairly predetermined. "I didn't have much else really to want to do. I'd got the bite for writing songs and I loved it, and I didn't want to stop that." However, a new Lydon-fronted group would be one with different parameters. "In many ways it was a free-thyself-up-young-lad, because I knew there were some serious restrictions in the Pistols, and there wouldn't be in anything that I would do in the future."

Lydon recruited mellifluous ex-Clash guitarist Keith Levene and beginner bassist Jah Wobble (John Wardle to his mum). Canadian student Jim Walker was installed on drums. Though a peculiar lineup, Lydon says that the collective songwriting worked "instantaneously in rehearsal." He explains that they were "just messing about. Wobble was learning. That was fine. We're all amateurs, really. The best thing you can be. And bits just fell together. The very first song that we created was the 'Public Image' theme, which was just absolutely perfect. The words just flowed straight out of my mouth. Unlike in the Pistols, this was people that I hung around with socially. This was an open house for all of us, and freeform and fun. Structure sort of crept in there accidentally." However, recording sessions for PiL's first album were somewhat chaotic. "The record company wanted to pull the plug almost continuously," claims Lydon. "There was a constant reminder that Steve and Paul were trying to put a band together called the Professionals, and 'Here's a cassette, wouldn't it be nice if you sang on it.' That kind of nonsense was going on. It was an uphill struggle, and finances played a serious role in it. Never really got a total session block-booked."

"Public Image," a stomping but stately put-down of the Pistols camp, became a UK Top 10 single in late 1978, and the *First Issue* album, which followed in December, had much to recommend it. The stage was set for PiL to be a major player in a music scene that had been utterly transformed by Lydon's previous band. Lydon was certainly not lacking for inspiration. "I'm always writing. Always. My brain's just flooded with ideas. I'll springboard and hop on anything. If you throw an accordion down the stairs, I'll have a rhythmic pattern to put into that with some sensible choice words."

On PiL's second album, Richard Dudanski—formerly of the 101'ers, Joe Strummer's pre-Clash band—took the place of Atkins. The first fruits of the record were a quite unnerving single released in June 1979, "Death Disco." Many assumed it was a denunciation of the titular musical genre. "I love disco," denies Lydon. "Not the Bee Gees, funnily enough. Them I preferred before they went disco." In fact, the song concerned nothing so petty as musical tastes. "It was about the strange and tragic slow demise of my mother dying of a very, very painful stomach cancer, which tore me apart emotionally," Lydon explains. "I suppose it was shout therapy before Tears for Fears." The track was a most unlikely Top 20 hit. When it resurfaced in a slightly different form on album, the song had been renamed "Swan Lake" in acknowledgment by Levene of an unintentional melodic crib from Tchaikovsky.

Metal Box appeared in November, housed in a round tin designed to emulate a film canister, with PiL's acronym logo embossed on the front. The package contained three discs, one of which had a side with a locked groove. It was a beautiful artifact but destined not to remain so for long: the records were fiendishly difficult to extract without touching or dropping them. As such, it soon became even more of a collector's item than its limited-edition run of sixty-thousand copies might suggest, as mint copies are scarce. Design aesthetics were not the only reason for the format, however. The band sought audio clarity and the most powerful bass sound possible, hence the twelve-inch discs playing at 45 rpm. The album made No. 18 in the UK. Promoting the release, the band were at pains to state that they considered it a collection of singles, not an album as such. Inevitably, however, *Metal Box* was reissued in a more conventional way. Renamed *Second Edition*, and with its tracklisting slightly rearranged, it appeared as a double LP the following February, when it also became the band's first US long-player.

The music to be found across *Metal Box*'s sixty-minute playing time had elements of both Jamaican dub and the avant-garde but was essentially uncategorizable. The ten-minute "Albatross" was skeletal and unearthly. "Memories" was also unearthly but featured skittering guitar lines and key shifts that disconcertingly threatened to be mainstream. The eerie music of "Careering" backed a Lydon lyric that tackled much the same territory as Elvis Costello's "Oliver's Army." Instrumental "Graveyard" gave rise to the suspicion in places that it was quoting "Shakin' All Over" and the *Peter Gunn* theme but still remained resolutely weird. "Radio 4" ended proceedings on an unexpectedly soothing, semi-classical note. Whenever the suspicion arose that all this quasi-formlessness stemmed from a lack of talent, an example of considered layering or canny juxtaposition of sound made clear the musical intelligence behind the project.

Some critics noted that, with *Metal Box/Second Edition*, it was almost as if PiL had decided to ignore all the things people liked about their first album and give them more of the things they didn't like. "No, although that sounds great, ha ha ha," says Lydon. "That's the mood we were ascending to. And spending slightly longer evenings in studios. And slowing the tempo down somewhat. And the subject matter always shape-shifts the track. There's no point in just being dead fast for the sake of it, which is what punk rock sadly turned into. Just a high-speed emptiness. One journalist described it once—and I loved it—as a slow-moving juggernaut of an album. I think that's fairly accurate."

Scared to Live: The Tragedy of the Skids

By 1979, a distinct new form of popular music had begun to take form. Artful, distant, cold, angular, and very European, this music could in no way be described as punk, being far too technically competent and emotionally calm for that. Nor was it new wave, a descriptive bracket which had hitherto been useful for mopping up the likes of the Jam, the Boomtown Rats, and the Stranglers—bands who had come in the door with punks but didn't have much more in common with them (or each other) than the fact that they would have previously been denied entry by the bouncers. In the early 1980s, this new form of music would be given a name, one that initially smacked of a placeholder but eventually—as with so many dummy names—became "official" simply because familiarity seemed to give it a validity. The term was "post-punk," a reference to the fact that without punk's pacesetting rejection of musical and lyrical traditionalism, the genre would never have come into existence.

"We get lumped in with all the post-punk bands, but we were there pretty early, and we always saw ourselves as essentially a punk band," says Richard Jobson of the Skids. Many would take issue with his claim, for the Skids' sophisticated music always seemed well beyond the limits of punk. One thing about which there is no dispute, though, is that the Skids were a band with the type of demons that wouldn't be out-of-place in the punk universe. The severe epilepsy of vocalist and guitarist Jobson gave him, by his own admission, a death wish. Jobson's woes were added to by tragedy when, early in the Skids' career, his girlfriend committed suicide. Guitarist Stuart Adamson's skills saw him likened to Jimi Hendrix, but he was constantly sabotaging his own talent and the group's career. Adamson's demons would later consume him. Amid all of this chaos, however, the Skids made some fine music. Their stature was never greater than in 1979.

Jobson describes the geographical origins of the members of the Skids—who played their first gig in August 1977—as "the rural backwaters of Fife." As for their name, in late 1978 Adamson explained to Garry Bushell of *Sounds*, "To skid means to slide forwards or backwards or sideways. Well that's what we're about—we don't want to be limited by 'direction' or labels." (Note: as with the Buzzcocks and the Eagles, there was technically never a definite article in the Skids' name but, as with those groups' appellations, it would read oddly if "the" didn't precede it, not least because band members didn't practice in interviews what their album typography preached.) Whether punk or post-punk, the Skids were a precocious bunch. Adamson was still a teenager at the inauguration of their recording career. Jobson was even younger, having still not turned nineteen by the time the group released their second album, *Days in Europa*.

The Skids made their recording debut in February '78 with an eponymous EP on new Scottish independent label No Bad. The contents were all written by Adamson, but from this point he and Jobson forged a songwriting partnership—one that involved clear demarcation of roles. "I was the lyric writer and Stuart was the guy who wrote the tunes and the structure of the songs," Jobson explains. "I'd have a melody in my head for the way that the song would work, like 'Saints Are Coming,' and he would take that idea and improve on it."

After being championed by John Peel (the man who made the Hendrix comparison), the Skids snagged a deal with Virgin Records, for whom their debut was the 1978 single "Sweet Suburbia," which inaugurated the band's chart career, climbing to No. 70 in the UK. Follow-up EP *Wide Open* made No. 48. Although "The Saints Are Coming," its lead track, was inspired by anti-war sentiment, the distressed phone call to a father the lyric described was rendered in sufficiently vague terms as to make the song more one of inchoate dread. The broiling, at times electrifying arrangement only deepened the sublime foreboding. The group's first release of 1979, meanwhile, was the single "Into the Valley." It shot them into the big time.

"Into the Valley" was the quintessence of one of Jobson's then obsessions: the use of the working class as cannon fodder. While both Elvis Costello and John Lydon also noted that year that, for many of their peers, joining the British Army seemed their only viable career option, Jobson's observation of this process was a firsthand one. "The area I came from was a series of villages in Central Fife. Most young men followed their fathers into jobs like the coal mines or the shipyards, and those jobs were slowly but surely closing. . . . They ended up in places like Northern Ireland during the height of the Troubles." This had a big effect on Jobson, the only Catholic in a group of Protestants. "They came back quite bigoted and were very anti the nationalist community, and very anti-Catholic." He was also moved at this juncture by his reading of the work of war poets like Robert Graves, Wilfred Owen, and Siegfried Sassoon.

The supreme irony, however, is that "Into the Valley" and similarly themed Skids songs like "The Saints Are Coming" and "Melancholy Soldiers" were stirring, anthemic, even martial. Jobson explains the paradox thus: "A lot of the tunes that I was familiar with were hymns." He also invokes the anthemic chanting patterns he had absorbed on soccer-ground terraces: "I was a big fan of Celtic."

"Into the Valley" highlighted another Skids paradox: the band could be both musically engaging and lyrically impenetrable. A study of the song words reveals a posturing but articulate denunciation of young men "deceived and then punctured." Those without access to the inner sleeve of the band's debut album, however, would not be fully cognizant of that, for Jobson's stylized-cum-yowled diction did not do justice to his lyrics. "It was more about the atmosphere of the song for me than enunciating every syllable," he shrugs. Disconcertingly, though, this may mean that the public consumed the Skids' music in the same way they did "Be-Bop-A-Lula" and "Chirpy Chirpy Cheep Cheep," with the lyrics viewed as nonsense syllables whose meaning was an irrelevance to overall enjoyment.

Jobson paid a further price for this approach in the early 1990s, when Maxell decided to highlight the superior fidelity of their audio-cassette tapes with television commercials that drew attention to songs with infamously unclear lyrics. Thus for an entire generation did the first verse of "Into the Valley" become one that talked of peas sounding divine, suffering sissies, and ironing being done by someone called Viv. The licensee, song publisher, and record company reached an agreement without approaching the artist. Jobson thinks he knows why: "I was quite shocked when I saw it, and I absolutely hated the ad. I don't mind other people having a laugh about these things, but I'm not joining in with it . . . the song's quite a serious song."

Whatever the general public's exact thoughts on Skids lyrics, they made "Into the Valley" a UK No. 10. The record's ascent was helped by an extraordinary performance on BBC TV chart show *Top of the Pops*. Following a seizure, Jobson had missed the program's rehearsal. "The director—who had done rehearsal with the band—had no idea that I was going to be jumping about doing high kicks and flying about the stage. I said to Stuart before, 'Let's just go for it and see what happens.' The camerawork's all over the place, 'cause they didn't know what was going on. That adds to the madness of that performance." The Skids didn't see their own "mad" performance because it was transmitted while they were en route back to Scotland. Once there, though, they realized their lives had been transformed. Because Britain was a country that could only boast three television channels, popular music was barely in evidence on the small screen. *Top of the Pops* was therefore the entire nation's meeting place for modern music. "We got to our rehearsal space to work and there was hundreds of kids, all skipping school."

"Into the Valley" kicked off *Scared to Dance*, the Skids' first album, released the week after the single. It was a record that had come perilously close to not seeing the light of day after Adamson—angry about the multiple-overdubs approach of producer David Batchelor—walked out of the sessions. "It was a regular occurrence with him," says Jobson of his colleague. "He had dark things in his soul. You never really knew where we were on a day to day basis." Adamson sent an open resignation later to music paper *Record Mirror* in which he fulminated, "Music only exists in the free meals and handouts of high-powered business executives. I don't need it, that's all." Says Jobson, "Stuart had this sense the business end of the music industry was cynical and exploitative." Because his bandmates and session guitarist Chris Jenkins finished up *Scared to Dance* without him, there has been some speculation about how much guitar Adamson played on the album. "There's probably only one song that there's overdubs on, which was actually 'Into the Valley,'" says Jobson. "We tried that on 'Scared to Dance' but it really ruined it, so we just went back to Stuart's playing."

Although Adamson's behavior was clearly frustrating to his colleagues, Jobson notes, "We had a fatalism about it. Punk kind of had that, anyway." Another possible reason for Jobson being resigned to the Skids having unstable foundations is that he had issues of his own. "I had a health condition that was quite serious and severe . . . I didn't really feel that I was going to be around for long, so I'm just going to squeeze the juice out of life. . . . Everybody thought I would be the first one to die." Jobson says that Adamson was very respectful of his epilepsy and understood his existential lifestyle. That Adamson may have felt he was being as tolerant of Jobson's foibles as the latter was of his is suggested by Jobson's observation, "I think it also frustrated him, 'cause he wanted something calmer and deeper. He wanted a home, a mortgage, a wife, children, family, all those things."

The stirring, pounding, and larger-than-life songs on *Scared to Dance* were infused with rock history—Adamson's virtuoso playing betrayed worship at the feet of all the usual guitar heroes—but sounded like little or nothing within that history. There was also a Caledonian timbre in both Jobson's lyrics and Adamson's somehow bagpipe-redolent fretwork—a sound the latter would expand on in his next group, Big Country. "Stuart's guitar playing was unique," says Jobson.

Scared to Dance was a Top 20 album in the UK and critically acclaimed, but there was little opportunity for the Skids to rest on their laurels. In 1979, it was still felt reasonable and commercially feasible for serious pop artistes to release more than one album in the same year, and, just like Joe Jackson and Gary Numan, the Skids released an LP brace. In the Skids' case, though, the idea was more their label's than their own. "It was a different era, and you just got on with it . . . we never had management. That was one of the great failings of the Skids."

However, the band did get to choose their own producer in the shape of Bill Nelson, a cult artist through his leadership of pop-rock outfit Be-Bop Deluxe. "It was my idea," says Jobson. "Because Stuart had been so unhappy during the *Scared to Dance* period, and he really loved Bill Nelson." The first Skids music on which Nelson worked was a song called "Masquerade." "Bill Nelson came to our little shitty rehearsal space in Dunfermline. He didn't really do a huge amount to 'Masquerade,' but he brought the keyboard into it. The keyboard line gives it a kind of anthemic quality." "Masquerade" rose to No. 14. "Everybody loved 'Masquerade,' so everybody felt we were onto a winner," says Jobson.

Jobson found Nelson pushing him even further in the direction of the obscure. "He read the lyrics to 'Masquerade' and was intrigued that I'd managed to get 'Guernica' into a pop song." In some cases, Jobson now employed the cutup techniques of author William Burroughs, that had been made famous by David Bowie, which involved slicing up lyrics and randomly reassembling them.

Days in Europa was released in October '79, with Rusty Egan the credited drummer after Thomas Kellichan had renounced the rock 'n' roll lifestyle for married stability. Apart from "Peaceful Times"—a self-indulgent closer that would only have been excusable or listenable if nobody had ever heard backward tapes before—it was another strong collection. It achieved a reasonable chart peak of No. 32, and spun off another pair of hits. The jerky "Charade" stalled just outside the Top 30. "Working for the Yankee Dollar"—which made No. 20—was possibly Jobson's best anti-war broadside yet. Contradictorily as ever, it had a marching beat and a parade-ground chorus. It also caused lyric-printing pop mags like *Smash Hits* to play host to audacious lines like, "Saw Vietnam as a partisan and wished I'd never been."

However, that something was afoot was revealed by the fact that the label of the single version of "Working for the Yankee Dollar" declared that it had been produced by Mick Glossop. The song had been re-recorded and made shorter and punchier. "The keyboards are much lower in the mix, and it's much more a guitar-oriented song," says Jobson of Glossop's "Yankee Dollar." The same could be said for a remix of the entire album by Bruce Fairbairn, released in March 1980. Quite extraordinarily, the Fairbairn iteration did not replace the original Nelson album but would sit in the racks alongside it. The explanation is complicated. "They were disappointed with the record we gave them," says Jobson of Virgin. The new version was rejigged as well as remixed, with the hit "Masquerade" added and "Pros and Cons" dropped. Jobson explains of the latter, "I think people felt it wasn't adding up to the sum of its parts." Unfortunately, the retained "Peaceful Times" seemed to escape this objective revaluation process.

"We actually took a backseat," says Jobson of the Fairbairn remix. The only active participation the Skids took in the preparation of the recalibrated album was Jobson's sleeve design. Some had considered the first edition of *Days in Europa* controversial for reasons other than Nelson's mix. The LP came housed in a primary-colored cover featuring a woman with a 1930s hairstyle adorning an athlete with a laurel wreath, all beneath gothic lettering. At first glance—or even protracted scrutiny—it resembled nothing so much as Leni Riefenstahl iconography. Moreover, some were beginning to perceive Jobson's lyrics not as nonsensical but as something much more sinister. "One of the myths that go with that whole strange little melee was that the record sleeve was removed or banned," says Jobson. "Neither is true." For the record, he states, "I hate fascism, as any reasonable member of society would . . . the songs that we'd written that used any of that terminology were criticisms." Fair enough, perhaps, but their next album came with a free limited-edition disc whose unwise title was *Strength Through Joy*—a Nazi catchphrase.

After *Days in Europa*, Jobson followed what might be termed the Bowie trail by moving to Berlin. Another reason for the relocation was the German nationality of his girlfriend, Caroline. His new start came to a tragic end after eight months when Caroline—who suffered from drug dependency and depression—killed herself. A devastated Jobson returned to the UK and began drifting around London. "That was the beginning of the end, without even realizing it. Stuart and I were four hundred thousand miles apart because my life was going in a completely different direction, and he was in many ways putting the shutters up, 'cause he had found a girlfriend, wanted to have a family." The band was disintegrating in other ways, too, with bassist Bill Simpson departing.

The Skids' third album was *The Absolute Game*, released in 1980. Recorded with Russell Webb on bass and Mike Baillie on drums, its songs were shot through with Jobson's recent traumas. Jobson opines of the record, "It captures the energy of the first album and inventiveness of the second album." It was the Skids' highest-placing LP, making No. 9.

Adamson actually fired Jobson just before they started recording the band's fourth album, *Joy* (1981). "Then two weeks later called me up and said, 'Oh no, I made a mistake, sorry about that, let's get on with it.' That's what you're dealing with." Worse was to come: Adamson departed before the end of the album's recording. *Joy* has its admirers but failed to chart. The Skids shortly disbanded, with Jobson and Webb teaming up with John McGeoch and John Doyle of Magazine in a sort of post-punk supergroup, the short-lived Armoury Show.

Adamson, meanwhile, made a most unlikely transition to stadium-filling superstar, Big Country effecting the lucrative Stateside breakthrough to which the Skids had never come close. "They were very successful in a much wider sense than the Skids ever were," says Jobson. "But even that wasn't enough." Big Country split in October 2000 after eight LPs. In 2001, Adamson was found hanged in a hotel room in Hawaii. He was forty-three. Even with all the trauma he'd seen firsthand with Adamson, Jobson says, "I never saw that coming."

While Jobson didn't match Adamson's post-Skids musical success, he has made successful ventures into several other areas of the arts, including spoken-word recording, television presenting, record production, prose writing, scriptwriting, and film direction. Music, however, clearly continues to form an important part of his DNA: in the twenty-first century, he revived the Skids' name, recording and gigging with a lineup that featured ex-Skids and Big-Country members.

Whatever the difficulties and ultimate tragedy of the Skids' story, it can't be denied that it contained triumph, and nowhere more so than in that frenetic last year of the seventies. "Seventy-nine was an amazing year," says Jobson. "There was so much competition. Every night there was a band playing somewhere." He is proud of the Skids' place in this glittering firmament. "The band made a stamp."

3
MARCH

It's noteworthy how many miserabilist works were considered worthy of critical attention in 1979 and, in the UK at least, even made the charts. It's difficult to imagine such studied glumness finding favor today, especially when aligned with not particularly stellar music. March, for instance, saw the release of Magazine's second LP, *Secondhand Daylight*, which, although a UK Top 40 album, was—as well as being glum—a rather static affair. It certainly had little of the vitality of "Shot by Both Sides," the excellent single from the band's 1978 debut album, *Real Life*. Some critics, noticing that "Shot by Both Sides" was co-written with Pete Shelley, postulated that Howard Devoto's defection from the Buzzcocks had deprived him of Shelley's pop acumen.

Meanwhile, the era was one in which it was generally felt that any act that left a gap longer than a year between studio albums was running the risk of being forgotten by its fans. That risk was considered even more acute in the wake of the public declarations by punks that such periods of inactivity were typical of the rock establishment's decadence. Roxy Music were one of five behemoths whose 1979 album came after what was—for the time—a long hiatus. The Rolling Stones and the Who excepted, it had seemed in the previous two years as though the rock aristocracy were sitting out the punk revolution that had declared them irrelevant, although in truth there were unrelated and complex reasons for the respective absences of Roxy, the Eagles, Fleetwood Mac, Led Zeppelin, and Pink Floyd. However, the sales of the 1979 returnees seemed unaffected by either their recent low visibility or the disapproval of the new wave. Roxy Music's comeback album, *Manifesto*, made the UK Top 10 and No. 23 on *Billboard*—their highest US album chart placing ever. It opened with defiant artiness in the shape of two and a half slow and instrumental minutes. Even so, the pointer to their future (and one of the few highlights of a dull set) was "Dance Away," a glittering but conventional ballad. By the time of their next LP, the hit-packed *Flesh + Blood* (1980), they were—apart from their perennial sophistication—unrecognizable as the band whose suave fare was once completely at odds with their platform-booted, teen-idol image.

"Glad to Be Gay" by the Clash-alike Tom Robinson Band induced a lot of discomfort in 1978, ironically the year at the tail-end of which the cheerful homosexual innuendoes of the Village People's "Y.M.C.A." topped the singles chart in TRB's native Britain. ("Y.M.C.A.'s" three weeks at the summit gave the Villagers the first UK No. 1 single of 1979.) The track that led off TRB's *Rising Free* EP, "Glad to Be Gay," undermined people's prejudices by quoting them at them ("The buggers are legal now—what more are they after?"). Like "Y.M.C.A.," it had a memorable sing-along chorus but, with it laboring under an unofficial BBC ban, stalled at No. 18. The leftist ensemble were much too value-for-money (VFM)-oriented to include either that track or their Top 5 hit "2-4-6-8 Motorway" on their 1978 debut album *Power in the Darkness*, but it was nonetheless a rewarding and exciting collection of hard-riffing, melodic, literate agitprop. Regrettably, the potential for an equally powerful follow-up was handicapped by personnel upheaval.

Robinson was an excellent bassist and Danny Kustow a guitarist who galvanizingly sounded like he was wrenching every note out of his very viscera, but the band were severely depleted by the successive losses of *wunderkind* keyboardist Mark Ambler and blistering drummer Dolphin Taylor. On *TRB Two*, big-name producer Todd Rundgren couldn't disguise the fact that replacements Ian Parker (keyboards) and Preston Heyman (drums) had plenty of skill but none of the departed pair's gutsiness. Meanwhile, Robinson had shot his lyrical bolt, his song words no longer possessing the verisimilitude that gave the first album's songs such streetwise resonance. Piano-based love songs like "Hold Out" and the female-vocalist decorated "Sweet Black Angel" flirted uncomfortably with the more insipid end of the mainstream, the Peter Gabriel–co-written Taylor putdown "Bully for You" had an incongruous electro beat, the comedy numbers "Crossing Over the Road" and "Law and Order" felt like makeweights, "Days of Rage" was a pedestrian and unconvincing recounting of proletarian teenage fury, and "Let My People Be" was a generic condemnation of US imperialism. Only the stately, seething "Blue Murder"—easily the best of a spate of late-seventies songs by various British bands about the *cause-célèbre* death, post–police custody, of a man named Liddle Towers—reached the heights of anything on the first album. Later in '79 came the execrable disco single "Never Gonna Fall in Love (Again)," co-written by Robinson with Elton John. Although it has turned up on TRB compilations, the fact that it was formally credited to Tom Robinson with the Voice Squad mercifully prevented it from being a pitiful swansong for a great group: the Tom Robinson Band had split by the summer.

In their native United States, Sparks are merely a cult, but in Britain they were chart regulars from 1974 onward. The pair of brothers who comprised the act had a peculiar image: vocalist Russell Mael was a tousle-headed heartthrob, while keyboardist Ron cultivated a look of Hitler turned to stone. Their brand of Bizarro World pop (e.g., the falsetto, breakneck "This Town Ain't Big Enough for Both of Us") was, by late '75, reaping fewer dividends. To revive their fortunes, they turned to Giorgio Moroder. The mastermind behind Donna Summer's success was possibly the producer of 1979, helming Summer's *Bad Girls*, *3D* by the Three Degrees, and, for Sparks, *No.1 in Heaven*. Sparks' transformation from an act backed by organic instruments into a synth-dominated, electro-beat-propelled proposition was bound to alienate some. Although jumping on the disco bandwagon was a common enough occurrence for the period, it was usually for just one track, and not usually executed by artists whose catalogue pronounced their iconoclasm. However, the pair couldn't really be accused of compromising their art. The music of the majority of the six songs on *No. 1 in Heaven* may have been written by the brothers with Moroder, but their lyrical playfulness was way beyond the imagination of Summer. Their grooves, however, weren't as enjoyable as Summer's. Cut-down versions of "The Number One Song in Heaven" and "Beat the Clock" took Sparks into the upper echelons of the UK hit parade again, but the album only made No. 73 in its sole week on the chart, while across the Atlantic it didn't crack the *Billboard* Top 200.

The same emphatically could not be said for Supertramp's *Breakfast in America*. Supertramp started out in the late sixties as prog-rock before gradually evolving, after lineup changes, into a contradiction in terms: prog-pop. Keyboardist Rick Davies and guitarist/keyboardist Roger Hodgson were the quintet's songwriting crux, though they tended to write separately rather than in collaboration. They'd had a series of hit singles and albums in their native UK since '74, but Supertramp's progress Stateside had been more incremental. *Breakfast in America* didn't sound much different from what preceded it, consisting of smooth-rolling melodies and sardonic lyrics decorated by both elegant electric piano—an instrument popular in the seventies for its perceived modernism, now rarely heard—and John Helliwell's sublime saxophone solos. On the debit end, their soundscapes were as emptily ornate as their famously arty album covers and were slathered with harmonies that were like Queen's massed vocals taken to their logical, effete conclusion. Enough people liked that brew to send the album to No. 3 in the UK and to the very top in the States, where it remained for six weeks. The syncopated catchiness of the enlightenment-seeking "The Logical Song" made it a Top 10 single both sides of the Atlantic.

Squeezing Out a Career: Graham Parker

By 1979, Graham Parker's time in the sun had actually come and gone. Only recently the hot new thing, unexpected outside events had served to make him seem lukewarm. Yet it was in '79 that he released the audacious "Mercury Poisoning"—a track that was an extraordinary attack on his previous record label—and *Squeezing Out Sparks*, an album that for most aficionados constituted the peak of the remarkable four-album creative arc he had begun in 1976.

Parker was born in 1950 in Hackney, London, but grew up in Deepcut, Surrey, "a little village surrounded by provincial towns." An exception to the standard pattern of artists who harbored goals of stardom from an early age, he lived an aimless, itinerant life until he was approaching his mid-twenties. It was at this point that he began taking seriously his guitar noodling and repudiating contemporaneous prog-rock in favor of old Eddie Cochran, Rolling Stones, and Otis Redding records. "I suddenly became this totally different person," he recalls. "It started to become this belief system: I had to reinstate the old ideas of pop music."

When Parker took his first steps toward a professional music career, his manager, Dave Robinson, put together for him an incredibly accomplished group that would ultimately be named the Rumour: Bob Andrews (keyboards), Martin Belmont (guitar), Andrew Bodnar (bass), Stephen Goulding (drums), and Brinsley Schwarz (guitar). It was this ensemble that backed Parker on his April 1976 debut album, *Howlin' Wind*. The American iconography of tracks like "White

Honey," "Gypsy Blood," "Back to Schooldays," and "Soul Shoes" was rather generic, and Parker readily admits this: "I was just taking all that great stuff and rewriting it. It wasn't that original, but I was doing it in my own way." However, the verve and the richness of the music— which included horn charts—was often irresistible. Moreover, in the tormented, simmering title track and epic broiling reggae closer "Don't Ask Me Questions" (later a minor UK hit in a live iteration), he found his own voice in vistas of apocalyptical despair that—crucially—were alien to the escapism and complacency of the mid-seventies rock scene.

Buoyed by rapturous reviews on both sides of the Atlantic, Parker put out his follow-up only six months later. Consequently, and predictably, *Heat Treatment* was much the same as the first LP but not quite as good, even if the snarlingly anti-careerist "That's What They All Say" was right in tune with the emerging punk zeitgeist. The rough-and-ready timbre of *Stick to Me* (1977) was a shock to those who loved the slickness of the first brace of albums. Others were converted to Parker precisely because of that, having found those records slightly staid. It certainly proved that Parker's songwriting well hadn't run dry, with coruscating reggae "Problem Child" and romance-demystifying "Thunder and Rain" particularly impressive.

It was the last studio album Parker would release in the States through Mercury Records, which—like his British label Vertigo—was a subsidiary of Phonogram. Robinson lays the blame for Parker's failure to become a Stateside star directly at Mercury's feet, and in fact effectively credits the label with inspiring him to set up Stiff Records. "[Managing] Graham Parker had taught me that the major record companies really didn't know what they were doing," says Robinson. "He really should have taken off. He had a career in America that was going great guns. Even Bruce Springsteen had come to a couple of gigs and was depressed that Graham was taking the space that he thought he was going to get into it." Robinson claims that the Chicago-based Mercury was oriented not toward Parker's rock but to jazz and funk. "That was the market in that particular part of the country. Graham was really happening on the East Coast and started to happen on the West Coast, but Mercury didn't see him, and so they didn't support his tours with promotion, etc."

Robinson's response wasn't only to set up the primary independent label of the age. "My manager said, 'Write a whole album of hate songs about Mercury,'" Parker recalls. He composed "Mercury Poisoning." Parker's UK record company refused to issue it in the UK, but his new US label, Arista, released it as the B-side to an incongruous cover of the old Jackson 5 hit "I Want You Back." Taken at face value, "Mercury Poisoning" was a searing onslaught against a record company that the artist claimed was trying to "cripple" him and that constituted "the worst trying to ruin the best." Except Parker sees the song—and Mercury—very differently to how Robinson does. "They couldn't help it," Parker says of the label. "They had nowhere to place my music in 1976. There was no category." As for the putative album of Mercury putdowns, he explains, "I wrote one and thought, 'That's a lot of fun actually, it's a funny song,' but I said to Dave, 'That's it.' We didn't even put it on an album." Parker, in fact, bears no grudges against any of the labels with which he has been associated. "Quite honestly, the record companies gave me more money every fucking year. I haven't really been hard done by. I had fans in record companies. They believed in me."

Parker and Robinson parted company after Parker's third album on what Robinson says were "reasonable terms," but not before Robinson had set in motion *Squeezing Out Sparks*. It was Robinson who suggested Jack Nitzsche as producer. The veteran studio man—famous for his work with Phil Spector, the Rolling Stones, Buffalo Springfield, and

Neil Young—had helmed "Mercury Poisoning," but the album itself got off to an awkward start. Recalls Robinson, "Graham gave me a call and said, 'We need to have a talk, 'cause Jack is not that keen on the tracks. So I went down to the studio. He didn't dislike the tracks. He liked them, but he thought the band were all playing far too much. He wanted to pare back their playing, which was probably a very good thing. At that point the Rumour maybe overplayed on the basis that they had been around longer than Graham. He wasn't the kind of guy that would say, 'Don't play that, don't play this.' Jack Nitzsche had a real attitude and the band were a bit grumpy, but after they tried a few of his ideas they realized they were great."

"It's stripped down," Parker says of the sound Nitzsche conferred on *Squeezing Out Sparks*. "There's no horn section. The keyboards are buried a bit." This defenestrated musical landscape helped give *Squeezing Out Sparks* its extraordinary intensity. The album never let up, its ten tracks seething and simmering—indeed, giving off sparks— whether they were rockers ("Discovering Japan"), ballads ("Love Gets You Twisted"), or exercises in whimsy ("Waiting for the UFOs"). Parker's lyrics were, as ever, high grade. In "You Can't Be Too Strong," he howled of an abortionist, "He wishes to God that he was dead," the music descending in perfect tandem with the protagonist's spirits. It created a moment of genuine drama and thoughtfulness rare in popular music. Ditto for his comment about a sexually exploited woman in "Discovering Japan," "Seeing a million miles between their jokes and smiles." Robinson is by no means alone in thinking the album an "incredible record." Celebrated American rock critic Robert Christgau described it as "perfect, untamable rock and roll . . . ten songs so compelling that you're grateful to the relative lightweights for giving you a chance to relax."

Once again, though, the contrast between the respective points of view of Parker and Robinson is startling. While acknowledging the "quality of the writing," Parker dismisses the album overall as lacking authenticity. Said falseness stems from the very simplicity he enabled by hiring Nitzsche. "It's a total anomaly," Parker says of the LP. "It's not me at all. It's me trying to catch up with new wave two years after the fact." He states that he engaged Nietzsche's services not because of his illustrious past but because he'd worked on Mink Deville's "Spanish Stroll," which he describes as "one of the earliest things that was called new wave."

That Parker should want to jump on the punk/new wave bandwagon is understandable, for it had somewhat stolen his thunder. In his first year as a recording artist, he had seemed something analogous to the future of rock 'n' roll. "Graham was a very tough exponent of the music," says Robinson. "A reaction against the platform shoes and the haircuts and the satin trousers and things. He was singing about a different England, a different world." That status ended almost as quickly as it began when, the very same year, the emerging UK punk scene served to make Parker's shtick—romanticism and epic anger backed by a virtuoso band and delivered in an American accent—seem suddenly old-fashioned. Robinson: "The musical moment had moved. Punk got in the way of a lot of people's careers." Ironically, Robinson bears some responsibility for that fact because it was Stiff that issued quintessential punk records "New Rose" (the Damned), "One Chord Wonders" (the Adverts), and "Another World" (Richard Hell).

Yet for all that, *Squeezing Out Sparks* was Parker's commercial peak, making No. 18 in the UK and No. 40 in the US. It was only with the lackluster *The Up Escalator* (1980, the UK release through the aegis of Robinson via Stiff) that a reputational decline set in, as Parker began to be perceived in his native country as something of a sellout for gravitating to American producers and session musicians. "It seemed like a typical English thing," shrugs Parker. "They loved me for a bit, then they got something more interesting, and now they fucking hate me. I'd seen that happen before. I'd read those music rags for years." However, it has to be said that the hackneyed approach of his new American associates was a bizarre counterpoint to his knowing and scabrous lyrics. The US breakthrough for Parker that the ditching of the Rumour seemed designed to secure never came to pass. His critical free fall continued. The solemn passion that had once made Parker such a breath of fresh air on the smug, pre-punk music scene now ossified into a generalized animus that even had long-term admirer Christgau (who awarded him an "A" grade for three of his first four albums) shovel him into an irrelevancy garbage bin he termed "Everything Rocks and Nothing Ever Dies."

Parker, though, has kept on rolling at a lower level, regularly issuing albums and continuing to play gigs, sometimes with the re-formed Rumour, sometimes with other bands, and sometimes accompanied only by his guitar. He has even branched out to some acclaim into prose writing. He has a much mellower perspective on his professional journey than the snarling persona that emanates from his peak-era works would lead one to expect. "I've got tons of fans who think that *Deep Cut to Nowhere* [2001] is my best record," he says easily. "I've got tons who think that *Struck by Lighting* [1991] is my best record. I've got quite a lot that think that *Don't Tell Columbus* [2007] is my best record. There are a lot of people that have moved with me."

I'm the Man (Well, Sometimes): Joe Jackson

That Joe Jackson released two albums in 1979 is, on the surface, impressive. If truth be told, however, neither *Look Sharp!* (March) nor

I'm the Man (October) were inordinately remarkable. Both, however, contained classic singles.

The lyrics on the debut were consistently above average but were also cheerless. They also often stooped to generic putdowns. Meanwhile, the music was slightly dull, even as it irritatingly affected a hipster cool. The unequivocal exception was "Is She Really Going Out with Him?" Issued in September 1978 as Jackson's entrée, it was something special from its inaugural strutting bassline onward. Its lyric found the narrator seething from his window at the spectacle of pretty women out walking with gorillas down his street. The track contained a chorus that seemed ingeniously to circle back on itself and an infectious exchange—*"Look over there!"* / *"Where?"*—that became a call-and-response between performer and audience at Jackson concerts. It finally became a hit in August '79, making No. 13 in the UK. Although it only reached No. 21 in the US, symbolically it entered the *Billboard* chart the month before it did the UK table, while the album reached No. 20 Stateside, twenty places higher than its UK peak. From the start, America—a country to which he ultimately relocated—was more receptive to Jackson.

I'm the Man was like a sharper, more nuanced version of the first long-player. Once again, though, it was just a tad boring and unlovable. Also once again, there was a diamond in the rough. When released on single, the blunt, colloquial language of the smoldering "It's Different for Girls" truly jumped out of radio sets, starting with its attention-catching opening line, "What the hell is wrong with you tonight?" What seemed merely a startlingly frank acknowledgment of the downsides of relationships, however, turned out to have even greater depths. The composer explained of the title to the *NME*'s Charles Shaar Murray, "[It's] a phrase that you hear a lot. It reverses the stereotype relationship: in this song the girl just wants a fuck and it's the bloke who's getting all sensitive." *I'm the Man* made No. 12 in the UK and No. 22 Stateside.

"It's Different for Girls" failed to crack the *Billboard* Hot 100, but—as with "Is She Really Going Out With Him?"—became a UK hit in the calendar year after its first appearance, making No. 5. Idiotically, Jackson destroyed his chart momentum by following up the single with an untitled EP fronted by a version of Jimmy Cliff's "The Harder They Come" that was not only apropos of nothing but sung in a ludicrously stylized American accent. On this slightly bizarre note, Jackson's brief era of greatness came to an end.

4
APRIL

Several critics placed the Roches' eponymous 1979 debut album in their "Albums of the Year" lists. A trio of Irish-American sisters, their acoustic-based songs quirkily and humorously addressed the minutiae of ordinary life, like disapproving of a friend's new boyfriend or regretting being fired, all sung in incongruously heavenly harmony.

At the other end of the career scale, *Black Rose: A Rock Legend* was Thin Lizzy's ninth studio album. The purveyors of melodic, anthemic hard rock propelled by twin-guitar riffs had proven themselves capable of classics, particularly the fist-clenching "The Boys Are Back in Town," but with their 1979 long-playing outing they unexpectedly came the closest they ever had to consistency across the course of an album. "Do Anything You Want To" and "Waiting for an Alibi" were high-notch outlaw anthems and UK hit singles. While front man and chief songwriter Phil Lynott displayed his traditional awkwardness with the female sex on the grisly, would-be endearing "S&M," he redeemed himself a little with the tribute to his daughter "Sarah," even if it was melodically generic and incongruously synth-poppy. The seven-minute closing suite, "Róisín Dubh (Black Rose): A Rock Legend," was a pleasing reminder of the band's breakthrough hit, "Whiskey in the Jar," which had been the world's first intimation that Celtic folk could be married to kickass rock 'n' roll.

April also saw the release of two noble failures. *Y* by British sort-of punks the Pop Group featured agonized vocals, funky guitars, staccato tunes, disconnected fragments of instrumentation, unsettling sound effects, and sampled media voices. It was sometimes compelling but ultimately unlistenable. Meanwhile, Lou Reed was currently recording for Arista Records. Following the albums *Rock and Roll Heart* and *Street Hassle*, he now issued the jazz-inflected *The Bells*. Like his other efforts for the label, it was hampered by a then-voguish recording process called "binaural," which supposedly had a 3-D effect on headphones but was a muffled experience for anyone listening without their benefit. However, and also like his other Arista LPs, it found him in a thoughtful and tender mood not seen since the days of the Velvet Underground, something underlined by several collaborations with sensitive rocker Nils Lofgren. Only the self-lacerating "Stupid Man" and the atmospheric "City Lights" came close to Reed's previous greatness, but, for many, it was just a relief that he'd laid off being so ornery.

45 rpm to the Rescue: The Year in Singles

The biggest-selling single in Britain in 1979 was by Art Garfunkel. Many of his US compatriots will not even have heard of "Bright Eyes" but, though it failed to make the *Billboard* Hot 100, the six weeks the record spent at No. 1 in the UK from April 14 made it one of those hits so omnipresent that eventually its opening notes inspired groans even from onetime fans. Written by jobbing composer Mike Batt, "Bright Eyes" was a track from the previous year's animated cinema adaptation of the anthropomorphic rabbit novel *Watership Down*. Its potentially laughable premise—it described the despair of a character whose fellow warren dweller had been shot by a farmer—was provided a pathos by the combination of a lush arrangement and Garfunkel's soaring vocal. It was certainly a contrast to the American top seller that year, the Knack's randy, even distasteful "My Sharona," which also sat at the summit for six weeks.

Whether they were Garfunkel or the Knack, wholesome or dubious, corny or edgy, singles were the music industry's savior that year. Nineteen seventy-nine was the biggest year ever for sales in the 45 rpm format, and the culmination of a surprising spike. The years 1973 to 1975 had seen an incremental decline in singles sales—one that was expected, even desired. Since the turn of the decade, both recording artists and record companies (as the businesses purveying music for sale to the public were then known) had effectively been insisting that single-song consumption was only for little kids or non-serious, "casual" music consumers. Artists insisted that albums were the real deal, the aesthetic statement to which they wanted the public to pay attention. For their own reasons—"price-performance ratio"—record companies were also keen on this perception.

Then something odd happened. In 1976, sales of singles didn't follow the pattern of year-on-year decline but instead increased, rising from 483 million units globally to 516 million. They then continued that annum-on-annum rise, culminating in the decade's final year in a plateau of 624 million units sold worldwide. Theories on why varied, ranging from the renewed importance of singles as a standalone entity in the VFM-oriented age of punk to the fact that the "second oil crisis" had triggered a worldwide recession that simply meant people could only afford a couple of singles with their weekly pay packet, rather than an album. There was also the influence of disco. Although it was said by detractors (and some devotees) to be bearable only on single, disco's phenomenal domination of shorter-format releases in the late seventies, particularly 1979, meant that it, more than any other genre of music, was responsible for the medium's continued health.

Those disco releases are dealt with in the genre's own section in this text. Many other important 1979 singles are addressed in this book's chapters on individual artists. Which leaves us with novelties, miscellanea, and singles by artists not renowned for notable albums—none of which descriptions, note, are intended as pejoratives, and none of which necessarily preclude listenability.

For instance, B. A. Robertson, a long-faced purveyor of lightweight pop. In the UK, he made No. 2 with "Bang Bang" (a galloping, hook-laden examination of the way the highest and mightiest can be felled by love) and No. 8 with "Knocked It Off" (a sort of British equivalent of Joe Walsh's "Life's Been Good"), both delivered for some reason in a London accent that was nothing like his natural Scottish burr. Surprisingly, he proved capable of much more heavyweight material, albeit in conjunction with Terry Britten, with whom he wrote most of the contents of *Rock 'n' Roll Juvenile*. The latter was Cliff Richard's album of 1979, one of several in the pioneer British rocker's long career considered to be a comeback record. The track "Carrie" was a smokily atmospheric tale of a man searching for the missing (implicitly murdered) woman of the title that, when released as a single early in 1980, went Top 5. The album's 1979 hit was "We Don't Talk Anymore," written by Alan Tarney. A sober, mid-tempo, highly melodic dissection of a decaying relationship, it spent four weeks in the UK top spot across August and September.

"*Uh-ooh! Uh-ooh!*" was one of the most nagging refrains of the first months of 1979, embedding itself in radio listeners' helpless brains with its infectious mindlessness. Not that its vocal refrain was the only singular thing about Lene Lovich's "Lucky Number," which peaked at No. 3 in the UK in March and became a cult favorite in her native United States. The record featured a lyric that mixed colloquialism with lines that sounded like they were lifted from a psychoanalysis manual ("The object of the action is becoming clear"), all delivered in a chirruping and quasi–Eastern European style. Witnessing Lovich perform her song on television added an extra dimension of weirdness to what was already a peculiar experience, for—with her bug eyes and mouse-ears headgear—she was a decidedly strange character, possibly one unprecedented in pop, where eccentricity was then usually the preserve of male artists.

In October, Buggles mounted the UK summit with "Video Killed the Radio Star." Though much about Buggles revolved around now outdated futuristic imagery, their debut single was the reverse: genuinely prescient. At the dawn of promotional films that evinced more craft than the songs they were promoting, guitarist Trevor Horn sensed that an era was about to pass. He wrote down his thoughts in a song with keyboardist Geoff Downes and early Buggles member Bruce Woolley. Some have likened the melody of "Video Killed the Radio Star" to a series of jingles, but that seemed more conceptual than deficient, and the lyric—which depicted a former professional musician shattered by a world whose affections had switched from sound to screen—had real poignancy ("Pictures came and broke your heart"). Although the record only just crept into the US Top 40, it became famous Stateside in 1981 when its video (as promos were now called) was the first played on MTV, the television channel that was pretty much the embodiment of all Horn's fears.

Boney M. continued to be a sales sensation in the United Kingdom, although inevitably not quite as much of a sensation as they had been the previous year. A four-piece black vocal group, they were put together by West German producer and songwriter Frank Farian. Marcia Barrett, Liz Mitchell, and Maizie Williams hailed from the Caribbean, while Bobby Farrell, the sole male member, was Dutch. Farian actually sang the lines lip-synched by Farrell, while Williams is also thought to have not appeared on the records. When glimmers of this situation of semi-puppetry reached them, the public cared not—especially in Britain, where Boney M. had nine consecutive Top 10 hits. Some classify them as disco, but their repertoire was too inchoate to define them as that or anything else, as demonstrated by their apparently random 1978 cover of "Rivers of Babylon," a biblical reggae number that had become known in the West from its inclusion on the soundtrack to Jamaican movie *The Harder They Come*. Boney M.'s interpretation made No. 30 on *Billboard*—their only record to go higher than No. 65 on the Hot 100. In Britain, it was No. 1 for five weeks, and, in a country whose relatively low population makes million-sellers rare, sold two million.

As 1979 began, Boney M. occupied the No. 2 spot with "Mary's Boy Child / Oh My Lord," the Christian ballad that had given them the coveted Christmas chart-topper. Four further hits followed that year: "Painter Man" (No. 10), "Hooray Hooray It's a Holi-Holiday" (No. 3), "Gotta Go Home" / "El Lute" (No. 12), and "I'm Born Again" (No. 35). Their album *Oceans of Fantasy*, which appeared in September and topped the UK chart, didn't mop up all the relevant singles even though it clocked in at nearly fifty-five minutes, making it almost a third longer than the average vinyl LP of the era.

Unexpectedly, Boney M. provided one of the most heartwarming music-related stories of 1979. "Painter Man" had been a sixties hit in West Germany for British band the Creation, vendors of freakbeat whose guitarist, Eddie Phillips, pioneered the practice of playing electric guitar with a violin bow. In 1966, "Painter Man," an anthemic lament for the pitfalls of the freelance illustrator's life written by Phillips with Creation vocalist Kenny Pickett, was released as the band's second single. It climbed into the lower reaches of the UK Top 40, but in West Germany made the Top 10, which is presumably why Farian was cognizant of it. Strange material to require their female vocalists to declaim, it was one of Boney M.'s lesser hits. However, as it was also included on the group's 1978 *Nightlight to Venus* LP, Farian's choice had a profound effect on Pickett and Phillips, who had in recent years become a jobbing songwriter and a bus driver, respectively. Phillips described what occurred next as a "little bit of a fairy story." After having gone through crushing experiences in the music industry, he suddenly found that fortune had come his way without him even trying. "It was unbelievable, 'cause I think the album sold, worldwide, millions," he observed.

Herb Alpert's "Rise" was appropriately named. The trumpeter's Latin sound was once so popular that at one point in 1966 he had an astonishing four albums simultaneously in the *Billboard* Top 10, but he had disappeared from the charts after 1968. When he reappeared with this mellow, disco-inflected instrumental, which spent two weeks at the US summit (and reached No. 13 in the UK), Alpert became the only artist ever to reach No. 1 on the *Billboard* Hot 100 as both a vocalist and an instrumentalist.

"Pop Muzik" was the work of Robin Scott, who traded under the name M. With its catchy riffs, arch female backing vocals, hipster lyric, and Kalashnikov lead vocal, it was almost as if Scott had managed to distill the very essence of great pop. The record's success was therefore unsurprising, it making No. 2 in his native Britain and going one higher Stateside.

Two records stay the hand of anyone inclined to mock the rather conservative and treacly tastes of American singles purchasers of the era in comparison to the far more eclectic British singles-buyer's palate. "One Day at a Time" had been a Top 40 US hit for Marilyn Sellars in 1974. As Kris Kristofferson was known for bringing countercultural values to country, it was somewhat surprising that he should have co-composed (with Marijohn Wilkin) a number that implored Jesus to "give me the strength to do every day what I have to do." It was equally surprising that, when Scottish singer Lena Martell revived the song, it should in October '79 make the top spot in the UK, a nation far less religious than the US, and stay there for three weeks. Dr. Hook's "When You're in Love with a Beautiful Woman" was a US Top 10 hit but actually spent three weeks in the UK top spot from November 17. It continued the rather schizophrenic career of a band who often went in for innuendo and zaniness on album tracks but consistently made the hit parade with stylized love songs like this Even Stevens composition.

The natural order, however, was recognizable in other songs that had lesser appeal for the British and maximum for Americans. Boy-girl duo Peaches and Herb's "Reunited"—a slow, sweet, but corny soul number celebrating resurrected love—made the Top 5 in the UK but spent four weeks on top of the *Billboard* chart. The Commodores' ponderous piano ballad "Still" made No. 4 in the UK but climbed all the way to the summit across the Atlantic. The Doobie Brothers' staccato-riffed, sweetly cooed, slightly sickly "What a Fool Believes" (from their 1978 LP *Minute by Minute*) didn't quite make the Top 30 in the UK but was a chart-topper in their native United States. Exactly the same happened with Robert John's soporific ballad "Sad Eyes."

No juxtaposition more perfectly summarized the transatlantic divide than the discs that inhabited the top of the respective singles charts at the end of the year. While Britons "celebrated" Christmas and the New Year with Pink Floyd's wrist-slitting "Another Brick in the Wall (Part II)," Americans were favoring "Escape (the Piña Colada Song)." This Rupert Holmes release—which climbed only as high as No. 23 in the UK—featured an almost conversational vocal that told the story of a man who, bored with his relationship, placed a news-paper personal ad. In it, he described himself as someone who liked drinking Piña Coladas, getting caught in the rain, and making love in cape dunes at midnight. The respondent to his "seeks similar" callout turned out to be his current partner, and their mutual treachery reig-nited their love. Although well crafted and reasonably intriguing, it was all as hokey as any of the notoriously formulaic American made-for-TV movies of the era.

Record companies, of course, cared little about such issues. Instead, they were simply thankful that something was selling. Singles were the only glimmer of hope for the music industry in a year in which it seemed the album might soon very well be dead.

The Wide-Boy Demi-Monde: Squeeze

Come 1981, Chris Difford and Glenn Tilbrook were being hailed by *Rolling Stone* magazine as the Lennon and McCartney of their generation. In 1979, however, their group, Squeeze, was perceived merely as a quirky outfit with a brace of inconsistent albums to their name. Yet Squeeze's promise was glaringly apparent, not simply in the shape of their major UK hits that year but in the fact that "Up the Junction" was a cast-iron classic that—even had they never recorded another note— would have secured them a place in the ranks of pop's immortals.

Guitarists Difford (born 1954) and Tilbrook (born 1957) met as teenagers when Tilbrook answered Difford's shop-window advertisement, ostensibly for a guitarist for a band but in reality for a writing partner. It didn't take long for the pair to establish a composing pattern to which they would cleave: Difford would provide the lyrics and Tilbrook would "set" them. "I stopped writing lyrics when I met Chris," explains Tilbrook. "He was a much better lyricist than I was." Difford says, "I was a lazy backseat driver, really. Glenn would write the melodies and produce and work hard to get the songs out. It became very co-dependent, but it worked very well." Difford's lyrical style would ultimately be a storytelling one. Furthermore, those stories—at least in the early days—would be inflected with the experiences and slang of proletarian London. Difford thinks this inevitable: "If you grow up in South East London, like I did, and you're surrounded by working-class families, you go to school with working-class kids, it's going to rub off on you as you write." However, though many great songwriters hailed from the same sort of background as Difford, few of them had allowed their hinterlands to leak into their lyrics. One of the exceptions, pre-punk, was the Kinks' Ray Davies, whom Difford says he was "definitely influenced" by.

Squeeze were signed to A&M with a lineup of Difford on rhythm guitar, Tilbrook on lead, Jools Holland on keyboards, Harry Kakoulli on bass, and Gilson Lavis on drums. Although Difford occasionally sang, Tilbrook handled most vocal duties, and did so with an attractively lilting voice. The band were assigned no less a producer than ex–Velvet Underground member John Cale. Cale, though, was not enamored of the songs he heard from Squeeze. "All of the good songs that we'd written up to the first album [were] stuck in the bin," says Difford. New songs were assembled. However, the album's single, "Take Me I'm Yours"—which crept into the UK Top 20—was of an even later vintage, being an addendum hastily recorded after A&M complained that there were no obvious 45s. Squeeze's eponymous debut LP was released in March 1978 but failed to chart.

Both Difford and Tilbrook assert that *Cool for Cats*, released a year later, was the first true Squeeze long-player. Not that the second LP was initially any better as far as A&M was concerned. Tilbrook: "We delivered an album to them which they rejected, so we had to go and think again and part of the thinking again was dumping some of the tracks and recording some others." John Wood was brought in to address the difficulties caused by the band's self-production. "*Cool for Cats* was really the culmination of what we'd been doing before that," Tilbrook says of the readjusted record. "It felt like a pop album, and our writing was getting stronger. It was pretty much about our London low-life at the time, which was intriguing."

A case in point is the title track, a stream-of-consciousness of utterly working-class London vernacular, delivered by Difford in an almost comically deadpan style. It's easy to imagine a lot of Squeeze's compatriots—let alone Americans—being befuddled by references to people being in and out of Wandsworth with numbers on their names, and likely lads swearing like how's-your-father. Nonetheless, its clever rhymes and insight into a "wide-boy" (smooth-talking con artist) demi-monde—along with pop smarts that included cooing female backing vocalists and a jaunty keyboard break—sent the track all the way to No. 2 in the UK singles chart.

"Cool for Cats," though, was merely the *hors d'oeuvre* before the banquet that was the album's second single. "Up the Junction" was an utterly convincing depiction of the course of a South London couple's relationship, from bantering first meeting to the joy of parenthood to bitter separation. Its title phrase alluded to a famous novel set in Battersea, the London district in which the busy Clapham Junction is situated. However, Difford co-opted the phrase to mean "in dire straits." Part of the song's verisimilitude stemmed from amusingly recognizable domestic notes. When the narrator was given a job starting on a Monday, he noted, "So I had a bath on Sunday." Baths were still often weekly affairs for Britons in the seventies, while showers were not common household fixtures. Meanwhile, the narrator's final-verse assertion that he would seek reconciliation with his former partner if only begging was his business summed up in one terse couplet an entire sweaty, alcohol-soaked, recrimination-drenched wreck of a life.

The achievement of "Up the Junction" was hard earned, however. Although Difford and Tilbrook resisted the entreaties of their manager, Miles Copeland, to insert a chorus, they did take some structural advice from their record company. "When I was writing my bit, I was thinking it was going to be like Bob Dylan and the Band, like 'Positively

Fourth Street' or something," says Tilbrook. "Just an ambling story. I thought that was good enough. It went through a few changes at A&M's insistence. I have to say they were right, because they spotted a pop song there that I hadn't. The backing track and the track that we recorded was the same, but they said, 'How about a bit of a tune at the beginning and the end, for instance?' We just had chords there. So I went back to the studio and it sort of gave it a focus."

In July '79, the song sailed up the charts. Unfortunately, it ran aground at No. 2. Despite the image they have of hit merchants, Squeeze in fact never had a No. 1 on either side of the Atlantic. Gary Numan (trading as Tubeway Army) was the artist responsible for consigning "Up the Junction" to the badlands oft mentioned in this text of great records that stalled in Britain at No. 2. His "Are 'Friends' Electric?" was as cutting-edge as Squeeze's record was steeped in classic pop values.

The *Cool for Cats* album made No. 45, but anyone who bought it based on those two hits was in for a disappointment. The rest of the material was mostly as leaden-footed as the singles were nimble. Meanwhile, "Touching Me Touching You" ("When I'm touching myself I'm always thinking of you") demonstrated a smuttiness that often ran oddly alongside the band's sensitivity. Perhaps the same could be said of "It's So Dirty" ("She is the business for a bit of old skirt"), although in fairness it sounds more like an example of Difford's penchant for adopting a persona than a personal manifesto. Tilbrook has fond memories of the track because its extended guitar solo revealed another dimension to him. "I thought I was a guitar god earlier on, but I've always put songs first," he reflects. "I think that affected how I'm perceived as a guitarist."

However, it was the songcraft rather than either plank-spanking or "Gorblimey" lyrics that were going to effect a breakthrough for Squeeze in the US. A radio-play version of *Cool for Cats'* penultimate track,

"Goodbye Girl"—a narrative in which a man is robbed by a one-night stand—created a lot of Stateside goodwill, but it was upon the release in 1981 of fourth Squeeze album *East Side Story* that Americans really sat up and took notice, chiefly because of "Labelled With Love," another superb Difford character study, this one ingeniously set by his writing partner to a poignant country arrangement. A UK No. 4, it vies with "Up the Junction" for status of Squeeze's signature song.

By this time, Squeeze were mutating into something quite different. John Bentley had taken over bass duties on the third album, *Argy Bargy* (1980). More significantly, when Holland subsequently departed he was replaced by Paul Carrack, who was seasoned enough to have appeared on the 1975 US Top 3 hit "How Long" by Ace. Carrack not only played keyboards but also had a fine voice that added a tinge of soulfulness hitherto missing in Squeeze's new-wave pop sound—a soulfulness epitomized by the smoldering tale of romantic betrayal "Tempted." Tilbrook: "Gradually, as our horizons expanded, so the pool of knowledge that everyone has that they draw on for their writing expanded as well. A song like 'Tempted' had nothing to do, really, with London boys. It was accidentally a very universal song. He definitely took us up another level." Another way of looking at that, of course, is that Squeeze were losing touch with their hinterland and divesting themselves of the personality that had been a large part of their appeal.

An upside of that draining away of character was that the band were more comprehensible to Americans. Although "Tempted" only just crept into the US Top 50 (they wouldn't start having bona fide US hits until 1987), it was in '81 that Squeeze sold out Madison Square Garden, as well as garnered that Lennon/McCartney comparison. Tilbrook says the comparison was damaging: "That was a quote that was much bandied-about, and I think that our writing became just a little too self-conscious. It took a couple of years to drift back down to earth." It's difficult not to conclude that Squeeze's split after 1982's *Sweets from a Stranger* was partly down to the hubris engendered by that comparison. However, the inevitable *Difford & Tilbrook* album (1984) tanked. Squeeze subsequently began the reformation-split-reformation merry-go-round, but the momentum and the magic were gone.

Difford has been on his own merry-go-round with his masterpiece. "I love 'Up the Junction,'" he says. "I think it's a fantastic song." This might seem a self-evident fact, but he has gone through the same process as many other songwriters have in resenting reminders of the fact that some perceive his greatest works as behind him. "I really enjoy 'Labelled with Love,' and all the hits. Once upon a time I couldn't run fast enough away from some of the stuff that we'd written, but now I enjoy it all."

The Dancing Queen Finally Goes to the Disco: ABBA

"Waterloo," the track with which ABBA achieved their breakthrough by winning the 1974 Eurovision Song Contest, was—like all bubblegum—delicious but devoid of nutrients. Yet in their subsequent recordings, the Swedish four-piece continually developed and experimented, embracing power-pop, synth-pop, and even rock opera. Guitarist Björn Ulvaeus later noted to journalist Jim Irvin, "We would have our ears to the ground all the time, knowing exactly what was happening." It should be no great surprise then that in 1979, ABBA, like so many that year, decided to unleash their disco album.

They had as much right to jump on this bandwagon as anyone: the opening notes of their 1976 hit "Dancing Queen"—though not technically a disco record—instantly fill dance floors worldwide to this very day. Unlike others who were jumping on the bandwagon, ABBA had no credibility to lose: the age was yet to come when critical rehabilitation would confer on them a heavyweight status that would have been almost laughable at the time. However, far from this inducing complacency in ABBA, *Voulez-Vous*—released in April 1979—was a record of some imagination.

The album took an entire year to assemble ('78 was the first calendar year without an ABBA album release since their 1973 long-playing debut). During that time, the quartet moved from Glen and Marcus Music studios to Polar, their own new Stockholm recording base. Because ABBA were never a self-contained group, they were always obliged to hire bassists and drummers. However, the fact that Sweden had a little-known repository of highly skilled sessioners meant that they were not penalized by this: many is the non-Swedish musician who will extol the virtues of ABBA's long-term bassist, Rutger Gunnarsson, and drummer, Ola Brunkert. In Polar, they were for the first time in the pleasing position of not having to watch any clocks. Having said that, time must often have hung heavy in the studio for Ulvaeus and vocalist Agnetha Fältskog after December 1978, when Ulvaeus moved out of the family home, pending their divorce. At the same time, the band's other couple—keyboardist Benny Andersson and vocalist Anni-Frid ("Frida") Lyngstad—moved in the opposite direction, making their union formal in October.

This was the first album where the Andersson/Ulvaeus songwriting axis was not provided assistance by band manager Stig Anderson. Unchanged, though, was the fact that they acted as producers of their own compositions and proffered a formula of sweeping strings and mellifluous keyboards oddly counterpointed by rigid rhythms and clinically arranged vocal harmonizing. On songs like "As Good as New" and the title track, they married that style to pulsating bass lines and four-on-the-floor drums. As noted elsewhere, such disco concoctions could be as suffocating as they could be exciting, but ABBA had an advantage over the "genuine" disco merchants in the shape of their pop craft. With tracks like "Chiquitita"—a beautiful, vulnerable, Latin-inflected ballad—and the chanted utopianism of "I Have a Dream," they were able to provide a pocket of air on the sweaty and stultifying dance floor. The album's only real clinkers were "Lovers (Live a Little Longer)," a would-be-saucy anthem that was merely shrill, and "Does Your Mother Know," a slab of generic rock that would be risible even without memories of Björn performing it onstage in a clinging silver jumpsuit.

Despite the odd American hit—including a No. 1 in "Dancing Queen"—the US was never quite as taken with ABBA as was the rest of the world. *Voulez-Vous* confirmed this fact, managing a mere No. 19 in the *Billboard* album chart and bequeathing only two minor hit singles. Over in the UK, ABBA's record company was able to gleefully milk the album (No. 1 for four weeks) for everything it was worth. "Chiquitita" made No. 2, "Does Your Mother Know" No. 4, the double-A-sided "Angel Eyes" / "Voulez-Vous" No. 3, and "I Have a Dream" No. 2. This meant that precisely half of the album's ten tracks had technically charted. A brace more appeared on B-sides. For those who objected to the plundering of albums for singles—a species far more numerous in the UK than the US—Epic Records was even able to supply a sop in the form of standalone single "Gimme Gimme Gimme," which climbed to No. 3 in November. "Gimme Gimme Gimme" was perhaps the purest of ABBA's forays into disco. Considering its earthiness ("a man after midnight" was what was being demanded in the title phrase), it possessed an absurd degree of solemnity, helped by its frantic timbre and swooping synth riff.

Voulez-Vous was the sixth of ABBA's eight albums. When the group's career dribbled to a close at the end of 1982, they were—whisper it lightly—on the way down: their final clutch of singles only reached chart positions around the No. 30 mark in the UK, a country that had always venerated them.

ABBA arrived at a time when it was not yet quite acceptable for serious musicians to be pop-oriented. However, they showed by sheer example that pop did not rule out substance. An additional, unintended contribution provided by ABBA was the breaking down of barriers in music. Come that posthumous reevaluation of the group, a certain watershed was reached, and a discernible relaxation of standpoint brought about. The concept of guilty pleasures is dying out in a culture where people have been given permission to like what they want on the grounds that, to use a current phrase, "It's all good." In ABBA's case, it was better than most.

The Unsmiling Face of the Future: Gary Numan

In the summer of 1979, the living rooms of Great Britain resounded with incredulous bellows. The cries of "Bloody hell—how did that get to No. 1?" came from people who simply could not get their heads around what possible appeal might be possessed by "Are 'Friends' Electric?," the nation's best-selling single, or the artist who purveyed it. The record was the product of a weird-looking, dead-faced young man with a prematurely high hairline. The song he rendered in a monotone had a doomy lyric and instrumentation that resembled sound effects from a science-fiction motion picture. Those people bewildered by the song and the artist were by no means all old fogies.

Like all things that are a complete departure from the past, Tubeway Army's "Are 'Friends' Electric?" mystified those whose frame of reference it lay beyond. Although it may not have conformed to the prevalent understanding of what constituted a hit, it soon would. It was the very start of the electro-pop revolution that would dominate the coming decade, and which would transform popular music forever.

Tubeway Army was really Gary Numan, the stage name—plucked from a Yellow Pages—of Gary Webb, brought up in Wraysbury near

Slough, an hour's drive from London. Numan was from a supportive family: his father, a British Airways driver, gave him £6,000 (around $11,000 at the time) from his life savings for musical equipment. Despite such nurturing, he had relatively severe psychological issues. "I'm over the top paranoid," Numan told Paul Morley of the *NME*. He could have added that he was also painfully shy, sometimes barely audible in broadcast interviews.

Originally a punk guitarist, Numan's conversion to synthesizers was Damascene. "It was just pure good luck," he confessed to *Q*'s Tom Hibbert in 1991. Working in a recording studio, he happened upon a Minimoog that had obviously been utilized in the session preceding his. "I just had a quick go. I couldn't play keyboards or anything . . . it could have gone *ik* and sounded really crap and I'd have gone, 'Fuck, them synthesizers are a complete pile of shit, I won't get involved with them.' But it sounded great, like a hundred guitars all going at once, such a powerful instrument." It should be noted that although Tubeway Army's sound proceeded to undergo a profound change, it retained a punch often lacking in the tidal wave of synth-pop it engendered because Numan's punk grounding meant that he ended up juxtaposing the synths with gutsier "real" instruments.

Tubeway Army's eponymous first album was released on independent label Beggars Banquet in late 1978. It made few waves at the time, but Numan—moving on at a rate of knots—may barely have noticed. Within less than a year he had released two further albums, on one of them, impressively, acting as his own producer. *Replicas* appeared in April 1979, recorded with a hired synthesizer because Numan still couldn't afford to buy one. The album was preceded by the single "Down in the Park." The latter was unsuccessful, but in May "Are 'Friends' Electric?" was lifted from the album. Plenty of people had as Damascene a conversion about "Are 'Friends' Electric?" as Numan had

had about the instruments it was played on. Such was the newness of its glistening, sterile soundscape that only people who had encountered the likes of Kraftwerk and Ultravox were not liable to be left befuddled or even repulsed by it. Once over the shock, though, it was impossible to deny that the song was giddily stuffed with hooks, melody, and countermelody. The fact that they all had a cold, artificial tone was, puzzlingly, something that didn't seem to matter. The single remained at the summit for a month. Naturally, the parent album followed it up the charts, and on July 21, when both LP and single were at the top, Britain had a new pop sensation. Numan was just twenty-one.

The backlash started early. "Electronic music wasn't considered to be real music at the time," Numan reasoned to j. poet of the *San Francisco Chronicle* in 2006. "Since I was the biggest act in the genre, I got the brunt of the hostility. Even as it became more popular, that hostility stayed focused on me. I also said some arrogant things and that didn't help." One of these arrogant things was an assertion that he thought David Bowie was frightened of him. This was a contemptible point of view for the many who considered Numan a purveyor of secondhand decadence and dystopianism picked up from Bowie records and interviews. However, even at the time it was clear that there was one area where Numan unequivocally trumped Bowie. While Bowie had contracted out the electronic work on his recent "Berlin Trilogy," Numan played all the synth parts himself. Although he admitted to being a one-finger operator, he was audibly dexterous and savvy, knowing enough about contrasts and movements to create electronic mini-symphonies.

In truth, "Are 'Friends' Electric?" was the only "crossover" track on *Replicas*. The rest of the ten cuts were far less pop, being relentlessly bleak and often repetitive. As such, the album was mostly of interest to Numanoids—the mushrooming army of fans who quickly adopted his pancaked, eyelinered, boiler-suited image. The same could be said of the following album, *The Pleasure Principle*.

Released in September 1979, it saw the dropping of the group pretense/name. All of the ten tracks had one-word titles, and several were informed by technology-related toy-town dread. Once again, the identikit stretches of musical droning and verbal whining made it a work palatable only to those with a fanatical penchant for the style. The one glorious exception was "Cars." The song's lyric suggested that an automobile was the safest place to live because its doors could all be locked. Numan didn't seem to understand that he was revealing a subconscious hankering for the comfort of the womb. However, much pop is predicated on risible ideas made palatable—even enjoyable—by good music, and "Cars" had plenty of that. A belching main riff, a gliding counterriff, and crashing percussion all combined to give Numan's neurotic terror the authority of wisdom. "Cars" made No. 1 in the UK singles chart in late September. The week previously, not only had *The Pleasure Principle* scaled the album summit but Numan had secured the feat of having three LPs in the Top 30. Moreover, he'd done all this with minimal promotion. As journalist Bob Woffinden noted, "Probably no major rock star of recent years has received less music press coverage." It's possible that this revelation about how unimportant they could be is another reason why journalists were keen to ridicule Numan.

Cannily, the album's second single—"Complex," released in November—was also equidistant between synth-pop and conventional pop: while graced with the usual robotic vocals, it featured piano and classical strings. Numan's all-conquering year didn't end when it made No. 6. At around the same time, a television commercial for Lee Cooper clothing featured Numan's unmistakable tones singing the refrain, "Don't be a dummy—use your money!" Although it was sung to a piece of electro-pop utterly in his vein, the jingle in fact was written by John Du Cann. It had been recorded in Numan's now-distant days of obscurity. Beggars Banquet's distributors, WEA, inevitably asked Numan to record an extended version for single release, but he resisted the pressure. While Numan might have dismissed the jingle as an adjunct to his art, the fact of his sound leaking into mainstream culture via said commercial was an important development. It indicated that media power brokers understood that synth-pop was not an anomaly but the coming thing. As if to confirm that, the following year "Cars" made the Top 10 in the States.

That Numan failed to capitalize on his US success and, moreover, would never be as big again in the UK would have been predicted by many in 1979. His music seemed at the time a plasticky flash in the pan. The five behemoths who returned triumphantly to the music scene that year certainly gave the impression that the oncoming 1980s were going to be dominated by traditional rock music, just like the seventies had been. In fact, in the next decade, rock started its long slow decline while synthesizer music ballooned. Its originator, though, was left behind. In the eighties, Numan was in the galling position of having to stand and watch as the likes of Depeche Mode, Soft Cell, and Yazoo proceeded to capitalize on his breaching of the electro-pop dam while his sales went into free fall. He also became even more of a figure of fun, mocked by the media for his mishaps in his airplanes, his hair transplant, his comic book–style musical concepts, his unhip public yearning for a wife and two kids, and his conservative politics.

It all eventually turned around. By the new century, Numan was being sampled, covered, and hailed as an influence by the likes of Basement Jaxx, Foo Fighters, Little Boots, Marilyn Manson, and Nine Inch Nails. Such people didn't know or care that he had never been perceived as cool like them. In 2017, his album *Savage* secured Numan his first Top 10 UK album chart placing in thirty-five years.

Nothing, though, could ever replicate the impact Gary Numan made in 1979, not just in terms of success but in being something never seen before.

5
MAY

Wave was the last album by the Patti Smith Group before their lead singer disappeared for a protracted period into the type of domesticity totally unexpected for a prototype ballsy female rocker. Following her critically acclaimed 1975 debut, *Horses*; her tediously experimental follow-up, *Radio Ethiopia*; and her commercial breakthrough, *Easter*, Smith now came up with a Todd Rundgren–produced record that was perhaps a logical synthesis of her apparently conflicting penchants for musical boundary-pushing and conventional rock structures. Opening track "Frederick" was an anthemic song of devotion to her soon-to-be husband that never betrayed the "side" her long-term fans kept expecting. The beautiful "Dancing Barefoot" approached the same subject in a more elliptical way. The latter was one of four tracks co-written by Smith with bassist Ivan Kral. Another pair saw her collaborating with guitarist Lenny Kaye. After that opening brace, the album descended into cuts with rather one-dimensional melodies and meandering lyrics, but at least ended on a high, and unearthly, note with the title track. A cinematic spoken-word piece with sparse keyboard accompaniment and ambient sound effects, it found Smith standing on a beach, delivering a monologue that could have been a piece of Shangri-Las-style coquetry, but could just as easily have been an awed encounter with Christ.

Electric Light Orchestra were designed by songwriter, singer, and multi-instrumentalist Jeff Lynne to pick up where the Beatles had left off with "I Am the Walrus." Rock songs with sumptuous orchestral arrangements seemed to some critics "naff," to employ a pejorative from the band's native Britain, especially in conjunction with ELO's penchant for aviator shades, beards, bubble perms, and faceless album-cover art. However, the results were sometimes majestic—something assisted by Lynne's knack for gliding melodies and imaginative lyrics. The public certainly loved them—between 1972 and 1986, ELO scored a staggering twenty-five Top 30 UK hits. That *Discovery* was the band's disco album (the clue in the punning title) didn't endear them to their critics, but it was their first chart-topping album in the UK, and more than half the album's tracks were Top 10 UK hits, if one counts both sides of the double-A release "Confusion" / "Last Train to London." It also garnered them two US Top 10s. For all that, the album was nowhere near as good as 1976's *A New World Record*. Lynne's helium-gas vocals, the gimmicky techie sound effects, and the florid arrangements were now combining to often suffocating effect. Only the pounding closer "Don't Bring Me Down" offered vigor.

Independence Day: The Specials and the 2 Tone Revolution

In early 1979, Jerry Dammers—keyboardist and spiritual leader of the Specials—anxiously asked Rick Rogers of his PR company whether five thousand copies was too many to press of "Gangsters," the Specials' debut single, which was about to be released on a label established especially for that purpose. By October, the record had sold 350,000. Although the label quickly blossomed into a multi-artist proposition, its roster was restricted to acts that played ska. Yet by February 1980, it had racked up seven consecutive Top 20 singles, five of them Top 10. There had been phenomena in independent record labels before but nothing like 2 Tone.

Dammers hailed from England's Midlands. Although not from poverty—his father was a vicar—the piousness of his household led to a rebellious outlook. The rock and reggae hybrid he had dreamed of since the age of fifteen properly crystallized when he saw the Sex Pistols. Dammers' genre preference, ska, was a precursor to reggae that was chunkier and livelier than the style it spawned, although it shared reggae's emphasis on the offbeat. Many in Dammers' homeland still refer to ska as "blue beat," the term by which it was colloquially known because so many examples of the genre were released on a UK label of that name.

Dammers's band of brothers in this musical endeavor were the Coventry Automatics, who became the Specials. In July 1978, the group—then a quintet—played their debut gig in Aylesbury. Their definitive lineup would comprise seven. In addition to Dammers was bassist Horace Panter, rhythm guitarist Lynval Golding, lead guitarist Roddy Byers (a.k.a. Roddy Radiation), drummer John Bradbury, toaster Neville Staple, and lead vocalist Terry Hall. In an ostentatiously egalitarian band, Dammers no more came across onstage like the leader than did the mordant-faced Hall, but his gap-toothed grin soon became famous.

The band were taken under the wing of Clash manager Bernard Rhodes, but three frustrating, neglected months in Rhodes' London rehearsal space saw them return, disillusioned, to hometown Coventry. From frustration came inspiration. "Personally, I think that had a lot to do with Jerry's decision to take the bull by the horns, as it were, and get the group to handle as much of its own business affairs as possible," Bradbury—who joined at that very point—later told Deanne Pearson of *New York Rocker*. "We recorded the first single at the end of January '79, and then Jerry came up with this idea of forming our own label, called 2 Tone." The label's name was designed to reflect the group's punk-ska hybrid and racial blend (two blacks, five whites). Dammers also thought up the label's soon-to-be iconic logo of "Walt Jabsco," a besuited, shades-sporting character rendered in monochrome and sharp angles.

It was decided that the Specials' debut would be "Gangsters," a Dammers-written number that was partly a sideswipe at their former manager. However, the band's grand, self-sufficient dreams looked like crashing and burning when they realized they didn't have enough money to record a B-side. Their solution was odd, and even smacked of amateurism. The released record's flip featured an old track by Bradbury and friend Neol Davies, titled, and attributed to, "The Selecter." Moreover, the sleeve featured hand-stamped titles. Yet upon its release in July '79 (distributed by Rough Trade), "Gangsters" proceeded to create a major buzz.

Although the Selecter were then more notion than reality, their presence on the debut's flip planted the idea of expanding 2 Tone to include other acts in the same vein. EMI, CBS, Island, and Virgin lost out on the new label's distribution rights to Chrysalis Records because they wouldn't grant the requisite creative control. By September, the reissued record was No. 6 in the UK charts.

From there, 2 Tone could do little wrong for an entire year. The deal with Chrysalis gave the label a budget to record up to ten singles a year by other artists, with Chrysalis obliged to release at last six. Londoners Madness were the first beneficiaries of this arrangement, their September debut, "The Prince," making No. 16. Meanwhile, Neol Davies had put together a proper band to go with the Selecter name, with Pauline Black their charismatic front woman. Their October release, "On My Radio," made No. 8. The Beat and the all-female

Bodysnatchers would also soon secure healthy chart placings under 2 Tone's aegis.

The Specials' own second single appeared in October, in the shape of "A Message to You Rudy," credited to "The Specials (Featuring Rico)." The latter was trombonist Rico Rodriguez, who—along with cornet player Dick Cluthell—would be a *de facto* Specials member for a while. Rodriguez had played on the song's original recording, then called "Rudy, a Message to You," a 1967 Jamaican release by Dandy Livingstone. The song—like several of the period—had sought to capitalize on the controversy about "Rude Boys": unemployed rural males who gravitated in search of jobs to the capital, Kingston, whose denizens mocked them for their uncultured (rude) ways. The term was now assuming a different meaning in the UK, as 2 Tone acquired a fan base instantly recognizable by its Walt Jabsco–redolent smart suits and porkpie hats. A record label had become a movement. These "rudies" were to be seen out in force that month on the 2 Tone Tour, where the Specials, the Selecter, and Madness (replaced by arrangement by Dexys Midnight Runners halfway through) undertook forty dates at venues selected for their low entry prices and tolerance of dancing. "Rudy" made No. 10. On November 8, the Specials were performing it on an edition of *Top of the Pops* that constituted a remarkable milestone. All three of the first bands signed to 2 Tone—the Specials, Madness, and the Selecter—had racked up sufficient sales to appear that week. They comprised a fifth of the featured acts. As Madness had by now left the label, it wasn't the complete triumph for 2 Tone that it might first appear, but only the most churlish would deny the minnow its moment of glory on such a technicality.

The following month saw the release of the Specials'—and 2 Tone's—debut album. It was eponymous, but it still managed to provide another variant of the group's name by not attaching a definite article to it, at least not on the cover. The Specials had loyally insisted on their LP being recorded in Coventry. Production at Horizon Studio was handled by Elvis Costello. "Rudy" kicked off a fourteen-track set, roughly a third of which was comprised of covers. The originals bore various publishing credits, but only one—Byers's stomping, mean-streets anthem "Concrete Jungle"—didn't involve Dammers. The latter also technically merited a credit on some of the non-originals. For instance, "Do the Dog" found him co-opting a number by American Rufus Thomas to address the British issue of youth-cult infighting—a hot topic of the day that had been discussed the previous year in the Clash's "Last Gang in Town" and Sham 69's "If the Kids Are United." At first, the problem didn't apply to Specials gigs, at which skinheads, mods, punks, blacks, rudies, and the unaligned all mingled peacefully. However, as time went on, they were increasingly afflicted with their own audience unrest problems.

Elsewhere, the album's lyrics alternated between calls for racial harmony and calls to resist conformity. "Doesn't Make It Alright" opened with the nigh tear-making sentiment, "Just because you're nobody, it doesn't mean that you're no good," before going on to tell white and black youth that their enemies were not each other. "Stupid Marriage" (whose swirling organ was one of the only times Dammers asserted himself musically) and "Too Much Too Young" (at six minutes, the only song on the album not trading on brevity) both indicated a terror of being prematurely tied down. Covers-wise, "Too Hot" was a composition by Prince Buster, enjoying a bumper year thanks to his Anglo fan club. Closing track "You're Wondering Now" (Coxsone Dodd) was—with its creamy harmonies—almost a lullaby, soothing the listener's emotions after a riotous forty-five minutes.

The album never improved on its entry position of No. 4, but it bobbed up and down the UK album chart for forty-five consecutive weeks. During that time, 2 Tone secured its greatest triumph when, in the first two weeks of February 1980, a live EP featuring a sped-up, cut-down version of "Too Much Too Young" topped the UK singles chart. It was rare enough for an independent label to achieve this feat, let alone with either an EP or an in-concert recording. The label also punched above its weight in the States. Despite not having the benefit of an attached hit single, *Specials* sold around 100,000 and reached No. 84 on *Billboard*. The US iteration included "Gangsters" (not on the UK original), accommodated by a shortened "Too Much Too Young" (different to the EP version).

From there, 2 Tone's demise was swift. In August 1980, "Mantovani" by the Swinging Cats became the first 2 Tone single not to make the UK Top 50. By now, the Specials were the only other act on the label: their non-proprietorial attitude toward signings meant that artists used 2 Tone as a springboard to deals with majors. Dammers probably wasn't heartbroken. In mid-1980, he was lamenting to Paolo Hewitt of *Melody Maker*, "2 Tone has become a monster. . . . There's such a great danger of it becoming too commercialized. You've got to stop it somehow."

The Specials' own demise was slower and more complicated. By this point, Dammers was already tiring of the ska sound, publicly saying that he wanted to take the Specials' music in the direction of easy-listening and movie soundtracks. It seemed a bizarre idea, but *More Specials* (October 1980) saw it fulfilled quite enjoyably. The Specials secured UK Top 10 hits with "Rat Race," "Stereotype," and "Do Nothing"—a trio of increasingly depressive, non-conformism anthems—before in June 1981 unleashing "Ghost Town," probably the definitive musical critique of Thatcherism.

When Margaret Thatcher's Conservative administration was elected into power in the UK in May 1979, some saw her as a savior, and by no means all of them were from high-income households. The number of working days lost through industrial action was running at 900,000 a month when she assumed office. Partly as a result of her outlawing secondary picketing and strikes without ballots, by 1985 it was down to 169,000 per month and continuing to fall. Meanwhile, by 1982, inflation was consistently in single figures for the first time in almost a decade. It would largely remain that way. Yet there was a price to pay for this economic miracle. Thatcher cut public spending to the bone in the middle of a recession, sending unemployment skyrocketing. Her monetarist policy, in fact, was partly dependent on unemployment: in a country where inflation had hit 25 percent as recently as 1975, it was adjudged that wage demands needed to be suppressed, and one of the most effective ways of doing that was to make people fearful for their jobs. Moreover, it was felt that over-manning in industry was making British firms uncompetitive and needed to be rectified.

The Skids' Richard Jobson notes of Thatcher's election, "The world was about to change forever more." While that might be true, its timing meant that it didn't make much impact on the music released that year: the vistas of decay heard in '79, in works by the Clash, the Jam, Sham 69, *et al.*, were more related to age-old proletarian grievances, and even the sense of chaos engendered by the previous five-year reign of the leftist Labour Party. By 1981, however, the effects of Thatcherism were beginning to be visible, and it seemed to people like Dammers that the growing prosperity of some was counterpointed by the increasing hardships of others. In "Ghost Town," Dammers described a Coventry—a boomtown in living memory—now pocked with shuttered shops and abandoned factories, its clubs closing down because bands refused to appear in venues where violence was always simmering below the surface. His colleagues devised a suitably eerie accompaniment to this vista of ruination. With perfect synchronicity, as the record made No. 1, British streets saw rioting by the frustrated unemployed youth to which the song referred.

Far from being triumphant, though, the Specials camp was an unhappy one, with some elements accusing Dammers of dictatorial methods. The public was shortly amazed to hear that "Ghost Town" was a swan song. While Hall, Staple, and Golding found success as the Fun Boy Three, Dammers embarked on the long, leisurely, and idiosyncratic process of recording *In the Studio* (1984). Credited to the Special AKA, it was essentially Dammers and hired hands. Much of it had already been heard on singles, but it was nonetheless an impressive work. Moreover, it contained, in "Free Nelson Mandela," one of those rare recordings that becomes something more than a mere song and takes on a cultural, even political, import: some people had never heard of the imprisoned anti-apartheid campaigner before they encountered this Top 10 hit. Its rousing chorus became a rallying cry at demonstrations the world over. Once again, though, in a moment of great triumph, the Specials splintered. The astronomical costs Dammers had run up during *In the Studio*'s extended gestation were responsible for bringing the band's career to an end.

At least for a while. At the time of writing, a version of the Specials is recording and touring, but it doesn't include Dammers. The latter is as perplexed as most people will be by the notion. As he noted to Nick Hasted in 2009, "At the end of the day, it's my words coming out of their mouths."

The use of the Specials' name as a meaningless trademark cannot take away their achievements at the turn of the eighties, when they—as both artists and record company—proved that neither big money nor corporate muscle were requisites for conquering the charts.

Spasticus, Mr. Funky, and Second-Album Blues: Ian Dury

Do It Yourself adhered to the clichés relating to the "Difficult Second Album"—up to a point.

As with so many recording artists attempting to follow up a successful debut LP, Ian Dury had to write a collection of songs in a time-frame whose briefness was in sharp contrast to the way the contents of his first album had percolated and developed over an extended period—in a sense, even a lifetime. However, while Dury could probably never have hoped to match the reception to his celebrated entrée, *New Boots and Panties!!*, its successor, *Do It Yourself*, was not a flop either critically or commercially. Yet it is also that peculiar proposition: an album that managed to go platinum while leaving no trace on the public consciousness.

Dury was born in 1942 and largely grew up in Essex, a county adjoining London. Although not from the impoverished background people often assumed, Dury was underprivileged in other ways. "He had a very difficult childhood with the polio and the fact he'd gone to a special-needs school," notes Dave Robinson, who would be his record-label boss. "In those days, special-needs schools were an incredible mixture of lunatics, bright people, people with distorted bodies. They put them all in the same place. Ian was a very bright, intelligent guy, but if he fell on the ground he couldn't get up. He had a very difficult life from that point of view."

"Being in that place is one of the reasons I talk the way I talk," Dury told journalist Will Birch of his time at special needs–oriented Chailey Heritage Craft School. "Before that, I talked not-quite BBC. It was a very tough place, very cold and very brutal." Dury was game to take life on, however. His withered left leg was addressed with a prosthetic, a walking stick, and a baleful attitude toward head-patting sympathy. (The latter was epitomized by his scowling 1981 single "Spasticus

Autisticus.") He gained the qualifications necessary to become an art teacher and commercial designer. By night, he indulged his love of music—in his case oriented around old-school rock 'n' roll—by forming Kilburn and the High Roads, for whom he sang and provided lyrics.

"He was a punk before punk" is a frequently and sometimes fatuously used superlative, but in Dury's case it's indubitably true. Kilburn and the High Roads purveyed songs that explored British culture, ones rendered in an indigenous accent. Moreover, there was much of punk's scatology and rudery in their lyrics, while Dury's scruffy-cum-menacing image was a precursor to punk's visual confrontationalism, even an inspiration. For instance, the razor blade Johnny Rotten sported in one ear was cribbed directly from High Roads–era Dury.

Despite a support slot for the Who and a record deal that resulted in the (generally disappointing) album *Handsome*, by 1975 Kilburn and the High Roads had split up, exhausted by arguments and money issues. Guitarist and keyboardist Chaz Jankel, a member of the High Roads in their dying stages, would proceed to be Dury's songwriting foil in his new venture. Robinson says, "Chaz Jankel was the great thing that happened for Ian." Of Dury, the Stiff man says, "He wasn't a very good singer, and he had no real music." What Dury did have, though, was great lyrics. His new collaborator could frame them perfectly, if on the surface somewhat incongruously. Robinson: "Chaz is Mr. Funky. He made that style for the Blockheads, that kind of rough punk-funk."

Dury had recently been adopted by Blackhill Enterprises, a management company run by Peter Jenner and Andrew King. Under their aegis, Dury began demoing songs co-written by him, Jankel, and American Steve Nugent. The demos turned into recording sessions for a full-blown album, on which Dury and Jankel were abetted by Geoff Castle (Moog), Edward Speight (guitar), Norman Watt-Roy (bass), Charlie Charles (drums), and Davey Payne (saxophone). (The latter three would become permanent fixtures of the Blockheads, the name ultimately given to Dury's backing band.) The result was extraordinary and frequently unprecedented: slick rock and funk with a dash of music hall (vaudeville, in American parlance) provided the backdrop to character sketches and street vignettes shot through with Dury's singular humor, scabrousness, and nose for a pleasing rhyme. "Wake Up and Make Love with Me" was revolutionary not only for its sexual frankness but for combining it with convincing domestic notes. "Billericay Dickie" was sheer braggadocio, but only a "prannet" (to use one element of the vernacular it proffered) wouldn't be charmed by this richly detailed, linguistically inventive jack-the-lad's anthem. Beyond the overarching studied uncouthness sometimes lay surprising sensitivity ("Sweet Gene Vincent" and "My Old Man" were moving tributes to Dury's musical idol and father, respectively) and nuance ("If I Was with a Woman" sounded on the surface like a misogynist's rant before revealing itself to be mocking macho delusion).

There turned out to be only one problem with Blackhill's cunning plan to accrue unusual levels of wealth by leasing a prerecorded work to a major record label: nobody was interested in signing Dury. While anybody with ears could appreciate that the music on offer was high-grade, the delicate fact remained that no middle-aged "spastic" had ever become a pop star before. As an afterthought-cum-last gasp, Blackhill offered the album to Stiff, located in the same building, whose overtures they had previously rebuffed.

Stiff had formed in 1976, when Jake Riviera and Dave Robinson decide to switch roles from artist managers to music purveyors. That the two had a different mentality to major-label executives was made obvious by them naming their record company after music-industry vernacular for the opposite of a hit. Within a year or so of their first release—Nick Lowe's "So It Goes" (August 1976)—they had one of the most exciting stables in the land, including the Adverts, Elvis Costello, the Dammed, and Ian Dury. Just as importantly, they were having hits.

Stiff inaugurated Dury's second coming in August 1977 via the delightful standalone single "Sex & Drugs & Rock & Roll." Although it appeared at first glance a hedonist's anthem, closer inspection revealed a skeptical attitude toward irresponsibility. Whatever its nuances, though, the record was never going to get either airplay or chart traction in a highly censorious country where the BBC had a national radio broadcasting monopoly and where, as late as 1982, BBC Radio 1 DJs were ordered to refer to Marvin Gaye's "(Sexual) Healing" only by its second word. However, it was also destined to attract attention and notoriety, partly for the very fact of being effectively banned. The titular phrase, which had been knocking around largely unnoticed for nearly a decade, proceeded to become part of the general vernacular. The album was released the following month. Its incongruously American and slightly icky title, *New Boots and Panties!!*, was about the only misstep surrounding it. (*New Boots and Knickers!!* would have been perfect, being not only British vernacular but alliterative.) It was taken to the heart of the critics and the public alike.

Dury had re-emerged with perfect timing: with punk and its anti-convention values now established, the world was ready to accept a man who resembled the Artful Dodger grown old and crippled. While his music was never overtly political in the manner of much of punk, in a way it slotted right in with the genre's stances: merely speaking and singing the way Dury did, in a very class-bound country where "received pronunciation" dominated the media, somehow came across as subversive.

Initially, the record had a respectable but short seven-week chart run. "The album was kind of at an end of its selling cycle," recalls Robinson of its disappearance from the UK charts in early December

'77. That brief turn in the spotlight might have been it for *New Boots* but for the fact that, in late 1977, Jake Riviera dropped the bombshell that he was departing Stiff. His decision left the label in what Robinson recalls was "a very bad financial position." He explains, "Jake's man had been the accountant as well. That weekend, when I went around the office and opened the drawers and found his desk full of receipts that had not been accounted for, I realized that I'd have to act fast." Robinson's rescue plan involved trying to revive one of the company's main assets: "We really worked on Ian Dury's album with his agreement . . . I decided to spend whatever money we had in the bank on a new promotion campaign."

New Boots reappeared on the UK LP chart at the end of the following January. It remained there for all but five weeks of 1978, essentially making it more an album of 1978 than of '77. Amazingly, though, *New Boots* was more an album of 1979 than of either '77 or '78. Although its chart run was a "mere" thirty-five weeks in '79, that was the year of its highest chart placings. Its ultimate peak of No. 5 was achieved in February, but it didn't finally exit the list until the following October. Not for nothing did the album become known as "the working man's *Tubular Bells*," a reference to Mike Oldfield's 1973 prog-rock LP's marathon 287-week chart occupancy. This act of longevity was made all the more remarkable by the fact that, while the album contained songs that would become iconic, it featured no hits: "Sweet Gene Vincent" had been issued on single but hadn't charted, and Dury's next clutch of 45s were standalone releases. Moreover, as Robinson notes, "There was a lot of tracks on there that really weren't playable on radio." ("Plaistow Patricia" started with the poignant reflection, "Arseholes, bastards, fucking cunts, and pricks!")

"What a Waste," a percolating denunciation of humdrum employment, made the Top 10 in spring '78. Stiff didn't bother with a second

Dury single until November, when Robinson decided to issue "Hit Me with Your Rhythm Stick." When, in the final week of January '79, the British public placed this shimmering, innuendo-laden ditty at No. 1, Dury had finally beaten the censors. "Reasons to Be Cheerful (Part 3)"—a proto-rap list of artifacts and sensations Dury liked, or pretended he did to appear whimsical or make a rhyme—followed in July and made No. 3.

The hit-parade triumphs and the extended life enjoyed by *New Boots* worked to disguise the fact that the task of following up his debut LP was something Dury was finding to be, as he would doubtless have put it, "a bugger." "Ian had to write a lot of songs on the road with Chaz, and it didn't suit him," recalls Robinson. "He would fiddle with the lyrics for a hell of a long time." In 1981, Dury pointed out to Mike Stand of *The Face*, "From *New Boots*, where we'd done thirty-six demos from which we'd selected ten, we were going in for *Do It Yourself* . . . trying to construct an LP out of ten songs with no spares." Jankel told Dury biographer Richard Balls, "We pieced together what we had left, the songs which hadn't been used for *New Boots*. I also came up with a few relatively new ideas."

Recording the second album was also fraught, Robinson says, because "Ian was constantly bickering with Chaz and bickering with musicians . . . he had no real music, but Ian always wanted to be the boss and the instigator and the one who would come up with the idea." Robinson describes Dury as his own worst enemy. "Ian was a wonderful geezer, but he was an ill-mannered drunk and also smoked a lot of dope with brandy." That the public didn't see much of this nastiness was particularly ironic in light of the fact that, initially, the solo Dury had had a rather sinister image: although he often wore smart suits, his cropped head, Doc Martens, eyeliner, and "Do-you-want-it?" demeanor were genuinely disturbing. Lately, though, the blandishments of celebrity, the indulgence of broadcasting presenters, and the validation of success had seen him morphing into something more avuncular, even into that most harmless/tame of things—the professional cockney.

That celebrity, incidentally, was destined not to transfer to America. Trying to do deals with Arista Records' Machiavellian head Clive Davis, and having to negotiate the snarling egotism of Lou Reed on a six-week support slot, seems to have put paid to any Blackhill fantasies of Dury ever being anything more than a cult Stateside.

Half of the new album's songs did not bear Jankel's name, with the other Blockheads all getting a chance to compose. However, Jankel produced (with Laurie Latham engineering), and some might suggest he did so with a heavy hand. "We brought the musicians in when they were needed," Jankel told Daryl Easlea in a 2003 interview. "It was like the way Steely Dan make records." At one point, this exclusion of unnecessary personnel even extended to Dury. Jankel had tired of Dury's "theatrical" personality and, aware that "the meter was running," he rang him from the studio with some bad news. Jankel told Balls, "I . . . said, 'Look Ian, I think it would be a good idea if you stayed away from the session.' There was the longest gap ever and then he said, 'I don't fucking believe it, I have just been asked to stay away from my own session.'" After Jankel completed the recording of the backing tracks, Dury returned to finish his vocals in a "tense" atmosphere.

Do It Yourself appeared in May 1979, twenty months after *New Boots*, in an age where an album per year was standard and, as noted, two albums per year was not all that rare. The long wait made its artistic disappointment even more acute. It surprised many and dismayed some because it revealed Dury to be yet another artist—and surely the most unlikely one—to have attached himself to the disco movement. It felt like Dury was being cold-bloodedly projected against a mainstream backdrop with which his authenticity, unconventionality, and abrasiveness had nothing in common.

Certainly, the public liked the confection less than it did the first album. Courtesy of massive advance sales, *Do It Yourself*'s No. 2 UK chart peak was actually three places higher than that achieved by its predecessor. However, whereas *New Boots and Panties!!* racked up eighty-nine "Weeks on Chart," its follow-up was gone after nineteen. Moreover, while several of the tracks on the debut will be lodged in popular affection forever, few are able to name any of the tracks on *Do It Yourself*. Here, the standalone singles policy probably backfired, as an album-related hit or two always provides the consumer a mental landmark and the album a spike in sales. There again, the album had few if any tracks that could be imagined as singles, because of quality, profanity, or structural suitability.

There were some admirable tracks on *Do It Yourself*. "Sink My Boats" was a soaring exploration of the vicissitudes of a relationship. "This Is What We Find," a collaboration with Blockheads keyboardist Mick Gallagher, married sunny reggae grooves to a lyric that catalogued the harrowing self-harm of the troubled and distressed, poetically concluding that the hope that springs eternal "springs right up your behind." Closer "Lullaby for Francies" [sic]—another reggae track—was simply beautiful. Elsewhere, though, the relentless musical smoothness sometimes tipped over into a dullness from which not even Dury's sprightly wordsmithery could rescue the songs. Some felt it a shame that *New Boots* had ended with the less-tuneful triumvirate of "Blockheads," "Plaistow Patricia," and "Blackmail Man," but *Do It Yourself* could certainly have done with some of their musical grit. Not that all the blame should be placed at the feet of Jankel or the Blockheads. Dury's lyrics were a step down, lacking that Dickensian character and richness that had so distinguished *New Boots*.

The cover of the album was in some ways far more noteworthy than its contents. The *New Boots* sleeve bore an evocative street photograph of Dury and his young son, Baxter. *Do It Yourself* featured merely the album title, artist name (the Blockheads receiving credit for the first time on LP), track listing, and Blockhead logo superimposed on a sample of the wares of wallpaper manufacturer Crown. However, the variants of this simple design were collectibly numerous. "They had the same wallpaper in every known color, so my idea was, let's put out a different album in the thirty-six territories that we have licensees in," explains Robinson.

Dury's third album, *Laughter* (1981), peaked at No. 48 in its paltry three-week UK chart run. The record suggested that Dury was a negligible talent without Jankel, who had now departed for solo, soundtrack, and production work. Even so, with his three-album Stiff deal at a conclusion, Dury was now able to sign to a major, in his case Polydor. However, excluding compilations, *Do It Yourself* was his last Top 50 album in his home country. There were only five further albums between then and 1998, as Dury diversified into acting and stage writing.

"I should have done *New Boots and Panties!!*, 'Hit Me with Your Rhythm Stick,' and then fucked off out of it for a year or two," Dury told Chris Welch in a 1995 interview. "We did a massive tour in 1979 that lost money, and that's what knocked the bollocks out of us. We lost £40,000 doing eighty gigs, even though they were all sold out." It seems reasonable to conclude that the bollocks were also knocked out of Dury—and musical productivity adversely affected—by illness. In 1995, fate—as if it hadn't battered him enough—gifted Dury cancer. After a false dawn of apparent remission, he succumbed to it in 2000, aged fifty-seven.

Although that could never be posited as a happy ending, there were some gratifying moments along the way. In the early 1980s, Jenner and King went into bankruptcy. At the Official Receiver's auction of Blackhill Enterprises' assets, Dury bid for the master tapes of *New Boots and Panties!!* and *Do It Yourself.* With his commercial star having waned, his offer of nine pence did not attract a higher bid. As he gleefully observed to Welch, "I've been leasing them out ever since."

Two Out of Three Ain't Bad: David Bowie

In 1976, David Bowie abandoned Los Angeles, where he had been domiciled for the past couple of years, to retreat to the musical backwaters of Berlin. It was in the Western half of that then-divided city that he set about devising—if not always recording—his so-called "Berlin Trilogy." Berlin had a history of decadence that the likes of Bowie lap up. Said decadence was now shot through with the menace of contemporary geo-politics: Bowie adored the fact that when he was working on the first two parts of the trio in Hansa Studio by the Wall, rifle-toting border guards in the Communist East were observing him through binoculars. His triptych lived up—at least at first—to his audacious 1976 quote to *Rolling Stone*'s Cameron Crowe, "I really, honestly and truly, don't know how much longer my albums will sell. I think they're going to get more diversified, more extreme and radical right along with my writing. And I really don't give a shit." This musical adventurism, a world removed from the laurel-resting of the rest of the old guard, made Bowie immune to the scorn of punks in the season in which the movement made casualties of the reputations, and sometimes careers, of so many of his peers.

Many was the punk, in any case, who had a soft spot for Bowie. The first musical obsession for millions of youths who came of age in

'76–'77 was his fifth LP, *The Rise and Fall of Ziggy Stardust and the Spiders from Mars*, the 1972 quasi-concept album on which he pretended to be a sexually ambiguous alien. Since then, he'd adroitly managed to retain his fan base as he explored multiple musical styles on releases that shared little common ground other than aesthetic excellence and a certain archness of delivery.

It was absolutely logical that Bowie should hook up for his new project(s) with Brian Eno. Originally the techie responsible for the unlistenable bit in Roxy Music's suave pop songs, Eno with his solo work unexpectedly transformed himself into a merchant of pop, albeit pop that—like so much of Bowie's catalogue—left the listener unsure whether or not the artist was taking the piss. Eno would be Bowie's right-hand man on the trilogy, playing synthesizer, offering composing and recording concepts like Oblique Strategies (randomly chosen recording limitations), and sometimes co-writing. Tony Visconti acted as producer.

Low (January 1977) started as a soundtrack to *The Man Who Fell to Earth*—the 1976 film in which Bowie took the starring role—but was rejected by director Nicolas Roeg as unsuitable. The album was a mash-up of the angular, artificial, and weird-noise-punctuated sounds common to the nascent musical genre of electro-pop and Bowie's own melodic-but-mischievous style. Its first vinyl side was comprised of shorter tracks, its second given over to four glacial, almost completely instrumental epics. However, the idea promoted by Bowie at around this time that he didn't care if he became, to deploy a Bowie phrase, a rock 'n' roll suicide, was probably not quite the full truth. Each installment of the triptych happened to have at least one tuneful cut of radio-friendly length. In this case, it was the hook-stuffed "Sound and Vision," which became a UK No. 3.

The album—like all of the Berlin Trilogy—made the Top 5 in Bowie's native Britain. In the US it was a different story, as it always had been there. With no residue of goodwill to count on from hordes who had adored him in his early-seventies "pop" phase—*Hunky Dory* and *Ziggy* hadn't charted Stateside, while *Aladdin Sane* only made No. 17—the trilogy lost him some of the ground he had made in getting *Station to Station* (1976) to No. 3 on *Billboard*: all tranches of it were appreciated by the cognoscenti but never bought in sufficient quantities by the wider public to crack the Top 10.

Eno took a bigger role on the following October's *"Heroes"* (the quote marks are Bowie's own), often writing the music and leaving Bowie to concentrate on the lyrics. The previous album had been informed by cocaine hell, but now hope was beginning to appear in the song words. The title track was high-gloss and ultra-tuneful, although a surprising flop, only managing No. 24 in the UK. Album "deep cuts" like the ambient, vocal-less "Sense of Doubt" and "Moss Garden," meanwhile, made no concessions to commerciality but were still strangely compelling. The appearance of live album *Stage* in September '78 seemed an oddly conventional non sequitur to all this groundbreaking. It was reputedly issued at the insistence of an RCA worried about Bowie's diminishing American stock.

When *Lodger* appeared in May 1979, reviewers were apprised that it completed the sequence at pretty much the same time as they first learned it was a trilogy. Some, though, suggest that it actually wasn't part of the sequence at all. The experiments with synthesizers were fewer, and the instrumentals absent. Burroughs cutups were giving way once more to linear lyrics. It was also the only one of the three records that was not at least partly recorded in Berlin, instead laid down at Mountain Studios in Montreux and New York City's Record Plant.

There was another difference. "The previous two were a delicate balance, I think, one third each of David, Brian, and myself," Visconti told John Tobler and Stuart Grundy for their BBC series *The Record Producers.* "But on *Lodger*, Brian was very much in control." Visconti—like many—was unhappy with the fidelity of the record. "Some of the earlier, freer stuff ended up being masters, and they weren't recorded very well, but David was confident that I could do anything in the mix, and he's a bit oblivious to that sort of thing anyway, and more concerned with writing the songs."

Opener "Fantastic Voyage" (like five other tracks, a Bowie and Eno co-write) had that liquid, backward-sounding melody style that was uniquely Bowie's. On "African Night Flight," the artist rapid-fired his lyrics against a clattering backdrop. "Move On" (a solo Bowie composition) was a melodic wanderlust anthem that tied in with the loose travel theme across side one that saw his music taking in African, Turkish, Japanese, and Jamaican motifs. "Yassassin" (Bowie) was a semi-reggae shot through with Hollywood sonic clichés of the Far East. Side-closer "Red Sails" was influenced by Neu!, although Bowie later told the *NME*'s Angus MacKinnon that it departed from the krautrock template because of guitarist Adrian Belew's unfamiliarity with his source of inspiration. "He'd never heard them. So I told him the atmosphere I wanted and he came up with the same conclusions that Neu! came up with, which was fine by me." However, Bowie disavowed the other Germanic stimulus attributed to the trilogy. "I'd say there's very little Kraftwerk influence on the albums," he later told the same paper's John Robinson.

"DJ" was percolating funk co-written with Eno and the album's other guitarist, Carlos Alomar. It became a minor UK hit single. Alomar's talents were also loudly on display in "Look Back in Anger," an urgent tribute to a down-at-heel angel. "Boys Keep Swinging" had a punk spirit achieved by the musicians playing the "wrong" instruments: Alomar handled drums and George Murray spurned his usual bass for keyboards. Bowie's solo writing effort "Repetition" was musically boring—perhaps deliberately so—but lyrically daring, exploring domestic violence. Closer "Red Money" was a Bowie/Alomar co-write that reused the music from Iggy Pop's "Sister Midnight" to create an apocalyptical vista.

Lodger was released in a wraparound sleeve on which Bowie was splayed like a marionette whose strings had been cut. Some might suggest that this was painfully apposite. Although taster single "Boys Keep Swinging" made the UK Top 10, the song noticeably, and rather desperately, harked back to the gender-bending of Bowie's peak fame. Regardless of chart positions—it made No. 20 in the States, No. 4 in the UK—it was immediately apparent that *Lodger* was the least impressive of the Berlin triptych. It portrayed itself as being in the preceding brace's adventurous spirit, while in fact hedging its bets. It was, paradoxically, a conservative avant-garde work. The awkward straddling act Bowie seemed to be attempting—torn between being a cutting-edge artist and a pop star—was epitomized by the fact that he rounded out the year by becoming yet another artist to jump on the disco bandwagon, in his case with the single "John, I'm Only Dancing (Again)," a re-recording of a song he'd already released in two iterations.

Bowie's unconvincing 1979 output would have been bad enough on its own, but that year saw the arrival on the scene—in a furious burst of creativity and commercial success—of one of his disciples. From today's perspective, it's clear that Gary Numan is an artistic minnow compared to Bowie, and that much of his studied alienation and emotionlessness was cribbed from him. However, Numan's output made it clear that he was more conversant than Bowie with the synthesizer technology with which Bowie had lately been dabbling, with the uncomfortable implication being that this fact was due to Numan's youth.

That the archduke of innovation suddenly seemed old-hat only served to underline the fact that *Lodger* was a damp-squib ending to what had started out as an audacious journey.

6
JUNE

That June albums *Labour of Lust* by Nick Lowe and *Repeat When Necessary* by Dave Edmunds were released within a day of each other was appropriate. The albums essentially featured the same personnel. Lowe (bass and vocals), Edmunds (guitar, keyboards, vocals), Billy Bremner (guitar), and Terry Williams (drums) constituted Rockpile, one of the hardest-driving ensembles of the era. The following year they would issue under the group name the well-regarded *Seconds of Pleasure*. The Edmunds and Lowe albums, however, sounded very different to each other, courtesy of the two men's contrasting tastes and abilities. Edmunds didn't write much but expertly purveyed fifties-influenced rock 'n' roll. As well as the aforementioned "Girls Talk," *Repeat When Necessary* gave him a UK hit via a throbbing rendition of Hank DeVito's "Queen of Hearts." Lowe had been the lynchpin of the band Brinsley Schwarz, who despite six albums and much hype had never quite made a breakthrough. Although he'd latterly reinvented himself as a producer, in 1978 he released his first solo album. Its follow-up was one of the best LPs of 1979. *Labour of Lust*'s music was slick and pop-oriented, but its lyrics were whimsical and sardonic. The album's acoustic guitar–driven opening track, "Cruel to be Kind" (written with his ex–Brinsley Schwarz colleague Ian Gomm), was a No. 12 on both sides of the Atlantic. Although on the surface a heartfelt critique of a feckless lover, Lowe's decision to rhyme "bona fide" with "coincide" seemed as mocking as Williams's delightfully dropped drum beats. As if to prove

Lowe could be serious, though, the album contained "Endless Grey Ribbon," an exquisite description of aching loneliness.

On the US edition, the latter track made way for "American Squirm," a UK single. Said 45's B-side was the first place that Elvis Costello's version of Lowe's Brinsley Schwarz song "(What's So Funny 'Bout) Peace, Love, and Understanding" ever turned up. This had an "in-house" logic courtesy of the fact that the Attractions played on the A-side. The Lowe song would finally "take" third time around: when it was covered in 1992 by Curtis Stigers on the soundtrack to the film *The Bodyguard*, said album's sales made Lowe a wealthy man. Lowe wasn't doing too badly in '79, either. He was co-author of "Milk and Alcohol," a UK Top 10 in February for R&B revivalists Dr. Feelgood.

Joni Mitchell's *Mingus* was always destined to be hated by a large part of her fan base. Mitchell—the only distaff artist at the time considered on a par with male titans like the Beatles, Rolling Stones, and Bob Dylan—had experimented with jazz strains on her last three albums, but her audience was still essentially the rock and folk crowd picked up from her first half-dozen LP releases. The winding, tinkling, and frequently improvisational sounds of jazz simply weren't that demographic's cup of tea, but that is what Mitchell proffered them with this Charles Mingus collaboration-cum-tribute. Extended snatches of the titular dying jazz legend talking, and at one point wolves howling, would only have befuddled further those yearning for another "Big Yellow Taxi."

The history of popular music is littered with salutary tales of bands damaging their careers by issuing their second album too hastily. Dire Straits' *Communiqué* could have provided just such a lesson. It sounded exactly like it would be expected to sound considering it was released just eight months after the British quartet's well-received 1978 eponymous debut: a pale imitation of that record's collection of well-crafted, blues-based rock. In Dire Straits' case, however, the precipitousness wasn't momentum-destroying. Ironically, this was partly because 1979 saw their first album achieve belated success. Said debut's highlight was "Sultans of Swing," a stately but driving tribute to a fictional bar-band sung by Straits lynchpin Mark Knopfler in a ridiculously affected Dylan-esque drawl. Released on single, it made the Top 10 on both sides of the Atlantic, although not in the same rendering. The US single featured the album version, while—at the insistence of a record company nervous about radio-play prospects—the UK got a re-recorded, slightly rawer execution.

Upon the appearance of their eponymous 1978 debut LP, the Cars were hailed as a great American new-wave band. In retrospect, they seem more a heavy-rock band with new-wave (as well as pop) shades. They certainly didn't have a penchant for speedy new-wave tempos. Like the debut, 1979's *Candy-O* was helmed by Queen producer Roy Thomas Baker. The result was another LP destined to be liked by people with a penchant for chugging guitar riffs, herky-jerky melodies, and wriggly synthesizer noises. The album went Top 3 in the States, but Britain—always slightly skeptical about Yanks who weren't as reconstructed as they liked to make out—only sent it as high as No. 30.

The Who had quite a roller-coaster 1979. Although the veteran British quartet didn't release a studio album, they were busily semi-reinventing themselves as filmmakers. Cinemas played host to both the band documentary *The Kids Are Alright* and a dramatization of their 1973 concept album *Quadrophenia*, which detailed the life of the type of mod who in the sixties formed a large part of their fan base. (The following year, lead singer Roger Daltrey would star in Who Films' bank-robber biopic *McVicar*.) Both movies came with double-LP soundtracks. *The Kids Are Alright* (June) collected various live tracks, TV performances, and studio outtakes. Oddly, not all of the tracks were heard in the film. Even more oddly, *Music from the Soundtrack of the Who Film Quadrophenia* (August) featured three sides of remixed tracks from the original 1973 studio album—thereby jettisoning several elements of what was designed as a narrative—and a side of various non-Who songs included in the movie. Meanwhile, Kenney Jones had been installed in the band's ranks in place of their iconic drummer, Keith Moon, who had died shockingly young in 1978. Jones would go on to make two studio albums with them, but in December that possibility seemed remote when eleven fans were crushed to death at a Who concert in Cincinnati, a tragedy that left even man's man Daltrey in tears.

In November, Neil Young released the double-LP *Live Rust*. It wasn't, as the title implied, an in-concert version of his June studio album. In fact, there was no need for such because, curiously, *Rust Never Sleeps* consisted of live recordings of new songs, albeit subjected to studio overdubs. This process was typical of Young's penchant for ostentatious contrariness. As contrary recording processes tend to do, it weakened the songs, the material robbed of potential power by the traditional ersatz live acoustics. For everybody but Young fanatics it was an irritating missed opportunity. "My My, Hey Hey (Out of the Blue)" was at least left unscathed by Young's pretensions, being a moving and haunting tribute to the impact on music of punk. The so-called studio album did better than the live album on both sides of the Atlantic.

Back to the Egg was the seventh album by Wings (including those credited to "Paul McCartney and Wings," but not including one LP credited to him alone, and one credited to "Paul and Linda McCartney"). The album featured new members Laurence Juber (guitar) and Steve Holley (drums). The latter pair appeared on early '79 disco-ish single "Goodnight Tonight," the transatlantic Top 5 placing of which augured well for the new lineup.

Back to the Egg was broadly modernistic, boasting new-wavy bass and washes of synthesizer. However, while the ex-Beatle may have been keeping up with the trends, his craft was audibly falling behind that of the new generation of musicians who had been weaned on his onetime brilliance. The warning signs came quickly, with the listener's heart sinking as the first track proper, "Getting Closer," found McCartney addressing someone as "my salamander" in a lyric that was impenetrable but clearly mired in the whimsy that had been infecting his writing since the "White Album." "Old Siam, Sir" was equally random lyrically, while its cod-oriental music pounded away for four almost unbearable minutes. Meanwhile, the brass section on "Arrow Through Me" seemed there purely to distract attention from one of the insufferably bland melodies that McCartney was these days proffering increasingly often.

That some of McCartney's craftsmanship remained intact was a given: after all, less than a decade previously, he was one of the two best songwriters in the world. Accordingly, there were flashes of class, such as the pretty, enigmatic "Winter Rose / Love Awake." Overall, though, *Back to the Egg* more than ever raised the question perennially attending the release of a new Wings album: whether people would be buying this stuff in such quantities if it were someone else's name on the sleeve.

Not that, this time, they did buy it in great quantities. McCartney had received unprecedentedly big bucks to switch his wares in the States from Capitol to Columbia, and, doubtlessly because of this, engaged in unusually heavy promotion for the LP. Despite this, *Back to the Egg* was Wings' lowest-charting album Stateside since their 1971 debut, *Wild Life*. In the UK, it disappeared from the charts two months quicker than its predecessor, *London Town*. None of its singles became major hits. (Perhaps unwisely, "Goodnight Tonight" wasn't included.)

The rebirth of Wings went further awry the next year. Nineteen eighty started traumatically with the cancelation of Wings' Japanese tour, when McCartney spent ten days in a prison cell after being found with marijuana in his suitcase, and ended shatteringly with the assassination of John Lennon, the man with whom, in the public mind, McCartney was indivisible. McCartney subsequently, and understandably, seemed reluctant to make public appearances, which made the retention of a working band untenable. He retreated to the studio and the solo recording career he had abandoned to set up Wings. It was a terrible set of circumstances to bring about the end of the group, but that end was for the best. The Wings experiment was doomed to failure from the beginning by McCartney's insistence on the inclusion on keyboards of his non-musician wife, and his refusal, as a confused point of principle, to work with names as big as him, which in practice meant employing jobbing musos who, while perfectly competent, weren't in his creative league. Things were "off" from the get-go: *Wild Life* sounded like a studio-outtake bootleg, a shockingly slovenly way for a superstar to introduce his new group. Although McCartney's subsequent solo career hasn't lived up to the Beatles' legend—like Lennon, he found his perfect compositional foil and then lost him—it has at least been marked by an application and craft that was simply never fully there in Wings.

Fame Is a Fickle Food: The Knack and Sham 69

Californian power-pop merchants the Knack and UK punk ensemble Sham 69 might on the face of it have nothing in common. However, in 1979, both bands trod remarkably similar paths: achieving commercial triumph that would by the following year turn into utter rejection by a fan base that had so recently revered them.

California four-piece the Knack proffered a blend of sixties pop-romance motifs and hard-edged new-wave chops that had major stars lining up to jam with them, record companies tussling to sign them, and the record-buying public sending their wares to the top of the charts. That by 1980 they were washed up is chiefly explained by the fact that, despite their retro leanings, the Knack's music had a characteristic never seen before: they were the world's first vulgar pop band. There had, of course, been plenty of vulgar rock ensembles, but never a group aiming sex- and profanity-laced aural candy at thirteen-year-old girls. Although at first thrilled by this novelty, the public quickly became disgusted with it.

The Knack comprised Doug Fieger on rhythm guitar and lead vocals, Berton Averre on lead guitar, Prescott Niles on bass, and Bruce Gary on drums. Gary was a bit of a veteran, having played for Jack Bruce and several others. He reputedly turned down a job with Wings in favor of staying with the Knack. For his part, Averre says, "We started playing as a band in June of '78. I was twenty-four."

The group acquired a name when Fieger was leafing through a dictionary. "We wanted a singular and it looked cool (a "k" on either side) and it was one syllable, and it actually meant something—to have a knack for doing things," Averre explains. The Knack's melodic but edgy music, as well as their suits and short hair, caused them to be perceived as a Beatles/new-wave hybrid, but, Averre says, "If somebody had to put an epithet on our style, I think power-pop comes closer than anything else: the chewy goodness of pop with real balls in the performance."

The Knack's live work at the likes of the Troubadour quickly created a buzz. "As musicians, we were a tight band," reasons Averre. "It didn't hurt that, for whatever reason, a lot of teenage girls were coming to watch us." That "whatever reason" was probably not Fieger, whose high hairline, large nose, and persistent—even relentless—smile made him resemble an unctuous insurance salesman, but more likely the curly hair of Niles and the sharp cheekbones of Averre. However, teenage-girl appeal was not what got the band signed. "Some big names in rock would get up and jam with us," Averre recalls. The big names included Ray Manzarek, Eddie Money, Stephen Stills, and Tom Petty. Averre adds, "Springsteen got up and jammed with us and the next morning all the record companies were calling our managers."

It was fairly natural that the Knack's record company would approach Mike Chapman to produce its new charges. Australia-born Chapman had recently added a string of American hits to his UK glam-rock successes. As well as the triumphs he'd secured for Blondie in '78–'79, he'd written and produced a US No. 1 for Exile ("Kiss You All Over"), produced another US No. 1 for Nick Gilder ("Hot Child in the City"), and co-written and co-produced a *Billboard* Top 5 entry for Suzi Quatro and Chris Norman ("Stumblin' In"). "He was at that time a Midas-touch kind of guy," notes Averre. Not so natural is that this process happened before it had even been determined which record company would win the band's signatures. "I was approached by Warner Bros Records," Chapman recalls. "I got the same phone call from Capitol Records. Both Warners and Capitol thought they were signing them. So I knew that, whichever company signed them, this band was going to explode, if they had songs." Chapman asked to attend a rehearsal before making his decision. "Mark my words, this was a great band," he recalls of what he witnessed. "They could play their asses off. Bruce Gary was one of the best drummers in the world . . . it was one of those lucky things that as a producer you just get the next big thing dumped in your lap."

The final decision as to who would produce, however, was the Knack's. Averre: "Mike's pitch—and the reason we ended up going with him—is he said, 'My idea of recording you guys is to just turn the tapes on and you just play like you're playing in the club.'" Which makes it all the more eyebrow-raising that during the recording of the Knack's debut album, *Get the Knack*, the charts were playing host to

Blondie's "Heart of Glass," the drum track of which song had famously taken Chapman an entire day to record. "I produce the way the music dictates," Chapman says. "They'd been on the circuit for a couple of years, playing these songs in. These tracks were laid down in one or two passes and they played brilliantly, all of them. A lot of vocals were done live. What did I have to do? The production on that was an entirely different approach to producing a band like Blondie." At a point in history when an album was costing an average of $100,000 to record, *Get the Knack* came in at less than a fifth of that. "The legend on our album is that it only cost seventeen and a half thousand dollars," says Averre. "Which was true. It was a couple weeks. And a significant part of that seventeen-five was Mike's wine bill. He was a connoisseur."

The album was comprised of twelve songs. Four were solo Fieger compositions, some predating the Knack. The rest were Averre/Fieger collaborations, apart from one cover. "Let Me Out" was a frantic expression of a desire to hit the nightspots written when Fieger decided the band needed an opening number for their Troubadour sets. Averre's music utilized a mirror image of the "Carole King chord," currently to be heard in Cheap Trick's "Surrender." In the twentieth anniversary year of his death, Buddy Holly's catalogue continued to reveal the influence he'd had on musicians: the Knack's version of "Heartbeat" followed hot on the heels of Blondie's rendition of "I'm Gonna Love You Too" from the previous year. However, Averre points out, "Our cover of 'Heartbeat' is a lot closer to the Humble Pie cover." This latter fact is the sort of thing that led detractors to decry the Knack's retro tendencies as ersatz. "Siamese Twins (The Monkey and Me)" was a composition based on a piece of writing called "A Petition," about a squabbling pair of conjoined twins, written by Averre's then-favorite author, John Barth.

The remainder of the tracks were based around romance, with no fewer than three of them actually using girls' names in their titles: "Oh

Tara," "My Sharona," and "Lucinda." "Your Number or Your Name" was a pretty affair with a jangly riff that, if it put people in mind of the Hollies, was not accidental.

"My Sharona" is the composition that got people excited about the Knack. The excitement started among the band when Averre brought the riff into a rehearsal session. "I showed the riff to Prescott, and I told Bruce I imagined some kind of tom tom/snare thing, as opposed to just straight time with a hi-hat," remembers Averre. "We jammed on it and Doug was scat-singing over it. When we stopped, he goes, 'That's great—let's go back and write it.' So, after rehearsal, we go back to his apartment . . . there were these teenage girls who were big fans of the band. They were from Fairfax High. They actually dubbed themselves the Knackettes. They would dress in black-and-white like us and that kind of thing. One of them was this sweet girl—very smart actually—named Sharona. She'd caught Doug's eye, and I think he was looking for some way to start singing about her. Serendipitously, I was playing that riff and going to those chords, and he heard 'My Sharona.' Sooner than you can say it, he was channeling Daltrey's stuttering thing in 'My Generation': *'Mah-mah-mah-my Sharona'* . . . Doug was living with [his] girlfriend. When he started singing 'Sharona' about this young girl we knew that he had the hots for, I said, 'Hey, man, Judy's in the next room!' But Doug was the lead singer, and he said, 'I don't care, I don't care!'

"Everybody knew, from literally the first time we played that song in the Troubadour, that was the song."

"Forget about being a hit, that was a No. 1 song before I ever heard it," agrees Chapman. The version of "My Sharona" that began appearing on the airwaves circa June '79, however, wasn't quite the same as the live version, or even the album cut. "We couldn't have that long guitar solo on the single," says Chapman. "In those days, anything over three and a half minutes was tough to get on the air." "They hacked the solo to pieces," Averre laments. Regardless, the song's staccato rhythms—the production giving heavy emphasis to that "tom tom/snare" drum sound—soon began storming up the American singles charts.

The Knack were touring the UK when their records began breaking. However, their British gigs were, for Chapman, never going to secure them much success in that country. "They were so L.A., and such an American act," he says. "It was a bit too slick and a bit too arrogant for the UK marketplace." He adjudges the latter "much more discerning when it came to pop music." Sure enough, while "My Sharona" made No. 6 in the UK, the album stalled at No. 65.

In contrast, over in the States, *Get the Knack* earned its gold certification in just thirteen days. It sat at the top for five weeks and ultimately racked up two million sales. "My Sharona" was No. 1 for six weeks and ended up as *Billboard*'s "Single of the Year." At one point, the band achieved the uncommon feat of simultaneously holding down the top spots in both album and singles charts. "It felt very surreal," says Averre. Chapman was of course used to such all-conquering vistas. "I honestly thought what happened was going to happen," he claims. "'My Sharona' was the most obvious hit I'd had in years."

The Knack's euphoria, though, was never unsullied. "There was a guy named Hugh Brown, and he started something called 'Knuke the Knack,'" recalls Averre. Soon, T-shirts with that slogan began proliferating. Brown was tapping into a feeling in the air. Averre: "It just started snowballing, because a lot of the critics didn't like us at all. . . . Doug had personally rubbed some writers the wrong way by seeming a little above himself . . . and that didn't help. . . . Another thing that was happening is, our success was so disproportionate. There were a lot of really good young bands in the club scene and unfortunately they weren't able to follow in our footsteps, so I think there was a resentment that was kind of a jealousy."

There was also an issue of presumption. "In Doug's mind, they were the reincarnation of the Beatles," asserts Chapman. "That was his attitude all the way through the making of that album, and Berton was the same. That's why they chose to go with Capitol Records. And Capitol Records jumped on board and said, 'Well, let's market you that way.'" "That's a myth," says Averre. He insists that the band chose Capitol over bigger players like CBS and Warners partly because of its enthusiasm. He also points out, "If you did sign with a CBS, you could sell a million records and you'd still be like number sixteen on their priority list. It was a very pragmatic decision."

Yet if the choice of record company was hardheaded and the Knack's black-and-white kits and skinny ties only vaguely allusive of the Beatles, such alibis could not be said to be attached to their record designs. *Get the Knack*'s labels deliberately aped the Capitol sixties rainbow-ring design seen by umpteen millions of the Knack's generation on mop-top releases. Further, this tied in with the concept on the reverse of the jacket. "The back side, we purposely staged it to look like *Something New*," reflects Averre. "What idiot first band would try to throw themselves in the same light as the Beatles? It was a joke, and nobody got it."

Another problem some had with the Knack was that their anthems of adolescent angst and virginal frustration could hardly describe the realities of their lives. That in interviews the band fudged their real ages only added to the suspicion that they were older men trying to look like young bucks.

None of these things, though, are enough—individually or cumulatively—to explain the intense hatred felt by so many toward the group. Chapman sums up the additional, enraging ingredient when he notes, "Every song is trashy. The songs were all dirty songs. The whole album was debauched. You listen to some of those lyrics, they're filthy." "My Sharona" featured the line, "I always get it up for the touch of the younger kind." "Good Girls Don't" proffered a scene of teenage sexual frustration in the second person in which the protagonist imagined the object of his desire "sitting on your face." (It was doctored for release as the LP's second single, whereupon it made No. 11.) "(She's So) Selfish" talked of a rich "bitch" who didn't give a "shit" about anybody but herself, and culminated in a refrain that ran, "Fuck-a me today." Although Fieger's mouthpiece role as singer, as well as his pugnacious personality, would make him the hate figure in the Knack, Averre takes most responsibility for what he terms the "skeezy" components of their songs. "It would be a rhyme line and I would throw it out there, probably about to laugh it off, but Doug—who had a lot more balls than me—said, 'Yeah, that's great, we're going with it.' So I'd be stuck with it."

Perhaps none of this would be relevant in any other circumstances. After all, sex is hardly a subject verboten or even discouraged in popular music, while criticizing a female in a song should not be automatically assumed to prove misogyny or sexism. The problem ultimately was in the Knack's demographic, whether or not it was a demographic the band had intended. "I knew that the record company was going to market it to a very young audience," says Chapman. "I don't think it was the best way to market the band because they didn't have any sustaining power within that marketplace, and they weren't taken seriously." Richard Riegel of *Creem* summed up the distaste felt by many when he noticed several "subteens" at a Knack gig, and reflected on them being exposed to songs about "wheedling heavy face-sitting sessions out of the Sharona-types they're about to become." He concluded, "I shudder at the thought."

The upshot of all this is that the Knack were destined to shortly endure something more arduous than the difficult-second-album syndrome. Simply put, their sophomore effort was released into a world that to a large extent was hoping for them to fail.

It tends to be forgotten now, but if UK punk was a race for the twin prizes of success and authenticity, by 1979 Sham 69 were perceived by many as pack leaders. Both Caroline Coon (widely credited with giving the punk movement its name) and Mark Perry (founder of punk bible *Sniffin' Glue*) publicly stated that Sham—particularly lead singer Jimmy Pursey—were the real, guttersnipe deal in a way previous punk acts (implicitly the exalted likes of the Sex Pistols and the Clash) were not. Some derided Sham as punk cartoons, finding fault with things ranging from their simplistic plebeian anthems to the fact that Pursey seemed suspiciously resistant to gelling and spiking his clean, neatly parted hair. However, the fact that in 1978 Sham 69 had three Top 20 UK hits (two of them Top 10) suggested that, as they entered 1979, the supposed joker in the punk pack was turning into a trump card, and about to inherit the discarded crown of the Sex Pistols as leaders of the movement.

Sham 69 hailed not from a graffiti-bedecked inner city but the semi-rustic town of Hersham in the county of Surrey. However, they had their own issues relating to class and authoritarianism. Additionally, as Sham guitarist Dave Parsons points out, "Being from the suburbs, we really were living in Boredom Central."

Seventeen-year-old Parsons met twenty-one-year-old Jimmy Pursey in the fall of 1976. When they shortly joined forces, they retained the name of Pursey's band, Sham 69, which derived from a piece of time-eroded, graffitied soccer triumphalism relating to the fact that Walton & Hersham were champions of a local league in the 1968–1969 season.

The pair would be the new Sham 69's songwriting axis, Parsons writing the melodies and Pursey the words.

By October '77, the band had a single in the shops, "I Don't Wanna," on the independent Step Forward label. It wasn't long before they signed what Parsons terms "a really good deal" with Polydor. Said major label also happened to be the home of the Jam, another Surrey punk ensemble—the Jam's hometown of Woking is a twenty-minute drive from Hersham. However, whereas the Jam's chief songwriter Paul Weller was notoriously touchy about his uncool suburban roots, Sham 69 wore their geographical origins with defiant pride.

A condition of signing to Polydor was that the label fund the free distribution at gigs of a record containing their guttersnipe anthem "Song of the Streets." Sham's first proper Polydor release was the single "Borstal Breakout" in early 1978. By this time, Albie Slider had been replaced on bass by Dave "Kermit" Treganna (sometimes misspelt "Tregunna"). Drummer Mark "Dodie" Cain completed the lineup. (As Treganna was raised in Surbiton, this made him the only band member who wasn't a Hersham boy.) February brought debut album *Tell Us the Truth*, divided between a live side and a studio side. The record showed that there was something more to this group than generic punk motifs. In "What About the Lonely?," Pursey expressed compassion for the type of people punks were usually too busy exuding leather-jacketed cool to even think about, while in "Family Life" he cautioned about throwing off the shackles of home too readily. In fact, the value of mother would be a theme in his Sham career—nowhere more conspicuously than in his tendency to precede television performances with a variant of, "'allo, mum, 'oo's on *Top of the Pops*, then!"

Tell Us the Truth made the UK Top 30, as did *That's Life*. The latter was not only Sham's second LP of '78 but a concept album, no less. Its ten songs and bridging dialogue depicted a day in the life of an everyman working-class teenager. The album's keynote songs—and hits—were stomping prole chorales "Angels with Dirty Faces" and "Hurry Up Harry."

Sandwiched between the respective releases of "Angels" and "Harry" was a standalone single that alluded to a shadow on Sham 69's career—one that would remarkably quickly consume it. Although nothing in the group's lyrics—a general populism aside—could be interpreted as being simpatico with their worldview, anti-immigrant skinheads latched onto Sham. "The National Front and British Movement, who had all these thugs out at football matches and stuff, were using these people to bring violence into punk gigs," Parsons explains. "It wasn't just us. We had the most bad press about it. . . . There wasn't that many people there but there were enough to cause a huge, great fight." Gigs having to be abandoned due to violence and intimidation became a motif in the band's career. A nexus issue was the fact that it was a time of a multiplicity of competing youth cults, chiefly teddy boys, mods, punks, and skinheads. "A youth movement could have possibly had a much stronger voice if they had been united rather than fighting amongst themselves," Parsons says. He and Pursey appealed for calm and unity with the thumpingly contagious "If the Kids Are United." It powered to No. 9, although in no way rid the band of the problem it addressed.

The first Sham 69 release of 1979 was "Questions and Answers." It was a competent example of their usual style, but the fact that its defiance was expressed in rather vague terms ("Only a friend can know the you that's you") was significant. The period involving the preparation of their third album, *The Adventures of the Hersham Boys*, was one in which the band had to find a way to square their men-of-the-people aura with the undeniable reality that they were now men of means. "We were starting to have our own houses, and I was able to buy nice cars and stuff," says Parsons. "It did feel a little bit contradictory . . . Jimmy did develop quite a guilt complex. He probably was in quite a funny space by the time he got to *Hersham Boys*." Pursey was also upset that Cain had been dismissed for his bad timekeeping on his instrument, and furthermore replaced by an American, Rick Goldstein.

The album was recorded at the Château d'Hérouville in northern France. "Beautiful old place," says Parsons. "It was built in 1740. Van Gogh painted it." But what was a punk band doing there? "Probably due to our manager. It was probably a tax benefit from his point of view. . . . I'm not bothered by it . . . a studio could have been anywhere." Parsons even offers that the studio was a step down after having recorded *That's Life* in the luxurious environs of John Lennon's Tittenhurst estate.

In contrast to the previous year, when Parsons seemed to have melodies coming out of his ears, the group landed in France armed only with music for "Fly Dark Angel," "Joey's on the Street," "Susie," and "Someone's Gotta Help Me." The latter two songs were written for the Who's *Quadrophenia* movie before Sham were ousted from the soundtrack, possibly for drinking dry the cocktail cabinet of the tardy director. "Susie" was retooled as "Money," and "Someone's Gotta Help Me" was recast as "Cold Blue in the Night" (the latter's publishing gifted to Treganna). "I don't know why I wasn't prepared," says Parsons. "Maybe I didn't feel the same motive." Parsons's lack of productivity was compounded by Pursey's personal demons when he was finally presented with tunes to which to add lyrics. As with "Questions and Answers," Pursey gave the impression of adopting writing styles designed to avoid the contradiction of his increasingly rarefied lifestyle. To that single's generalized antiauthoritarianism, he added internal mythos ("Hersham Boys," "Voices"), poetic metaphor ("Fly Dark

Angel"), and Americana ("Joey's on the Street," "Lost on Highway 46"). Only "Money" seemed to address his growing prosperity, and even then did so allusively.

While Pursey was having to mold his lyrics to suit his new circumstances, Parsons was taking the music away from the primitivism of punk. Parsons knew that the music press was ever on the alert for signs of a sell-out of punk values but was clearly beyond caring. "We were getting so pissed off with all this right-wing stuff that was going on and increasingly not being able to play," he says. "It was certainly a subconscious thing of moving things away from where we'd been." While some punks might not have approved of this shift, the new florid melodic touches at least mitigated the sludge-like rhythm guitar with which Parsons burdened too many of the tracks. Further broadening was provided by the album's keyboard parts, which included harpsichord on "Lost on Highway 46." Said parts were played by Pete Wilson, who co-produced with Pursey all Polydor Sham fare, and of whom Parsons observes, "Pete was your archetypal hippie, but he was so enthusiastic. When things were sounding good, he used to leap around the studio like a mad thing."

Partway into making the album, Pursey surprised Parsons by suggesting the group record the old Yardbirds number "You're a Better Man Than I." Parsons admits, "We'd never have dreamt of doing something like that before." Perhaps underpinning Parsons's willingness to record only the band's second cover—acknowledging the worth of predecessors was somewhat frowned on by much of punkdom—was a relief that he didn't have to come up with more material. Certainly, the fact that the album featured more than one example of previous Sham material suggested padding. A re-recording of "Questions and Answers" made it onto the LP, of which Parsons says, "I didn't even like that version: the way he was answering himself on the chorus and stuff like that." The album closed with "What Have We Got (Live)," better known to Sham fans as "Song of the Streets." "Polydor were always a bit pissed off that we initially gave the track away . . . we were always under pressure from either the record company or the manager to put that track out, so we agreed to the live version." Of course, its inclusion also helped make up the numbers.

Although the reason for the presence of "What Have We Got" might be ambiguous, one track whose inclusion was definitely dictated by a need to fill out the LP was "Hersham Boys." "We got to the end of the album and Pete Wilson turned around and said, 'You're short of time. We need another track.'" Strangely, "I'm on the Run"—the third track intended for the *Quadrophenia* film—was not excavated, but instead a new song was written from the ground up. Parsons: "Jimmy had this chant of 'Hersham Boy.' I took an acoustic guitar and a few scribbled-down lyrics that he'd got [and] went back to my room. After about half an hour, I had enough of a structure to go back to the studio." Like "Hurry Up Harry," the song was a collision of punk rock and pub sing-along, its guitar riffs complemented by bobbing piano. The chorus line, "They call us the cockney caah-boys," alluded to the fact that the group members' "estuary English" is an accent common among the working class in a wide radius outside Britain's capital. Parsons: "People thought we were trying to pretend we were Londoners, and we never were."

The afterthought was transformed into an asset. "Hersham Boys" was released as a single in July, and its good-natured raucousness saw it sail to No. 6. The parent album to which it gave a name was released in September, in a lavish gatefold sleeve that depicted the band in gun-totin', Wild West costume. A free twelve-inch single of live tracks was thrown in. Like the "Hersham Boys" single, the album marked an all-time commercial high for the band, making No. 8.

Sham proceeded to tumble from this high point remarkably swiftly. The "Hersham Boys" single was followed by a gig at London's Rainbow Theatre at which Sham were onstage for all of twenty minutes before "argy-bargy" once again made continuing to play impossible. It would seem logical that this type of chaos was one of the reasons that Pursey decided to abandon Sham 69 to hook up with ex–Sex Pistols Paul Cook and Steve Jones. (Treganna was also on board.) Some were intrigued by the idea of the Sham Pistols (as they were, part-mockingly, dubbed); others felt that a punk supergroup was the epitome of the type of rock-aristocracy star syndrome that the new wave was supposed to be washing away. In early July (in other words, before *The Adventures of the Hersham Boys* was even released), Pursey was babbling his excitement about the project to Garry Bushell of *Sounds* ("Sham had said all they could say"). Bushell intimated that Parsons was glad Sham had finished on a peak and as mates, and was planning a new band with Goldstein and possibly Barrie Masters of Eddie and the Hot Rods. "I don't remember being fazed by it," recalls Parsons of the Sham Pistols machinations. "Again, it was probably our bloody manager. He could see that there would be a great big mega-deal and advance. Because that's how Jimmy's solo albums came about. Because he was about to join the Pistols, our manager went into Polydor and he got Jimmy a double solo-album deal which was for a hundred grand each, which in those days was a huge amount of money." By September, it had been announced that the Sham Pistols were finished. That the band never got beyond rehearsals and photo sessions was predicted by Parsons to Bushell: "I don't think it's gonna last that long, 'cause Jim always likes to be 100 percent in control."

As he now had a solo deal off the back of the abortive Sham Pistols, and as the very idea of Sham live work had soured so profoundly, it would seem unlikely that Pursey any longer felt much commitment to

Sham 69. This theory is borne out by Parsons's recollections about the release of the follow-up to "Hersham Boys," "You're a Better Man Than I." "Jimmy pushed for it to be released as a single, against our manager's wishes and the record company's wishes. I think that was Jimmy pushing a self-destruct button." The record only just scraped into the Top 50. Even so, in late '79, Pursey flew with the band to Super Bear Studio in the French Alps to record the follow-up to *The Adventures of the Hersham Boys*.

Whatever the hopes in some quarters for their failure, the fealty of the Knack's millions of fans could have been secured had the band come up with a second album that was as consistent as their LP debut. That they didn't was pretty much predetermined by the fact that the follow-up appeared just eight months after *Get the Knack*. "I remember saying to them at the time, 'Don't you think we should wait a little longer?'" says Chapman, who again produced, albeit billed as "Commander Chapman." "I knew going into that second album that the songs were 'B' versions of the first album. There wasn't a smash on there." As such, this time the Knack were far less able to withstand public opprobrium. Intensified strains of the latter were guaranteed by the decision to give the new record the title . . . *But the Little Girls Understand*. The line, co-opted from Willie Dixon's "Back Door Man," implied that the Knack could ignore critical brickbats because they got their validation from the Kids—i.e., people who were too musically unsophisticated to know any better. This was a deliberate red rag to those who thought their fan base inappropriately young. "Doug had an unfortunate aspect where, when somebody criticized, he doubled down," says Averre. He adds, "The first single off that album was 'Baby Talks Dirty,' and you can hear it in the title right there: that was Doug saying, 'You think we're smutty? Here's this!'" As well as being self-consciously provocative, "Baby Talks Dirty" was unimaginative, bearing a structural resemblance to "My Sharona." This self-parody of the Knack's grubby pop style peaked at No. 38. Its parent album only managed No. 15. Follow-up single "Can't Put a Price on Love" achieved a miserable No. 62. Mike Chapman says of the Knack's talents: "Could that have been parlayed into something that could have lasted years? It should have but you had a self-destructive leader of the band running the show . . . Doug was coked out of his mind most of that time I worked with him. . . . What Doug wanted, Doug got."

Sham 69's fall from grace was just as precipitous. Their fourth album, *The Game*, released in June 1980, was a respectable effort, even if Pursey's concerns were becoming ever more opaque—something underlined by an impenetrable sleeve design featuring a roulette wheel, a procession of toddlers, and cuffed hands. Yet while the commercial performance of leadoff single "Tell the Children" was a slight improvement on that of "You're a Better Man Than I," the album failed to chart at all. It seems logical to assume that fans were disgruntled by the disloyal and semi-farcical Sham Pistols interlude, and that they were bored by Pursey's repeated dramatic insistence-cum-threat that the latest Sham gig was the last. Parsons, though, feels the problem stemmed more from Polydor's unhappiness over the "You're a Better Man Than I" saga. "The record company were starting to cut their losses and say, 'Sod that, let's move onto something else.'" "Unite and Win," released in July 1980, was Sham 69's swan song. A second-rate "If the Kids Are United," it became the first Sham 45 not to bother the chart compilers since "Borstal Breakout."

. . . But the Little Girls Understand and *The Game* were to be found clogging up the cutout bins (or remainder racks, in UK parlance) pretty much simultaneously. Before long, it became difficult to find anyone prepared to admit to being one of the millions who had once bought

records by the Knack or Sham 69, and it became just as difficult for the public consciousness to reconcile the two bands' undeniable onetime success with the faults they were now unanimously perceived to possess. Jimmy Pursey himself was considered no less a joke than Sham 69: his solo career went nowhere. Nor ultimately did he have anything to show for his solo-deal mega-advance. Parsons: "He lives in a caravan now. He can't keep money. He's always been a big gambler." Because he would feel guilty if he was well-off? "Yes, there's definitely an element of that."

Music history has shown that tides come in as well as recede. It has also shown that late-seventies punk fans who held the established rock acts in contempt for living off past glories are no less susceptible to nostalgia than any other generation. "Sham re-formed in '86, and we've been back together ever since recording and playing, and never so successfully as now," Parsons says. Moreover, Sham 69 songs have taken on a new life. A surreal example is the fact that, in 2005, "If the Kids Are United" was used as walk-on music for British Prime Minister Tony Blair at a Labour Party political conference.

Sham 69's cachet may have long evaporated—the history books do not accord them the level-pegging status with the Pistols and the Clash that seemed evident to so many at the time—but their impact is undeniable. That impact was just as important to Sham as to their fans. "Punk was a gift," summarizes Parsons. "For the first time ordinary people like us had been given a platform to speak our minds, say what we thought, and possibly enlighten ourselves and others on the way."

The Knack are not in a position to mine the nostalgia seam. They split in 1981, after the poor reception to their Jack Douglas–produced third album, *Round Trip*. Although they attempted comebacks in 1991, 1998, and 2001, it wasn't the same band, because Bruce Gary was *persona non grata*. Reconciliation was ruled out by fateful turns of events.

When Chapman notes, "The story of the Knack is really a tragedy in many ways," he is not merely referring to the fact that they were perennially unable to recapture their once far-reaching fan base. Half of the lineup was cut down shockingly young. Bruce Gary died in 2006 of Non-Hodgkin lymphoma, aged fifty-five. Four years later, Doug Fieger succumbed to lung cancer, aged fifty-seven. Chapman says that Fieger and Gary took a mutual animosity to the grave: "Bruce always claimed that he should have been a writer on 'My Sharona,' because he came up with the drum riff."

These days, Averre composes in the field of musical theater. "I've been doing that for twenty years or so. Nothing you'd have heard of, but it's going well . . . I didn't want to be that guy who's fifty, and the one thing he does is still try to look like a rocker so he can get onstage and do the one song that people know him for." Whatever the vicissitudes of the Knack's fortunes, "My Sharona" has sustained a life of its own, becoming a staple of classic radio, commercials, sporting events, and karaoke sing-alongs. "You can't kill it with a stick," Averre marvels. "I live comfortably because of this one song."

Averre himself doesn't subscribe to the theory of the Knack as a tragedy. "How many people would give their left nut to have my 'problems'? That we weren't able to sustain—it's not good. But, on balance, I got to experience something few people can, and that's a beautiful thing."

Unknown Pleasures and Death Wishes: Joy Division

Joy Division were the kings of post-punk. However, although their music was the quintessence of that category, in truth their regency was as much to do with the perfect symmetry and—for want of a better word—integrity of their career. When their front man, Ian Curtis, committed suicide in 1980, after the band had recorded just two albums, it meant not only that Joy Division had left a legacy that would never be blemished by any subsequent group decline but that Curtis had been true to the depressive visions his songs had consistently purveyed.

"Not many people saw the Sex Pistols live, but most who did formed bands" is a mantra that cannot possibly be true but certainly is in the case of canal-company employee Peter Hook and graphic designer Bernard Sumner, who attended a Pistols gig in their hometown of Manchester in July 1976. This being four months before the Pistols released their first record, they were among an audience of no more than fifty people. Both men have reported that they didn't think much of the music they heard but were inspired to set up a group because they realized that, if these people could have the effrontery to perform, then so could they. Summer took up guitar, Hook bass. An advert in Manchester's Virgin music store procured them a singer and second guitarist, Ian Curtis. Like his new colleagues, Curtis had a respectable job, in his case in the civil service. The band—then called Warsaw—was completed in August 1977 when, having already been through three drummers, another music-shop recruitment card yielded them Stephen Morris.

That Curtis was drafted without an audition was a very punk act, but the group's days as a punk band were over not long after their debut gig in May 1977. Journalist Jon Savage became a member of the band's circle after moving up to Manchester from London in April 1979 and would later author two books on the group. He says, "They were very inspired by punk, but by the time they released their first EP, *Ideal for Living*, which was recorded in November '77 and then released in June '78, they were already moving away from punk thrash into something much more interesting, particularly on a track called 'No Love Lost,' which is quite cinematic and almost krautrock." Savage also says, "Tony Wilson always said that the difference between Joy Division and punk rock was that punk rock was 'Fuck you' and Joy Division was 'I'm fucked.'" The Warsaw appellation had been dropped to avoid confusion with London punk band Warsaw Pakt. Perhaps it could be said that the studied bad taste of the name under which that aforesaid EP was released was the group's last punk act: "joy division" was a phrase used in novella *House of Dolls* as slang for Nazi concentration-camp brothels.

It was symptomatic of this well-read band that they took their name from a book. Their taste was for alternative literature, something that in the seventies had to be actively pursued. "It was much harder to get information about things—obviously there was no internet—so you really had to hunt to find odd stuff, weird stuff," notes Savage. "Ian and Stephen spent quite a lot of time in the local alternative bookshop in Manchester picking up books by Michael Moorcock and J. G. Ballard and [William] Burroughs." The dystopian tenor of the works of the latter two writers would certainly find their way into the band's songs.

Joy Division records would attribute songwriting to all members. "They were all responsible for the music," says Savage. "Joy Division were four musicians, and they all had equal importance." "I'm more rhythm and chords, and Hooky was melody," Sumner said. "Ian was pretty good at riff spotting. He'd go, 'Oh, that bit's good, that bit's good.' . . . Ian would take it home, where he had a big box of lyrics . . . he'd come back next rehearsal and we'd have finished lyrics." Curtis's technique was not just prolific but elevated. As Joy Division road manager Terry Mason noted, "Everyone else in the country's doing simple rhymes, and Ian's putting these poems together . . ."

An Ideal for Living was self-produced and self-released, funded by money Curtis received for his twenty-first birthday. Joy Division had an in-concert track on *Short Circuit: Live at the Electric Circus* (June 1978) and a brace of Martin Hannett–produced studio tracks on the first release by Tony Wilson's independent label Factory, *A Factory Sample* (also '78). By now, the band had acquired interest from major labels, but that interest was never quite reciprocated. They decided to remain with minnow Factory. "They quite liked the fact that on an independent label you didn't have an advance to pay back, which you would on a major," says Savage.

Daringly, Joy Division spurned singles until after their first long-playing statement. This lack of way-pavers only made more surprising to their fans the sound—and made more appropriate the title—of *Unknown Pleasures*, recorded in 10cc's Strawberry Studios in April 1979 and released the following June. "Joy Division live were extremely raw and loud and distorted," Savage recalls. Such could not be said of the soundscapes of *Unknown Pleasures*, which, though powerful, were temperate, sometimes glacial. Morris had opted to use Syndrums. The placing of the rest of the band's sound in an adjacent clinical territory was more to do with producer Hannett. "Martin created something else," says Savage. This something else engendered a fissure in the group. Savage: "Ian and Stephen got it and realized that they were making a record, that it wasn't a straight reproduction of a live show, and Bernard and Peter Hook felt for quite a long time that Martin had toned them down. They did come to realize that it actually worked very well. By the time of the productions that Martin did later in the year, they were all definitely on the same page." Hannett is on record as saying, "They were a gift to a producer, because they didn't have a clue. They didn't argue." Can we infer from that that he was using Joy Division for his own ends? Savage: "No, absolutely not. He was bringing out what was in them. It was a collaborative exercise."

Unknown Pleasures came housed in a minimalist white-on-black Peter Saville sleeve featuring radio waves that, at first glance, resembled a mountain range. The record's contents were similarly spindly and monochromatic. The keynote song was "She's Lost Control," which proffered a lyric of sweaty paranoia set against instrumentation predicated on space, delay, and not-quite-identifiable noises-off. On the loping "Shadowplay," Sumner's guitar work keened and spiraled while Curtis attempted to get to grips with a never-defined dread. The tension between the band's old/live and new/studio sound was epitomized by the opening of "New Dawn Fades," where Sumner's growling rock guitar resembled a dog straining to get away from the stake it was tied to, in the form of the overarching sonic discipline. The album didn't work as background music or a casual listening experience but did reward concentration. Some might object to the uniformity of tone and lack of gaiety, but nowhere was there a rock cliché to be found—perhaps a capsule definition of post-punk.

However unexpected their stately, skeletal restyling, the *Unknown Pleasures* songs instantly struck a chord with music lovers seeking something cerebral. "It was one of those albums that defined the year," says Savage. Not that this was reflected in chart positions, of which originally there were none, something almost certainly related to the decision not to issue any singles from it. This, though, didn't mean that Joy Division were going unrewarded. "*Unknown Pleasures* was done quite cheaply, and they made money on it," says Savage. "Groups who were signed by majors in London, they racked up huge bills without even thinking."

In October 1979 came standalone single "Transmission." The band's first 45 was that epitome of pop: a song about the radio. Except this was not the usual airwave anthem but a creation refracted through Joy Division's mordant prism, its refrain of "Dance to the radio" dripping with ambiguity, if not scorn. Another new song, the brooding "Atmosphere," appeared in France in March 1980. The band's increasingly devoted UK fan base was frustrated at being unable to easily obtain it. They shortly had bigger things to worry about. Before it could appear on 45 in the band's home country, Curtis was dead, hence so were Joy Division.

That Curtis was not a well man might have seemed something that could be gleaned from his lyrics. However, many an artistic twenty-something has specialized in doom-and-gloom without taking it to its logical conclusion. Curtis's despair was real, and his problems many.

The Skids' Richard Jobson first met Curtis when Joy Division were still called Warsaw. Through his spoken-word recordings for the label Crépuscule, Jobson was also a close friend of Annik Honoré, the Belgian woman with whom Curtis was conducting an extramarital affair. That both Curtis and Jobson were epileptic gave them a connection, and, while not close, they socialized together. Both men took the medicinal drug Phenytoin for their condition. "It's a drug with immense side-effects," observes Jobson. Said side-effects included depression and receding gums. Nonetheless, taking the drug was vital for stability. Yet Curtis's behavior undermined any possibility of stability. "If you drink alcohol or take drugs, it can be very dangerous," says Jobson of Phenytoin. "His attitude to his epilepsy was different from mine. He drank and took recreational drugs. I think he had a bit of a death wish, unfortunately."

Psychologically, Curtis seems at this point to have been moving on from Joy Division and even music. He spoke to confidants of not having wanted to make a follow-up album to *Unknown Pleasures*, and of a dream of running a bookshop. That in itself, though, could have been upsetting: it's likely that he felt obligated to carry on with the band so as not to let down his colleagues.

These health and work travails were bad enough, but Curtis was simultaneously going through emotional trauma in his private life. He was torn about the idea of leaving his wife and daughter for Honoré. "I think he wanted to have both," says Savage. "He was being forced into some kind of choice by the pressure of events." Savage's feeling is that no single factor motivated Curtis's suicide but rather stuff "piling" up on him. "He must have thought there was no way out." Jobson feels that the reason for the suicide was a combination of the love triangle and "just being a bit lost," adding, "When you've got that condition as well, it makes you confused and vulnerable."

Curtis had tried to kill himself with a drugs overdose in the first week of April 1980, but lost his nerve and phoned an ambulance. On May 18, 1980, he went through with another suicide attempt, hanging himself with a clothesline. He was just twenty-three. For Joy Division's fans, especially those in thrall to his melancholy worldview, he was an instant martyr—a man who walked it like he talked it, much like Kurt Cobain did for Nirvana's fan base fourteen years later. "I wouldn't call Ian a martyr, because that slightly dramatizes it," says Savage. "It's actually a terrible, sad story, and it's had an appalling impact on all the band and, in particular, his family. It's not something to be celebrated and elevated into some kind of principle or romantic idea." For his part, Jobson feels that the "beautiful loser" image doesn't do justice to Curtis the man. "He was a good guy," Jobson says. "He was also a very funny guy. I went to see that movie that was made about him, *Control.* I just thought it painted him in the light of how people want him to be remembered. The guy that loved football and had an eye for women and was funny—that's not in that film."

What made Curtis's death all the more tragic was the quality of Joy Division's second album, *Closer.* (The title is meant to be pronounced with a hard *s*, for those who might assume it a statement about Curtis's suicide; the funeral theme of Saville's cover design was also a coincidence.) Issued in July 1980, the LP was a development from *Unknown Pleasures*, covering the same sort of territory as the previous record but building on it, especially melody-wise. The month before its release had seen the perfect valedictory in the shape of standalone single "Love Will Tear Us Apart." Curtis's lyrics had always been rooted in absolute sincerity, but the wider world hadn't actually been aware of that. As the facts became known about Curtis's love triangle, it was clear that this was a song harrowingly steeped in its composer's own experience—and a song that helped explain why there would be no more Curtis compositions. Incongruously, it was also rather pretty. It will never be known whether "Love Will Tear Us Apart" would have been a hit without Curtis's demise, but its un–Joy Division deployment of some of the trappings and vocabulary of standard pop numbers suggests that its No. 13 UK chart placing was not entirely a pity vote.

Curtis's surviving bandmates continued working together, adding Gillian Gilbert on keyboards and changing their name. New Order would be one of the most influential bands of the eighties, and in the shape of "Blue Monday" (1983) would release arguably the greatest piece of synth-pop ever recorded. Interestingly, its stridently pessimistic bent could have come straight from the pen of Ian Curtis.

Forgotten Icons: The Boomtown Rats

On January 29, 1979, Bob Geldof, lead singer of the Boomtown Rats, was sitting in a radio station at Atlanta University, preparing for one of the production-line interviews that are the lot of a recording artist's life. On the surface beside him was a telex machine, at the time a cutting-edge way of quickly transmitting large amounts of information over long distances, and, as such, favored by news-wire services and their media clients. The machine was spooling out a story currently unfolding in San Diego, California. The overarching facts were horrific enough for somebody like Geldof, from the sleepy Republic of Ireland, but the minutiae would alarm even Americans wearily familiar with such scenarios.

There had been a shooting at Grover Cleveland Elementary School in which nine children were wounded and both the principal and school janitor killed. *Chicago Tribune* reporter Steven Weegan had heard about what was developing and decided to call homes in the vicinity to try to establish some facts. The first house he rang was located directly opposite the school. Sixteen-year-old Brenda Spencer answered the phone and acquiescently told Weegan what she could see. Weegan then asked her where she thought the shots were coming from. It was when Spencer gave her own address that the terrible reality began to dawn. When Weegan pressed, Spencer admitted it was she who had done the firing. As Weegan further asked, "Tell me why?" the tragedy became tinged forever with a terrible banality. Weegan told NPR in 2009, "She said, 'Because I just don't like Mondays.'"

"I thought, 'How fucking weird,'" Geldof later wrote of the blend of horror and ordinariness. "Then I went back to the hotel and it was preying on my mind and I was actually playing Elvis Costello's 'Oliver's Army' on the guitar and it sort of turned into 'The silicon chip inside her head.'" Geldof averred that the song he proceeded to write was less about the incident—he would draw on the San Diego events as well as deploy phrases from the Weegan/Spencer conversation, but the locale and participants were never identified—and more about what he then felt to be a peculiarly Californian psychosis: not needing a reason for anything, even murder. The resultant song, "I Don't Like Mondays," cemented a period of seven or eight months—one now strangely forgotten—when the Boomtown Rats were the biggest band in Britain.

The Boomtown Rats sprang from the arid, covers-dominated music scene of mid-seventies Eire, as the Republic of Ireland tended to be referred to in those days. Middle-class Dubliners Bob Geldof, John Moylett a.k.a. Johnnie Fingers (keyboards), Garry Roberts (guitar), Gerry Cott (guitar), Pete Briquette (bass), and Simon Crowe (drums)

were originally called the Nightlife Thugs. They restyled themselves
the Boomtown Rats—inspired by a real-life gang mentioned in Woody
Guthrie's autobiography—upon the occasion of their first gig, on
Halloween 1975. Musically they took their cue from R&B revivalists
Dr. Feelgood but, as was common for young bands of the time, the
influence of punk began to audibly seep into their music when that
movement kicked into gear. Geldof was the chief songwriter. His compositions were marked by ferocious intelligence and wry wit, if not particularly a value system.

Signing to Britain's Ensign Records, the Rats moved across the
Irish Sea. Once in Britain, the incongruity of their mix of new-wave
strains and slick musicianship saw them dismissed by some on the then-
powerful weekly music press as inauthentic. There may have been some
condescension toward the Irish underlying the dismissiveness. The
by-your-own-bootstraps rhetoric of their August 1977 debut single,
"Looking After No. 1," didn't help their image, either. The public didn't
seem to care whether they were plastic punks, "Paddies," or Tories: the
record went to No. 11. That and subsequent schoolyard-crush anthem
"Mary of the 4th Form" (No. 15) featured on the group's 1977 quite-
good eponymous debut album.

With second album *Tonic for the Troops* (1978), the influence of
the group's assigned producer became so pronounced that some band
members felt Mutt Lange could plausibly claim co-writing credits. However, Lange had rich material with which to work, not least
"Rat Trap." The didactically minded punks may have disdained the
Rats for their general apoliticism, but with "Rat Trap" the Irishmen
trounced them all, for no song in the rock canon more acutely articu-
lates the soul-destroying dreariness of working-class life than this tale
of leather-jacketed loser Billy traversing the neon-dappled streets of
Nowheresville. Musically, the five-minute track was a veritable opera,

switching tempos and moods multiple times. Released on single, it became Britain's first punk/new-wave chart-topper. *Tonic for the Troops* revealed several more delights, with the ever-playful Geldof exploring themes like the insurrectionary potential of conservatives, the manifold suicide methods offered by residency on an island, and Hitler's hypothecated lack of feelings for Eva Braun.

Released in July 1979, "I Don't Like Mondays" was the Rats' first UK release of the year. Geldof had written the song in a soft-reggae style, but when he handed over his creation to his colleagues it was given a baroque and melodramatic treatment like nothing they'd ever recorded before, starting with Fingers' dramatic opening glissandos. As well as being piano-dominated, the track featured classical strings. If it has achieved the status of classic that it was patently tilting for, it is via notoriety, success, and smoke-and-mirrors, for its grandeur disguised a certain emptiness. Geldof's song words were rather lazy and glib (he observed that the telex was kept clean simply so that he could find a rhyme for "machine," and in any case the reference to the telex was irrelevant to the rest of the lyric). Moreover, as Garry Roberts notes, "He doesn't really try to get to the root of why that would have happened. It's just an observation of it, really." Meanwhile, Simon Crowe saw a drawback in the fact that the massive success of "Mondays" caused it to become the band's signature song: "'Mondays' did an awful lot of good, but it also did us some harm in terms of a lot of people only remember us for that now." The Rats' second consecutive UK No. 1, it spent four weeks at the top and won two Ivor Novello awards (the British equivalent of the Grammys). It also made No. 1 in dozens of countries around the world. Part of its success was due to its promotional film/video, which had a game-changing importance comparable to the promos for Queen's "Bohemian Rhapsody" and a-ha's "Take on Me"—an importance that, like so much of the Rats' one-time prominence, has been largely forgotten. Director David Mallet provided a cinematic vista in which demonic-looking children were seen chanting the chorus refrain in a rural church hall under an ominously overcast sky. "It started the mini-epic type of video, which I almost regret, but then it was new and different," wrote Geldof in his autobiography.

Crowe might have different feelings about the record if it had, as was then hoped, broken the band in the States. To this day, some people are under the bizarre impression that "I Don't Like Mondays" has much the same subject matter as the Easybeats' wistful hankering for the end of the working week, "Friday on My Mind." However, Geldof's disclosure of its inspiration in interviews apprised the Spencer family at least of the fact that it was about something much more serious and, to them, personally traumatic. They tried to prevent the record being released. In a nation with deeply entrenched free-speech principles and no law of *sub judice*, it was a quest doomed to failure. However, the band's American record label, Columbia, withdrew the record from sale after a week. Geldof was prepared to fight any notional court case, but lamented, "Columbia didn't have the courage." In fairness, the label was probably more concerned about widespread repugnance about the song's perceived exploitation and trivialization of a tragedy. The record peaked at No. 73 on *Billboard* in February 1980—the band's sole placing on the Hot 100. The Boomtown Rats were destined to remain a rest-of-the-world phenomenon.

Parent album *The Fine Art of Surfacing*, titled after a psychology article in a science magazine, was released in the UK on the same day as the single. Although lacking the broad sweep, consistency, and occasional warmth of its predecessor, it was studded with quality tracks. "Wind Chill Factor (Minus Zero)" and "Having My Picture Taken" were meaningless but exceptionally catchy. Although "Nothing Happened Today" once again explored Geldof's terror of the mundane, it unfortunately did so in a mundane way. However, the closing five-minute *tour de force* "When the Night Comes" covered the same territory far more impressively. Tracing the daily grind of an office Johnny, it featured a sweeping melody and galvanizing classical-guitar work.

One of the quality tracks was a relative flop on single despite featuring possibly Geldof's greatest-ever lyric. One theory has it that "Diamond Smiles" stalled at No. 13 because of a BBC technician's strike that took *Top of the Pops* off the air for several weeks just after the record's November release—the type of maddening industrial action that had helped get Thatcher elected a few months before. The theory is plausible, but so is the one that dictates that this tale of a high-society belle crushed by the emptiness of her glitzy life (after tying a lamé belt around a chandelier, she "went out kicking at the perfumed air") was too mordantly sophisticated for the hit parade. Something to which the British public could more readily relate was the album's third single, "Someone's Looking at You," released in January 1980. A fist-pumping anthem, albeit with the usual subversive Geldof lyric—this one concerned with paranoia—it made No. 4.

The Rats success didn't so much dribble as sprint away. *Mondo Bongo* (1981), *V Deep* (1982), and *In the Long Grass* (1984) found them struggling to regain their former (and still very recent) greatness. *V Deep*'s opener, "Never in a Million Years," was symptomatic. A passionate railing against God-knows-what, its epic but empty lyric showed a writer as confused and out-of-touch as "Rat Trap" had shown Geldof with finger fixed firmly on the public pulse. Astonishingly it was considered suitable for single release. Not so astonishingly, it only managed to struggle to No. 62.

It's conceivable that a band as talented as the Rats would have eventually regained their lost inspiration and thereby commercial

momentum. However, when Geldof helped launch a compassion juggernaut with the Band Aid project, it caused a bump in the road of the
Rats' career that proved impossible to negotiate. How could Geldof
concentrate on a fading pop band when the Live Aid concert project
of July 1985 offered him the chance to save lives on a gigantic scale? In
their time out of the limelight, the Rats faded to insignificance. "I don't
think we could get arrested after Live Aid," says Crowe.

The band was not just over but consigned to oblivion. That they
had scored nine consecutive UK Top 15 singles seemed to be washed
from public memory. The sensation—cultural and musical—that they
caused in mid-1979 with "I Don't Like Mondays" was suddenly almost
as implausible as a dream. By 2012, Crowe was lamenting, "I wonder
what do people really think about the Boomtown Rats now? There was
a time when we were very important and very noteworthy and that's
all gone by the wayside." The Rats' partial reunion in 2013 (Cott and
Fingers didn't participate) passed almost without notice, even though
it was ongoing at the time of writing. It was a painful contrast to the
financially triumphant in-concert resurrection in 2007 of their peers
the Police.

For many, the highlight of Live Aid was the Boomtown Rats'
Wembley Stadium performance, not because they were particularly
outstanding but because of Geldof's co-opting of a section from their
most famous/infamous song. He later recalled to David Roy of the *Irish
News*, "The line in 'Mondays'—'And today's lesson is how to die'—
pulled me up. I thought, 'Oh, I want to remember this,' because it was
so overwhelming. That's when I stopped and purposely looked all the
way around the stadium, taking it in and thinking about the number
of people watching." Geldof standing with his fist raised in the musical
lull achieved the same sort of resonance as the line, "Who's gonna plug

their ears when you scream?" from the video of the Cars' "Drive" when it was played the same day: a sort of enforced meaningfulness that was powerful nonetheless.

"I think 'Mondays' will be remembered by people when they're sixty," Geldof told Dave DiMartino of *Creem* in 1981. "They'll hear the song and it might evoke some memory of 1979." Whether he's right about that or not, the song's serious message remains valid. Speaking to the *Guardian*'s Dave Simpson in 2013, in the midst of the Rats' reunion, Geldof noted, "The first week into rehearsals some fucking clown killed his parents and his mates and another guy shot up a naval facility in Florida. This shit has actually got worse."

7
JULY

Rainbow—the band formed by ex–Deep Purple guitarist Ritchie Blackmore—never made much headway in the States, but in the UK they did well in both the album and single charts. *Down to Earth*, their 1979 effort, was their fourth studio LP, although the personnel had changed considerably since their 1975 debut. It was less baroque than previous releases, its eight songs comprised of fairly melodic, fairly sprightly heavy rock, two examples of which—the pile-driving, braggadocio "All Night Long" and Russ Ballard's lovelorn "Since You Been Gone"—were UK Top 10 hits.

AC/DC's *Highway to Hell* was heavy rock of a less nuanced type. The chorus of its title track simply consisted of the same line sung four times. However, many had a partiality to the Australian band's bludgeoning simplicity. In that title track and "Touch Too Much," *Highway to Hell* featured two of the band's most iconic songs, and it saw them for the first time break the UK Top 10 and US Top 20. However, the album also marked the end of an era due to the shock death shortly thereafter of lead singer Bon Scott. The new era with vocalist Brian Johnson was even more successful, though: follow-up *Back in Black* is calculated to be one of the three best-selling albums of all time.

Alternative popsters and funkateers the B-52's were a mixed-gender quintet hailing from Athens, Georgia, although they could just as easily have hailed from a tacky suburban home in the 1950s, what with their retro hairdos and antediluvian cultural references. They could also just as easily have hailed from Mars, what with their utter, if studied, weird-ness. Britain took to them before their home country. Their epony-mous debut album brushed the UK Top 20, while its single "Rock Lobster"—an apparently drunken exploration of the ocean bed to a backing resembling the "James Bond Theme"—was a Top 40 hit.

The Fall of the Glitterball

Nineteen seventy-nine marked the peak of disco. It also marked its bloody death.

The medium with the muffled, four-on-the-floor drumbeat and lyrical exhortations to dance—or at the very least not be downcast—had been slowly evolving within soul music since the early 1970s. It was a love-it-or-hate-it proposition. Its hooks and slogans made it infernally catchy, but it was sharp-edged and relentless: disco soundscapes were never softened with acoustic instruments or leavened with respites. As such, it was difficult to tolerate in anything more than short bursts. "It wasn't album music," admits journalist and disco fan Jon Savage. "It was twelve-inch singles. If you want a good disco album, you buy a simulation of what Larry Levan was playing at the Paradise Garage, or you buy a mix album of what David Mancuso was playing at the Loft, and then it really made sense, because it's a mix of the best songs by different artists."

Some had other problems with disco. The penchant of disco pro-ducers for using classical strings, however stylishly or rhythmically, seemed somehow inimical to the unkempt spirit of rock (which at that point was still an umbrella title for just about all post-Elvis popular music). Moreover, while some thought disco socially progressive for the way the white, male dominance of seventies rock didn't apply in a medium where women and minorities were highly visible, the piti-less admission policies of Studio 54 and other dance venues were felt in some quarters to be predicated on their own forms of prejudice. Many rock fans thought disco actively reactionary because it embraced apolitical hedonism. Its escapism was certainly a commodity many Americans desired in 1979, when daily television images implied the US was not a superpower but an impotent minnow, whether they be of the Sandinistas taking office in Nicaragua, the Iran hostage crisis, the Soviet occupation of Afghanistan, or fractious domestic tableaux that underlined the general feeling that the postwar economic boom was stuttering to an end.

At the start of the year, disco was pretty much all-conquering. In the UK, the first five No. 1 singles of '79 were all disco records. What is remarkable about this dominance is that not all of the acts concerned were disco merchants. In the latter category indubitably lay the Village People, whose "Y.M.C.A." hogged the top for the first three weeks of the New Year; and Gloria Gaynor, whose assertion that there is life post–bad boyfriend, "I Will Survive," became a *de facto* feminist anthem, proving that at least some examples of the genre had sociopolitical import. However, Ian Dury and the Blockheads ("Hit Me with Your Rhythm Stick") and Blondie ("Heart of Glass") were recording artistes of a greater depth who happened to be cashing in on and/or paying tribute to the medium.

The Bee Gees, who made the top with "Tragedy," were a more complicated proposition. Their career had started in the sixties with some of the most baroque and surreal pop ever recorded. The three brothers Gibb had gone through more than one identity somersault before alighting on the flashing disco floor in 1975 with *Main Course*. It was their ubiquity across 1977 that more than anything else was responsible for disco turning from one flower in the garden of popular music into a weed that threatened to strangle all other types of flora. The Bee Gees' 1979 album *Spirits Having Flown* wasn't really disco, but moved them into an area that might be termed "ornamental soul." However, in the imagination of a public that had unequivocally seen the *Saturday Night Fever* ballad "More Than a Woman" as disco, the same categorization-by-association applied for the multiple hits their new album bequeathed.

Over in the States, disco's supremacy was even more extraordinary. Even if *Spirits Having Flown*'s three No. 1s are excluded, for fully half of 1979, disco records were sitting at the top of the *Billboard* singles chart. "I Will Survive" and "Heart of Glass" got to No. 1 in the States, as they did in the UK. Amii Stewart scaled the summit with a discofied-cum-space-age recalibration of the old soul number "Knock on Wood." Anita Ward proffered the jingle-ish "Ring My Bell," a record pocked with idiotically enjoyable electronic bloops and pings.

Donna Summer, the veritable queen of the genre, made No. 1 with the pumping, horny "Hot Stuff" and prostitute's anthem "Bad Girls." There was more to Summer than met the eye: her producers, Giorgio Moroder and Pete Bellotte, created sophisticated, not-easily-categoriz-able soundscapes ("Hot Stuff" had a rockin' guitar solo and "Bad Girls" sweeping horn charts). Summer herself wrote much of her material and specialized in concept albums. *Bad Girls* was her second double LP in succession. Her association with disco, in fact, destined her to never be taken as seriously as she deserved.

Barbra Streisand shamelessly hitched up with Summer for "No More Tears (Enough Is Enough)," Summer's third US No. 1 of the year. In contrast, Michael Jackson could be given a free pass for his disco-bandwagon-jumping chart-topper "Don't Stop 'Til You Get Enough" on the grounds that there was a thin dividing line between soul and disco. Its parent LP, *Off the Wall*, was Jackson's first adult solo album, its flawless grooves marking the beginning of his transforma-tion from star to tortured immortal. *Off the Wall* inhabited a genre all of its own in its embracement of black music of every type, but it was unquestionably informed by disco. Though studded with other fondly remembered anthems like "Rock with You" and "She's Out of My Life," it did rather suffer from that no-room-to-breathe quality that consigned so much disco to places requiring limited attention, such as singles and radio.

"Le Freak" and "Good Times" confirmed Chic as the thinking man's disco. The fact that they were a "real" band in a field where producers were often king was a big help in this department, but the brawny bass lines of Bernard Edwards and *chinka-chinka* guitar of Nile Rodgers decorated records of elevated lyrical and musical intelligence. If Chic's records were ones even disco naysayers found difficult to hate, the same couldn't quite be said for Rod Stewart's "Da Ya Think I'm Sexy?" The opening track on his 1978 album *Blondes Have More Fun*, it had been released as a single that September. While it had climbed to No. 1 in his native Britain in December, it didn't make it to the top in the States until February 10 the following year (the same day, in fact, as its parent album). It wasn't so much that "Da Ya Think I'm Sexy?" was a bad record: its soaring synth riff was sublime, and its lyric, about a couple staving off the spiritual coldness of the city by finding warmth in each other's arms, was actually touching. Duane Hitchings, who co-wrote the song with Stewart and Carmine Appice (although Stewart has admitted plagiarism of both a Jorge Ben Jor melody and a Bobby Womack riff), has even claimed it was a "spoof on disco." Unfortunately, Stewart at this point in time had an execrable public persona, a sort of parody of Jagger's male-tart stage image that involved immodest public pronouncements, mascara, and the provocative wiggling of his backside in leopard-skin leggings. The record's title line played into the public perception of both Stewart as ickily pathetic and disco as a music for people who were obsessed with themselves.

Not all notable disco records made No. 1, of course, and not all even charted. Some contend that the best disco release of 1979 was Dinosaur's "Kiss Me Again," an almost avant-garde, thirteen-minute extravaganza written and produced by Arthur Russell and Nicky Siano (the first disco record where a DJ—a profession so important to the genre's infiltration of the culture—got to be a producer) and featuring guitar from the ultra-hip figure of Talking Heads' David Byrne. However, the fact that the above analysis doesn't even include the disco hits that didn't make the top spot only underlines the medium's dominance—a dominance that for many made the Knack's six-week occupancy of the summit with "My Sharona" such a blast of fresh air.

As such, the backlash against disco was probably inevitable. Its zenith was Disco Demolition Night. An event that took place on July 12, 1979, its reputation as the "Night Disco Died" is overplayed: Donna Summer was dominating the *Billboard* chart for the entire month after it, and hers wasn't the last US disco No. 1 of the year. However, the night stands as a symbol of the prevailing discontent with disco and all it was felt to stand for, and at the very least it hastened the decline that is always inevitable for anything that reaches saturation point.

Disco Demolition Night started as a gimmick designed to boost attendances at Chicago White Sox games. The baseball team recruited shock DJ Steve Dahl, well known for his on-air anti-disco tirades and his "Disco Sucks" slogan, to MC an event wherein the public were admitted to the Sox's Comiskey Park stadium for the bargain price of ninety-eight cents plus a disco record. The plan was to ostentatiously destroy the discs on the field between games. However, the event got out of hand. The fifty thousand people who turned up vastly exceeded the stadium's usual attendance of six thousand. (More were locked outside.) The implication that many of the attendees weren't baseball fans was confirmed by the fact that discs began skimming onto the pitch while play was underway, and underlined by people rushing onto the field in the demolition section between games, where they vandalized and set fire to the field. Riot police were called. The scheduled second game was abandoned—the first time in baseball history that any reason other than bad weather had caused this. The next day, the event was national news.

Jon Savage doesn't buy the idea that, before the carnage descended, Disco Demolition Night was rooted in nothing more sinister than banter. "It was so bloody homophobic it's horrible," he says. "One of the reasons disco was disliked in America [was] because it was 'faggot music.' There's an incredible amount of homophobia in American music culture, much more than there is in the UK." Many people have also claimed that racism lay at the heart of the sort of hostility to disco expressed on Disco Demolition Night. It's certainly true that, in late-seventies America, professing a love for disco was often a codified way of being "out," and it's certainly striking how disco gave black artists parity with white artists in the American singles charts in 1979. (More than parity, if one stretches the definition of disco to include Peaches & Herb, and the Commodores.) However, while no doubt many had a problem with either or both of these facts, the equally vitriolic "Knuke the Knack" campaign was given the benefit of the doubt and taken at face value. That some had a legitimate grievance about disco is underlined by the fact that, across the course of '79, many US radio stations switched over to an all-disco format that left rock fans feeling abandoned. In 2016, Dahl wrote, "I'm worn out from defending myself as a racist homophobe for fronting Disco Demolition at Comiskey Park. This event was just a moment in time. Not racist, not anti-gay. Just kids, pissing on a musical genre . . . just as they pissed upon Perry Como."

Whatever the truth of the reasons for the hatred, after the start of the new year/decade, disco was never as big again. Disco Demolition

Night made disco a pejorative term beyond the realms of the likes of Dahl. Music critic Vince Aletti was at the time working for the disco department of a record label. "We became the dance music department," he recalled to Tony Sclafani of MSNBC.com. "Disco became a dirty word." "Disco Sucks won," Nile Rodgers told *Q*'s Paul Stokes in 2015. "After Disco Sucks . . . we never [had] another No. 1 record."

"Disco was about escapism, but it became inescapable," Barry Walters told the *New York Times*' Bernard Weinraub, on the occasion of a 2002 disco exhibition of which Walters was co-curator. "In some ways it defeated its own purposes."

8
AUGUST

Plenty of music fans have heard of David Bowie's *Lodger*. Few on the other hand are even aware of *Ghostown*, another 1979 album bearing Tony Visconti's production credit. The LP was the product of the Radiators, the Republic of Ireland's first major punk band. Some who know both works actually prefer *Ghostown*. Whereas Bowie's album was often irksomely "difficult," *Ghostown* boasted a straightforward punk-pop hybrid, relatable lyrics, and an often-hilarious turn of phrase, the latter exemplified by the scabrous character study "Ballad of Kitty Ricketts."

Talking Heads were the brainiest and most eccentric of the bands that emerged from the CBGBs scene. Their first two albums were stuffed full of pop with odd lyrical perspectives. With their third album, *Fear of Music*, they varied the formula a little, making the songs looser and more percussive. As ever with their product, it was loved by those who favored lateral perspectives and disdained by people who found quirkiness little compensation for lack of a heart.

Drums and Wires was the third album by XTC, new-wavers hailing from the unfashionable English town of Swindon. Growing musical proficiency and the engagement of Steve Lillywhite as producer gave the record a layered and poised feel absent from their previous efforts. It also contained XTC's first hit, "Making Plans for Nigel." Unusually written by bassist Colin Moulding rather than guitarist Andy Partridge, it was a hypnotic denunciation of careerist parents who thwart romantic teenage dreams. It was also liquid and transcendent where XTC's music was usually designedly thumping and unashamed of obvious artifice.

Van Morrison's *Into the Music* was a return to form after a long dip following 1972's *Saint Dominic's Preview*. A mix of folk and soul, it didn't add any signature songs to his canon but was rich and likeable. The latter quality was partly predicated on its happy vibe, which was a refreshing contrast to the Irishman's grouchy, graceless interviews. Interestingly, a newfound Christianity was evident in the lyrics, but "Van the Man" kept the references subtle enough to not alienate fans the way his peer Bob Dylan would do the very same month.

Judas Finds God: Bob Dylan

In 1978, Bob Dylan was interviewed by Australian journalist Craig McGregor. The two had last met in 1966, when Dylan was on a journey in which he would transform popular music: within a couple of months, Dylan would unleash double album *Blonde on Blonde*, the final part of a stunning triptych that confirmed him—willingly or not—as king of the counterculture. It and its 1965 predecessors, *Bringing It All Back Home* and *Highway 61 Revisited*, had done something nobody had ever presumed possible: seamlessly married rock 'n' roll's primal energy to the intellectualism of folk. During the astonishingly short period of time those three albums spanned—fifteen months—Dylan and his imitators (who included artists normally perceived as trendsetters, like the Beatles and the Rolling Stones) forever consigned to history the idea that post-Elvis popular music was suitable only for adolescents. Not that Dylan's achievements were predicated solely on innovation: his lyrics were dazzling, and the sounds he coaxed from his backing bands magisterial. To this day, many consider *Highway 61 Revisited* the greatest album ever made.

Since then, Dylan had had a bumpy journey. Varying quality control, markedly declining productivity, and unconvincing comebacks had pocked the path to 1975, when he was able to proffer *Blood on the Tracks*, his first album of the seventies worthy of standing beside his great sixties output. Sadly, it was an artistic triumph wrested from personal failure, addressing the agony of the breakup of his marriage. So too—following the spotty *Desire* (1976)—did 1978's *Street-Legal*, although to the accompaniment of far less beautiful melodies and instrumentation.

One of the questions McGregor had for the 1978-vintage Dylan was whether he had "got into any religion" since they'd last met. "No, no dedicated religion, I have not gotten into that," Dylan replied. "I've never felt that lost." A 1979 book by Paul Williams on Dylan's conversion to fundamentalist Christianity was titled *Dylan—What Happened?* The bewildered tone of Williams's title was justified, for whatever did happen, it happened quick. *Street-Legal* was recorded a month after the McGregor interview. Its closing track, "Where Are You Tonight? (Journey Through Dark Heat)," revealed Dylan to have found a relief from his pain via "a pathway that leads up to the stars." Toward the end of his 1978 tour, Dylan could be seen sporting onstage a small silver cross. Meanwhile, his concert reworkings of his lyrics were now conspicuously speckled with Biblical references. Those members of Dylan's fan base who picked up on all this had their suspicions fully—and dismayingly—confirmed with the August 1979 release of his nineteenth studio album, *Slow Train Coming*.

Dylan approached the album with an unusual amount of application. His run of great LPs through the sixties had been—recording-wise—the result of instrumental spontaneity and a light production touch. On *Slow Train Coming*, he for the first time employed a famous producer, namely Jerry Wexler, responsible for landmark recordings by the likes of Ray Charles, Wilson Pickett, and Aretha Franklin. Also for the first time, Dylan jettisoned live-in-the-studio methods in favor of overdubbing. The result was an album of remarkable smoothness. Courtesy of crack musicians—guitarist Mark Knopfler, drummer Pick Withers (both from Dire Straits), keyboardist Barry Beckett, bassist Tim Drummond, and the Muscle Shoals Horns—the smoothness in no way prohibited gutsiness.

Yet the exquisite music was, for many, a spoonful of sugar that didn't make the medicine of the lyrics any less bitter. The keynote song on *Slow Train Coming* was "Precious Angel," which declared, "Ya either got faith or ya got unbelief and there ain't no neutral ground." The same song saw Dylan exulting in a future in which men would beg God in vain to kill them. The man who had written the definitive humanitarian anthem, "Blowin' in the Wind," and the quintessential broadside against using religion as a justification for wrongdoing, "With God on Our Side," was now proffering fire-and-brimstone judgmentalness. Across the nine selections, the only relief from the finger-wagging was "Do Right to Me Baby (Do Unto Others)," which featured sentiments like "Don't wanna judge nobody."

Only the most obtuse would aver that religion had never featured in Dylan's songbook. "Quinn the Eskimo (The Mighty Quinn)" (written in 1967) was supposedly nothing more than whimsy but, in the context of other spiritually themed "Basement Tapes" songs, it seemed more a Second Coming metaphor. *John Wesley Harding* (1967) was suffused with biblical imagery. *Desire*'s "Oh Sister" was about a couple who "died and were reborn and left mysteriously saved." However, "Quinn the Eskimo" was joyous, *John Wesley Harding* was underpinned by a tone of penitence, and the only chiding to be found in "Oh Sister" was the type to be heard in a lovers' quarrel. What made the doctrinaire slogans of the *Slow Train Coming* songs even more bewildering was that they simply did not sound like they originated with the same psyche as, say, the fiercely intelligent, self-knowing "It's Alright, Ma (I'm Only Bleeding)." They provoked contempt above and beyond disgust at intellectual decline: it seemed obvious to everyone but Dylan himself that his embrace of organized religion was simply a manifestation of the trauma caused by the rupture of his marriage.

Dylan's new piousness, plus the fact that none of the *Slow Train Coming* songs were up-tempo, hardly raised his stock with the punks who had for the last three years dismissed his generation of musicians as lethargic old men. New-wave ire, though, was to be expected. More important was the potential response of Dylan's fans. He was an artist who appeared to be committing commercial suicide. For all his cultural influence and the multitudinous hits he wrote for third parties in the sixties, Dylan's records didn't sell that well, making a big impact upon release but boasting only a short commercial tail. He was reliant on a dedicated audience largely comprised of people who it would be fair to describe as "alternatively minded." Essentially, Dylan's fans were the very type of people most contemptuous of God-fearing rhetoric—folks who were, in the main, old enough to remember that part of the reason for the stultifying authoritarianism of Western life before the 1960s was the hold that organized religion had over the culture.

Yet it wasn't quite as simple as that. Dylan's journey had mirrored that of his generation from the beginning, whether it be his youthful idealism, his drift away from political issues as he discovered the bliss of marriage, or his fractious custody battle when that marriage ended. To a large extent, that reflecting back of his cohort's progress was now happening again. Bob Dylan was going through what millions of Americans were at the time: born-again Christianity was sweeping the nation like wildfire. As such, with *Slow Train Coming*, he actually picked up new fans. The numbers of those people appeared to more than compensate for any concurrent shakeout of the faithful. *Slow Train Coming* was a Top 3 record on both sides of the Atlantic, while its first single, "Gotta Serve Somebody," was his biggest US hit for six years. The gloss conferred by Wexler and his colleague Barry Beckett must be assumed to have had something to do with that commercial success: however skeptical the reviews, all were compelled to note how easy the LP was on the ears. Meanwhile, being prepared to do more than one vocal take also reaped dividends: his singing on "Gotta Serve Somebody" garnered Dylan his first Grammy.

This apparent triumphant vindication of Dylan's religiosity, though, wasn't the end of the story. Over the next year, Dylan began to refuse to play his pre-conversion songs in concert. He also started to preach from the stage about the coming Armageddon and the sordid behavior of homosexuals. The press ridiculed him, and he was booed at his own gigs—something that hadn't happened since his mid-sixties switch from folk to rock (when—irony of ironies—he was famously called "Judas!"). It all came to a head with the appearance in June 1980 of *Saved*, his second Christian album and his second to be produced by Wexler and Beckett. The title was itself presumptuous and arrogant, but in conjunction with Tony Wright's cover painting—a celestial hand reaching down to dispense salvation by touching fingertips with a selected individual in a clamoring mob—caused revulsion. Although the album made No. 3 in the UK, it stalled at No. 24 in Dylan's home country. More importantly, though, it caused the tide to definitively change. This was the point where used record stores were suddenly flooded with Dylan albums dispensed with by disgusted ex-fans. Ironically, *Saved* was a fine album. It was also a far less judgmental and hence much more likeable record than its predecessor, exemplified by the humility of tracks like "What Can I Do for You?," "Pressing

On," and "Saving Grace." Also unlike its predecessor, it rocked: the title track and "Solid Rock" were galvanizingly up-tempo.

The damage, though, was done. On *Shot of Love* (1981), an apparently nervous Dylan downplayed the religiosity. The reining back might have worked, were the record not so banal (except—anther irony— "Every Grain of Sand," the most articulate and moving expression yet of Dylan's faith). After that, Dylan set about the task of working his way back into the respect and affection of the public and critics. Slowly, and with several false dawns along the way, he did it. *Time Out of Mind* (1997) was his first work universally hailed as a post-religious comeback. From that point on, he settled into a groove—albums of competent, rootsy music decorated by intriguing lyrics—that contrived to garner him an unassailable status as godfather of heritage music.

It was a limited—even Pyrrhic—victory. He has never publicly disavowed his vengeful brand of religion but, from 1983's *Infidels* onward, it was communicated in code (for example, in "Something's Burning, Baby," from 1985's *Empire Burlesque*, he spoke of flames and "a man going 'round calling out names"). In the 1960s, Bob Dylan had never needed to shield his opinions because they were utterly in tune with the zeitgeist. Post–*Slow Train Coming*, he could only persuade the public to buy his wares by hiding his true self.

Dinosaurs to the Rescue: Led Zeppelin

The late-seventies revival of the singles market brought some cheer to record companies, but not that much. In 1979, there was a feeling of crisis in the halls of the music industry, whose denizens were painfully aware of the fact that the overall trend for record sales continued to be dramatically down. In the United States, cumulative sales of recorded music decreased from 1978 to 1979 by 10.4 percent. The figures were even more vertiginous for the UK, where the drop between 1977 and 1980 was an astounding 26.4 percent. Once more, theories abounded as to the cause. As well as the oil-related global recession, it was conjectured that music was struggling to compete with other forms of media (including the nascent home-video industry). There was also the issue of the increasing prevalence of home audio taping, which only a decade previously had involved negotiating one's way around cumbersome apparatus based around large reel-to-reel tapes but now involved only a compact, user-friendly machine and a cassette small enough to fit into a back jeans pocket. The technology was getting better all the time: 1979 saw the release of the Walkman, the final evolutionary step from a contraption that was a nightmare to transport to complete portability and convenience. From 1981, sleeves or inner bags of some LPs came with an industry-approved declaration that "Home taping is killing music—and it's illegal." Some had a problem with the pious tone, some with the fact that the causality wasn't proven, but the mortal threat, at least, was real. If the rate of decline in the UK specifically should continue at its current rate, the music industry would literally cease to exist before the looming eighties were over.

The besieged music business needed a savior. An abrupt, wholesale turnaround in the industry's fortunes was hardly likely. However, a totemic knight in shining armor was feasible—some event or artist that could remind the public how much they enjoyed the role of music in their lives, and cause them to once more look benignly on shelling out on it some of their increasingly hard-won cash (or credit-card usage, for trendy people). That savior came along in August. The identity of this savior? Led Zeppelin.

On the surface, the proposition seems absurd. The veteran four-piece British rock act was supposedly one of the emperors whose lack of clothes had been belatedly exposed by the punk generation: theoretically, their unfashionable decadence, hauteur, and declining artistry had decimated Zeppelin's cachet and commerciality.

Prior to that, the years 1969 to 1975 had marked a relentlessly upward trajectory for "Led Zep." It started when guitarist Jimmy Page left the Yardbirds and decided to set up a new group. On vocals he recruited Robert Plant, a good-looking man with a remarkable voice that was simultaneously macho and feminine. On drums he added John Bonham, whose heavyweight sound many would find overbearing, but which perfectly fitted in with the larger-than-life soundscapes Page had in mind. John Paul Jones was enlisted on bass and keyboards. Even-tempered and well-spoken, Jones always seemed the odd one out in this debauched, dissolute, and demanding crew.

Jones says of the new band's sound, "It was Page's vision, really. He had this idea of acoustic and electric and blues and mixing it up a bit. Then the actual band's style and the sound came really from the members playing our interpretation of his idea." Did Jones feel he and his colleagues were—as has been claimed for them—creating a new genre? "Yeah, pretty much. We were playing the blues in a particularly characteristic sort of way." He does take issue with "heavy metal," a description he first noticed being applied to Zeppelin around the time of "Whole Lotta Love." "It used to be 'hard rock.' It was actually 'progressive rock' right at the beginning, but then that quickly changed meaning to be ELP, Soft Machine, King Crimson. I always thought heavy metal was Black Sabbath and Deep Purple and Uriah Heep— that sort of band." He is happy to accept the "cosmic blues" sobriquet conferred on that new genre, but adds, "Also, there was the light and shade. It would go from that to absolutely you could hear a pin drop. It was a very dynamic way of playing." It was also a way of playing that was relentlessly dramatic—something that could be tiresome and even ridiculous. At its best, though, it was sublime.

Whatever the nomenclature, the concoction was announced in the January of the last year of the sixties via Led Zeppelin's eponymous debut LP. It has to be said that the record also seemed to declare the band's contempt for the communality of the dying decade in the way it saw them steal other artists' song credits. Such behavior partly explained the critical disdain Zeppelin would endure pretty much throughout their lifespan. Another reason for press slatings was their lyrics, which often tipped over from flirtatiousness into macho posturing. Another was the stories that leaked out from their gargantuan, debauched tours, which ranged from sex with underage groupies to beatings administered to people who were deemed to have shown the band insufficient respect. Another was their unashamed avarice. Another was the Spinal Tap absurdities peppering their interviews, such as Plant's comment to *Rolling Stone*, in 1975, "What I heard coming back to me over the cans while I was singing was better than the finest chick in all the land."

Zeppelin's record sales proved that many didn't care about their transgressions, or perhaps even saw them as part-and-parcel of the strutting, groin-thrusting self-aggrandizement that defined so much of their sound. That sound was refined to its core on *Led Zeppelin II* (October 1969), which included the previously mentioned "Whole Lotta Love," the epitome of their hard-riffing, blues-plundering cock-rock. Their sound then took a surprising side turn with the largely acoustic *Led Zeppelin III* (1970).

Zeppelin's 1971 effort—which had a title that consisted of four symbols, but which inevitably colloquially became *Led Zeppelin IV*—is considered their masterpiece, not least because of the epic, majestic "Stairway to Heaven," which triumphantly lived up to the heavy/light ideal stated in the band's name in the way it segued from a slow, delicate opening into an up-tempo, bone-crushing second act. *Houses of the Holy* (1973) might be seen as a consolidation album, were it not for its forays into reggae and James Brown pastiche, which showed adventurism, even if refracted through Zeppelin's uniquely bombastic prism.

There was another two-year gap before the next album, but *Physical Graffiti* (1975) was a double set—one, furthermore, that could be postulated as providing a panorama encompassing everything the band stood for. However, the same album was beginning to make clear that the group's vitality and brutal majesty—as well as their ability to know when to stop—were now a little frayed.

During this ascent, Led Zeppelin set sales and concert-attendance records as they helped transform the very meaning of the rock business. Previously, it was an enterprise conducted in school gymnasiums and corn exchanges, where artists were subservient to promoters who held their craft in contempt. Now it became an enterprise where top acts filled stadiums and got their rightful share from people who knew their place. The record company, meanwhile, was apprised of its role as mere distributor. Zeppelin's success was made all the more remarkable by the band's lack of a presence in the wider culture. The names of John, Paul, George, and Ringo had been known to all society, regardless of whether they bought Beatles records. Elvis Presley and Mick Jagger were household names even in those numerous households that wouldn't allow their product across the threshold. Zeppelin's spurning of mainstream media meant that they were simply invisible to anyone who didn't read the music press.

In 1976, Zeppelin's fortunes began ever so slightly to turn. They released two albums that year, but both were underwhelming at precisely the point where they needed to be works that proved the band's spiky-topped, ripped-shirted detractors wrong. October's *The Song Remains the Same* was a ghastly live album, ostensibly a soundtrack to a deeply pretentious movie of the same name. Its twenty-seven-minute version of "Dazed and Confused" and thirteen-minute rendition of "Moby Dick" (a song that automatically racked up a black mark for consisting of a drum solo) epitomized the rock aristocracy's self-regard and self-indulgence. When Bonham sat in with the Damned—one of the rising groups who espoused rawness, approachability, and brevity specifically because of the absence of those qualities in the aristos' music and universe—he was booed by an audience who only months before would probably have besieged him for autographs. Ironically, Zeppelin's 1976 studio album, *Presence*, released seven months before *The Song Remains the Same*, was a back-to-basics effort. However, its quality was affected by injuries sustained by Plant in a car crash, and the unusual absence of Jones from the songwriting process.

It would be nearly three and a half years before *Presence* was followed up by *In Through the Out Door*, a shocking gap between studio albums even for nobility. This time they had a good reason: in 1977, Plant's young son died from a stomach illness. The new album was the second of two significant LPs of 1979 to be recorded at Polar Studios in Stockholm. In 2003, Page recalled to Barney Hoskyns of *Rock's Backpages*, "Somebody had approached me saying ABBA had this studio and they were desperate to get an international band in there and they'd give us three weeks' studio time for free." ABBA's overture has led to the circulation of surreal anecdotes about Agnetha and Frida driving around Stockholm trying to track down the dubious establishments to which Benny and Björn had been dragged by the kings of excess.

Tragedies such as the one endured by Plant are the stuff to make the vagaries of musical fashionability seem trivial. Nonetheless, the entertainment industry is predicated on the desire to be appreciated, and, when Led Zeppelin returned in the final year of the decade they had done so much to shape, they must have been determined to create a musical statement that demonstrated to their detractors that their best days were not behind them. For the second time in a row, though, they were handicapped by a less than optimum recording process. This time around it was Page's heroin addiction that posed the main problem.

The man who had always guided the group as musical visionary and producer was frequently absent. Bonham—who had his own, alcohol-related, issues—was also dilatory. This meant that for long stretches Jones and Plant were alone in the studio. "There were two distinct camps by then, and we were in the relatively clean one," Jones told Dave Lewis of *Tight but Loose*. "When that situation occurs you either sit around waiting or get down to some playing." Jones had recently taken receipt of a state-of-the-art Yamaha synthesizer. "I'd got this huge machine installed and I wasn't going to sit and just look at it," he noted to Lewis. What followed was in many ways a vindication for the band's "quiet one," who could sometimes be said to have as good a claim as several old blues masters to a share of the publishing on songs credited to Page/Plant. "I probably should have taken more care over the song-writing credits in those days, but that's those days," he says. "Page and Plant weren't really the main songwriting team except that Plant always wrote the lyrics, so he was always there on the credit." Now, though, there could be no dispute about Jones's contributions: his collaborator was a non-musician. Accordingly, the majority of the album's seven tracks were attributed to Jones/Page/Plant, and, in "All My Love" and "South Bound Suarez" (Jones/Plant), the album contained two tracks that—covers aside—were the only ones of Zeppelin's career that didn't bear a Page writing credit. Not that the songs the singer devised with Jones would much resemble what he'd previously composed with his guitarist colleague, as he explained to *Q*'s Mat Snow in 1990. "In '77, when I lost my boy, I didn't really want to go swinging around—'Hey hey mama say the way you move' didn't really have a great deal of import any more. *In Through the Out Door* is more conscientious and less animal."

It wasn't just the lyrics that had a different quality. Although Bonham appeared in the studio a sufficient number of times to ensure the recordings possessed Zeppelin's trademark thunderous bottom end, and although Page's characteristic virtuosic-but-disciplined guitar threaded the tracks (even if often via overdubbing at his home back in Britain), this was a new Zeppelin. Whether it was a good or bad thing depended on one's point of view. While it was understandable in the circumstances that Page's guitar took a backseat on the album to Jones's keyboards, that those keyboards constituted not the rootsy feel of a piano or organ but the space-age timbre of synthesizer was something that seemed wholly inconsistent with the sound/tradition/ mythology Zeppelin had spent a decade establishing. There was also another difference—one that some couldn't put a finger on at first. Page later remarked on it to Hoskyns: "The nature of the album took on a different movement from, say, the earlier albums, where we were consciously not trying to do choruses. All of a sudden we were, and there were things there with choruses, and we were just traveling along another route for a moment." His temperate-cum-generous comments a quarter-century after the events masked—according to some eyewit- nesses—a resentment at the way he felt his musical leadership had been usurped.

At first, nothing seemed too unusual. Album opener "In the Evening" married three Led Zep traditions—killer riffing, pile-driving importuning, and extended length. (It also had, in finest Jimmy Page tradition, a comically inept guitar-solo overdub.) After that, unfamiliar tones and styles abounded. "South Bound Suarez" was a jaunty, piano- dominated number. To be more accurate, it strived for jauntiness. As with so many examples before—ranging from the fifties-referencing "Rock and Roll" to the reggae "D'yer Mak'er"—Zeppelin were pre- suming to pastiche a form of music whose spryness was simply beyond them. The same inability to get in the groove also applied to "Fool in the Rain" (a semi-samba) and "Hot Dog" (a hoedown, and the only track bearing the familiar Page/Plant writing credit). For many of the band's fans, complaints about them not being limber had always laughably missed the point—people loved them precisely because of their lack of subtlety—but Zeppelin's ponderous rhythm tracks had now assumed a sociopolitical dimension: they sounded like the lumbering footsteps of dinosaurs on a scene now populated by younger, fitter, and studiedly more nimble descendants. The rules of evolution suggested that this was a fatal flaw.

The real sonic shocks occurred on side two. Across the course of ten and a half minutes, the epic suite "Carouselambra" moved between archetypal Zeppelin gothic rock, exotica in the style of their 1975 song "Kashmir," a form of music not yet known as electronica, and even pulsating quasi-disco. It sometimes gelled, sometimes didn't, but overall felt weirdly counter-demographic, while Jones's electronic bloops and whoops are now as irritating as only synths of that period can be in their mistaken insistence that this-is-the-future.

Although few had a problem with Plant's tribute to his dead child in the lyric of "All My Love"—which makes it surely the most vulnerable and heartfelt song of the Zeppelin canon—the track's music horrified those people (including Bonham and Page) who felt that the Zeppelin sound had always constituted a repudiation of the sort of pretty, soft-rock tones it proffered. Moreover, the album closed with "I'm Gonna Crawl," which was pleasant enough but opened with synthesized strings and proceeded to purvey an almost shockingly MOR sound. "She is my girl and she can never do wrong," meanwhile, were the sort of song words that, post–Sex Pistols, even post-Blondie, seemed laughably trite, something compounded by the drama with which the band sought to imbue them.

Zeppelin's grand comeback took place across two consecutive Saturdays in August 1979, at the UK's Knebworth Festival, albeit preceded by a brace of warm-up shows in Copenhagen. Zeppelin's million-pound performance fee was reported to be the highest ever paid, although that sort of financial landmark was by now commonplace in their career. Most of the approximately four hundred thousand people in attendance across the Saturdays were there to see Zeppelin, and those who were there on the 4th indicated how pleased they were by their return with an emotional sing-along of "You'll Never Walk Alone."

The album wasn't quite ready in time for Knebworth but appeared four days after the second concert, housed in one of the most elaborate (and at the same time dingy) of all sleeves by trendy album designers Hipgnosis, itself hidden by a plain paper bag. Its title was a reference to the band's long absence and the uncertainties associated with it: "In through the out door" was, Page said, "the hardest way to get back in." Some of the reviews certainly indicated that regaining their previous prominence was going to be an uphill struggle. In *Sounds*, Geoff Barton said, "Three years away from it all is far too long. How anyone could remain a fervent Zep fan during that period is beyond my comprehension, especially when so many new, vital and exciting things have happened in the interim." Reviewing Knebworth for *Rolling Stone*, Mick Brown sniffed, "In light of Zeppelin's prolonged layoff and the abrasive climate of the current British music scene to which they have chosen to return, the group sounded woefully complacent and anachronistic, even obsolete."

Critics sometimes do genuinely wield power, but what transpired over the following months showed how impotent they can also be. That the album instantly topped the charts worldwide didn't necessarily prove anything: advance orders were bound to be optimistic, considering Zeppelin's past sales performance, and many is the album that "shipped gold, returned platinum." However, without even the benefit of a tour to keep them in the spotlight—Plant wouldn't acquiesce to more live dates until nearly a year after Knebworth—*In Through the Out Door* sat atop the *Billboard* chart for seven weeks. Even in the UK, where the four music weeklies were considered to have considerable power, it mounted the summit and enjoyed a healthy chart run. Britain, though, was a sales minnow compared to the States. There, in the month of September, Atlantic sold a million back-catalogue Zeppelin albums, marking a resurgence of interest in the group's history that reached its climax during the two weeks straddling the end of October and the beginning of November, when the band's entire oeuvre occupied the *Billboard* Top 200.

In June 1980, Zeppelin finally returned to the road. Tour Over Europe was a short, tentative trek, but was also charged with significance. There hadn't been much evidence of punk on *In Through the Out Door*, which—despite the new territories it explored—was hardly their equivalent of the Rolling Stones' self-consciously amends-making 1978 effort *Some Girls*. Instead, Zeppelin's new wave–engendered revitalization came with their live work. On Tour Over Europe, they spurned the excess for which they were famed in venue size, spectacle, and song length. "We were reminded of the energy that we used to start off with," Jones says of punk's influence. "'Communication Breakdown' used to roar along. Maybe we'd sat back a bit. We'd done a ton of work as well by then. The stadiums had got bigger and bigger, and there wasn't that immediacy that there was at the beginning of the band [that] you can hear on things like the *BBC Sessions*, where it's really tight and it's really firing on all cylinders. Punk made everybody think, 'What is it all about and what are we trying to do here?' So we stripped the whole thing right the way back."

The band enjoyed themselves sufficiently to agree on an American tour, scheduled to start in October 1980. Rehearsals were booked for September. After the first rehearsal, John Bonham died after choking on his own vomit following a day of heavy drinking. He was thirty-two. The tour was immediately canceled. Although an announcement of the permanent dissolution of Zeppelin didn't come until December, it was inevitable: Bonham's sound had defined the band more than any other element, and the group's sonic chemistry-cum-codependency ruled out absorbing a newcomer. The disastrous turn of events rudely slammed the door on what had seemed stirringly fresh possibilities. "At the time it finished, we were about to go into a new phase," laments Jones. "It was all looking quite exciting." Did he consider joining another band after the split? "No. You can't follow Led Zeppelin with another band. And I'd had enough being with a band, to be honest." For anyone determined to prize something positive from the grim circumstances, it could be noted that they conferred a neat symmetry to Zeppelin's exactly ten-year recording career. Leftovers collection *Coda* (1982) posthumously rounded off the legacy with reasonable dignity.

As for *In Through the Out Door*, the consensus now is that, along with *Presence*, it is the least impressive of Zeppelin's studio LPs. For the industry at the time, however, it was manna from heaven. It's difficult to empirically quantify the fillip Led Zeppelin gave to a beleaguered music business in 1979. *In Through the Out Door* wasn't necessarily the year's biggest-selling LP. Accurate sales figures for an era before barcode-scanning are difficult to come by, but, for what it's worth, *Billboard* gave the "Album of the Year" award to Billy Joel's *52nd Street* (released in 1978), even though it held the US No. 1 spot for just a week in '79. Michael Jackson's *Off the Wall* never made the top spot but was a titanic record. The Eagles' *The Long Run* spent two weeks longer at No. 1 in the US than even Zeppelin's effort. However, *In Through the Out Door* may well have been the most important album of the year in the fact of it sparking the type of album-related consumer mania that many music-company executives feared was a thing of history.

9
SEPTEMBER

In 1979, Cheap Trick became perhaps the most unexpected beneficiary of the recently established capacity of double in-concert LPs to kick-start sluggish careers (see Kiss's *Alive!* and Peter Frampton's *Frampton Comes Alive!*). After achieving middling success with their first three studio albums, the Illinois pop-rockers hit big with their live album *Cheap Trick at Budokan*. The record had appeared in their biggest market, Japan, the previous year, and a by-popular-demand Western release saw it climb into the US Top 10. It was followed there by their next studio album, *Dream Police*, released in September. It was odd that the band achieved their greatest success just as the melody began draining from their increasingly bombastic music.

The Crack by London punks the Ruts found a band far more in touch with the streets than the Jam and the Clash, who—however studiously down-to-earth—were now ensconced in the rarefied environs of a successful recording career. Unfortunately, the Ruts were less musically adept than those bands, too often purveying gratingly abrasive guitar lines and muddy drum tracks. Nonetheless, the album showed them capable of greatness. "Babylon's Burning" and "Jah War" both explored the subject of recent race riots in the UK's capital, but in wildly differing styles: the first was a top-grade punk broadside while the latter was a nimble reggae. The group's potential, unfortunately, was never to be fulfilled, a consequence of the fatal heroin overdose of vocalist Malcolm Owen in July the following year.

By 1979, Kenny Rogers had been around for a dozen years, during which time he had made a journey from psychedelia to country to mainstream soft rock. While this ostensibly indicated an intriguingly eclectic artist, the fact that he'd abandoned along the way the songwriting for which he'd once shown a facility suggested, conversely, an artist of no particular ambition beyond making a living. Yet his operating as a characterless mouthpiece for a miscellany of outside composers found favor with a big section of the public. His 1979 effort, *Kenny*, was his most successful LP yet, making No. 5 in his native United States and No. 7 in the UK. The British success actually mostly came in 1980, due to closing track "Coward of the County" belatedly becoming a No. 1 single in that country. Possibly few who heard it as background on the radio realized that within its staid C&W folds resided a story of a revenge spree for a gang rape.

The musical mastermind of British sextet Foreigner was lead guitarist Mick Jones, but the fact that he was not to be confused with the Mick Jones who was lead guitarist of the Clash would have been detectable without even going beyond the cover of Foreigner's third album. *Head Games* featured a charming picture of a bobby-sox'd model stranded in a men's public lavatory. The album itself consisted of the sort of thing that would become increasingly popular over the next few years: shrilly sung riffing rock threaded with glistening keyboards purveyed by artists who sold millions but somehow managed to remain anonymous. It was the band's third successive US Top 5—heights that would only be reached in their home country with 1981 follow-up *4*, which itself was a US chart-topper.

Siouxsie and the Banshees and the all-female Slits were both punk groups that, though they had both started as far back as 1976, took what seemed an inordinately long time to get a record deal. Perhaps the fact that the Banshees were led by a former member of the Sex Pistols' outlandishly dressed entourage—the "Bromley Contingent"—made music executives perceive them as wannabes. Once they had persuaded Polydor to give them a contract, though, they triumphantly proved detractors wrong with their infectious 1978 hit single "Hong Kong Garden." Debut album *The Scream*, released the same year, showed some promise. Despite her slightly flat voice, Siouxsie Sioux (Susan Ballion to her mum) was—what with her explosion of black hair, defiantly unshaven armpits, and penchant for gathering her microphone lead like a spider's web—a mesmerizing front woman. However, the Banshees' 1979 follow-up, *Join Hands*, sounded like the very album those doubtful record-company executives had first feared, right down to the inclusion of a deconstruction of "The Lord's Prayer," a version of which Sioux had famously declaimed from the stage of London's 100 Club at the epoch-marking Punk Festival of September 1976. The largely war-oriented songs were unmelodic and tedious, although little of this can be gleaned from contemporaneous reviews, which—in an era when any lack of convention was hailed in some quarters as a synonym for excellence—were laudatory.

The critical reassessment that has seen *Join Hands* relegated to the status of a minor work has not been applied to the Slits' *Cut*, which is asserted to be a classic simply because it's considered a landmark for female participation in popular music. Its tinny, trebly, hesitant soundscapes were often dependent for any compelling element on the percussive production tricks of Dennis Bovell, who usually worked in the field of reggae. The band's critiques of consumerism and boys were comparatively novel, but they hardly offered profound insight. The bopping "Typical Girls" became the closest thing to a famous Slits song but was not much less slight than everything else on the LP.

Similarly simplistic politics could be heard on *Entertainment!* by Gang of Four. Its slick, angular funk was far more professional than the

Slits' music, but the level of insight in its song words could be gleaned from its embarrassing front-cover sloganeering: "The Indian smiles, he thinks that the cowboy is his friend. The cowboy smiles, he is glad the Indian is fooled. Now he can exploit him."

The mixture of Stones-y rock and synth-pop purveyed by Manchester band Sad Café now seems as quaint as their unwieldy seven-piece format, yet they had quite a following across the late seventies and eighties. Their third album, *Facades*, was a UK Top 10 and spun off three hit singles: the fluttering ballad "Every Day Hurts," the menacing "Strange Little Girl," and "My Oh My." The latter was an example of a phenomenon that was quite thick on the ground in the seventies: a track that—with its raggedy rhythms and uncouth vocals—aspired to nothing more than being mistaken for the work of the Rolling Stones. Yet it was also genuinely eerie: when the narrator looked in mirrors and found the devil looking back at him, it was enough to make the listener's nape come alive.

Between 1977 and 1979, UK quartet Wire released a trio of albums on EMI subsidiary label Harvest, *Pink Flag*, *Chairs Missing*, and *154*. *Pink Flag* was a classic, careening exhilaratingly between unsettling impressionistic soundscapes, gorgeous, if skeletal, pop numbers, and breakneck fury like "12XU." Wire insisted they weren't punk, which surprised many who thought the LP a keystone of the genre. An anxiety to distance themselves from punk presumably accounted for the fact that, since then, they had become incrementally slow and doomy. September 1979's *154*—their third album in twenty-one months—was the culmination of that depressing process of turning away from their own talents. They at least continued to revel in their knack for a postmodern pop song. In this case, it was the snappily titled "Map Ref. 41°N 93°W," which married a lovely tune to a deadpan recitation of geographical location. There was an additional element of subversion in the form of a cry of "Chorus!" just before that section of the track. Although some bemoaned the decreasing accessibility of their music, the band couldn't have been more content with their direction, or themselves. Wire bassist Graham Lewis later said, "When we made *Pink Flag*, we were pretty happy. When we did *Chairs Missing*, we were absolutely delighted . . . when *154* came out, then it was a little bit scary, because we understood how far ahead we were."

Triumph Through Turmoil: The Eagles

The Long Run, released in September 1979, was the exhausted conclusion of the meaningful part of the career of the Eagles. An LP informed by nothing much more inspired than the American country-rock outfit's bewilderment about how to follow up their phenomenally successful *Hotel California*, it was a pale shadow of previous achievements. Yet it was also one of the biggest albums of the year, spending more time in the US No. 1 spot than any other record.

The Eagles started life in 1971, evolving from a backing band for Linda Ronstadt recruited largely from musicians who hung out and played at the famous West Hollywood venue the Troubadour. The original lineup was comprised of Glenn Frey (guitars), Don Henley (drums), Bernie Leadon (guitars), and Randy Meisner (bass). All four sang. All men wrote, too, although from the second album onward Frey and Henley were the dominant composers, which created the peculiar situation of much of the band's live set being rendered by a man who was invisible to the audience behind his drum kit. "In the Hopi mythology, the eagle is considered a most sacred animal," Leadon said of the name chosen for the ensemble. "We wanted a name that would have mythological connotations. We're the fuckin' Eagles. Kiss my ass!" Although this origin is gainsaid, that pugnacious quote does rather give a flavor of the contradictions at the heart of a band made up of overly assertive characters who played music that was often very mellow, even soporific, and who purveyed socially enlightened politics that didn't seem to chime with their personal behavior or the caustic tone their lyrics reserved for women.

The Eagles' 1972 eponymous debut LP was helmed by big-name producer Glyn Johns, who has been credited with shaping the band's colossal but inchoate talent, and for pointing them in the direction of a meld of country and rock. The idea wasn't new, of course, but the difference between this ensemble and the likes of the Flying Burrito Brothers was musical grittiness and mass harmonies, both of which made rock radio amenable to them.

After the following year's *Desperado*, *On the Border* (1974) exhibited the first signs of evolution. Disagreeing with Johns over their hankering for a more rock-oriented sound, the band replaced him with Bill Szymczyk. They also absorbed into their ranks Don Felder, who handled various stringed instruments. The album gave them their first No. 1 single, the ballad "Best of My Love." The following year's *One of These Nights* turned the group from stars into superstars, making No. 1 on *Billboard* and bequeathing three US hits in the hard-hitting title track, the melancholic "Lyin' Eyes," and the yearning "Take It to the Limit." All three were also hits across the Atlantic, albeit on a lower level: the Eagles would only ever have one Top 10 single in the UK, where their increasingly Californian song topics had less appeal, especially after punk made anything slick and successful an object of suspicion.

That plateau was a departure point for Leadon. Post-Eagles, he was never as prominent again, but no doubt the royalties from *Their Greatest Hits (1971–1975)* provided a handy cushion against hard times. It would become officially the biggest-selling album of the twentieth century.

The country-loving Leadon was replaced by inveterate rocker Joe Walsh. *Hotel California*, the Eagles' fifth album, was their magnum opus, a concept piece whose subject Henley described to *Melody Maker*'s Chris Charlesworth as "the demise of the sixties and the decadence and escapism we are experiencing in the seventies." The six-and-a-half-minute title track—a Felder/Henley/Frey collaboration—was fit to rank beside "Bohemian Rhapsody," "Scenes from an Italian Restaurant," "Stairway to Heaven," "Won't Get Fooled Again," or any other classy rock epic one cares to name. The album itself was soon tussling with *Their Greatest Hits (1971–1975)* for the title of history's top seller.

The only drawback to these aesthetic and commercial triumphs was that it left the Eagles with the problem of how to follow them. They eventually did, but the process of making *The Long Run* effectively destroyed the group.

The band that recorded it, in five different studios across eighteen months with Szymczyk producing, wasn't quite the same one that had made *Hotel California*. Meisner left the group in 1977, tired of the strain of the road and inter-band argument. He was replaced by ex-Poco member Timothy B. Schmit. Another reason that the band wasn't quite the same was that, for the first time, their inspiration was lacking. "When we began the process of recording that album, we were completely burned out," Henley told David Browne of *Rolling Stone* in 2016. "Our collective tank was empty. We'd been touring relentlessly, even in between recording sessions. We should have taken a one-year hiatus, but . . . there were big bucks at stake, the corporate stockholders had expectations, jobs were on the line." If that sounds like self-mythologizing, it should be noted that Joe Smith, chairman of the board of the Eagles' record company Elektra/Asylum, noted to *Rolling Stone* in 1979, "We hurt when we didn't get an Eagles album last year. You fall $15 million short in your projections, you hurt."

Yet the group started the project with grand plans, intending to make their first double album. It eventually became obvious that they couldn't even scrape together among themselves enough songs of sufficient quality to assemble a single LP. In 1992, Frey told Lloyd Bradley of the UK's *Independent* newspaper that, during the making of *The Long Run*, he and Henley found out that lyrics are not a replenishable source. "We, Don in particular, said a mouthful on *Hotel California*, and a big part of the problem was, 'What do we talk about now?'" Showing an unusual level of self-awareness for a cossetted rock star, he noted, "Then, because of what we were as members of the Eagles, we had far fewer real-life experiences to draw on." Friends like Bob Seger and J. D. Souther—presumably more conversant with real life—had to be roped in to assist. Even some of the compositions that did get generated provoked the type of accusations of plagiarism that had repeatedly dogged the group. Some noted the similarity between the title track and "Trying to Live My Life Without You" by Otis Clay, while the riff of "The Disco Strangler" owed a clear debt to the Rolling Stones' "Fingerprint File."

"We called that 'the long one,'" Szymczyk wearily noted to John Tobler and Stuart Grundy on *The Record Producers*. "It had stopped being fun," Frey told Bradley. "There was considerable disagreement as we were for the first time considering what we ought to be doing. Also, working in close quarters for such a length of time without the distractions you get on a tour, we found out a lot about each other." Frey also noted that matters were not helped by the drug habits that he and Henley had picked up.

The Henley/Frey–written opening title cut was an anthem about mellowing, although it still contained a sideswipe at the punks who were questioning the band's continued relevance. Plagiarism issues aside, the lively slide guitar and Henley's likeable, quasi-falsetto immediately created an, as it were, peaceful easy feeling. The response, though, was Pavlovian. The track was actually Eagles-by-numbers, and what followed was worse.

"I Can't Tell You Why" (Henley/Frey/Schmit) was a keyboard-led ambiguous hymn of devotion. Like so many Eagles ballads, it tipped over from smoothness into dullness, something that had always been a primary reason why they were loathed by as many people as loved them. The Walsh/Barry de Vorzon composition "In the City" seemed included only to bulk out the contents. Although a decent-enough cut, when it was featured on the soundtrack to the controversial teen-violence movie *The Warriors* six months previously, it had been listed as a Walsh recording. If it could qualify as Eagles fare because of its composer and singer, some might have preferred that the LP include "Life's Been Good," Walsh's high-grade hit single from the previous year, which amusingly mocked (or celebrated, or both) Eagle-level rock-star excess. The circular, slightly menacing "The Disco Strangler" (Henley/Frey/Felder) was the Eagles' underwhelming contribution to the debate about the titular musical genre. Although Henley and Frey's "King of Hollywood" was musically nondescript, in its lyric's denunciation of the casting-couch process it supplied an unexpected touch of feminist philosophizing.

Side two opened with "Heartache Tonight" (Henley/Frey/Seger/Souther). Its dramatic stomping beat and chant-melody made it sound for all the world like a glam-rock song, and it was no worse for it. "Those Shoes" (Henley/Frey/Felder) could also have been interpreted as sympathetic to women's liberation, but could equally be seen as an overdramatic putdown of a promiscuous social climber. "Teenage Jail" (Henley/Frey/Souther) expressed sympathy for the oppressed adolescent but was no punk number. Slow, circular, and monotonous, it was curiously reminiscent of post-punk, even synth-pop. The up-tempo

Henley-Frey "The Greeks Don't Want No Freaks" was a nod to six-ties frat-rock. The track was not in the same league as "96 Tears" by ? and the Mysterians—the song it strived to conjure—even despite the Eagles' chops being so much more refined.

The latter track was at least a change from the Eagles' endless tilts at profundity—such as the album's five-and-a-half-minute closing cut, "The Sad Café." With perfect symmetry, the final song on the final (for now) Eagles album lamented the end of the age that had birthed them. "We could feel an era passing," Henley told Browne. "The crowd that hung out in the Troubadour and the bands that were performing there were changing." He might even have been referring to the club's latest darlings, the Knack. The lyric of this Henley/Frey/Walsh/Souther com-position reflected, "We thought we could change this world with words like 'love' and 'freedom.'" David Sanborn ramped up the mechanical but reasonably affecting pathos with a smoky sax solo.

For all the album's thinness, at the end of the day the Eagles had managed to deploy their professionalism and production know-how sufficiently well to proffer a collection that sounded, at least on shallow listening, cohesive and solid. The album might have been completely lacking in the gravitas of *Hotel California*, but a large number of the multimillions who had purchased their previous long-playing effort were unlikely to be disappointed by it. The only thing about *The Long Run* that hinted at the exhaustion and discontent resident in the Eagles' camp was its uninspired, minimalist sleeve.

The Long Run was released three months shy of three years after *Hotel California*. This meant it was almost as long awaited as Led Zeppelin's album of that year. As with their fellow behemoths, the Eagles' absence had accidentally ensured that they had leapfrogged the punk wars, and, as with *In Through the Out Door*, their new album's success made it seem like punk had never happened. *The Long Run* made No. 4 in the UK. In the States, it was the final No. 1 of 1979, and hence the seventies, monopolizing the top of the *Billboard* album chart from November 3 onward. Its nine weeks at the summit beat out all other releases that year, and was even one week more than *Hotel California* had managed. Unlike Zeppelin, though, the Eagles were also a bona fide singles band. The album spawned three US Top 10s: "Heartache Tonight" (a No. 1), "The Long Run," and "I Can't Tell You Why."

To the casual observer, then, it all would have seemed pretty much business as usual. The sniffy reviews were hardly a harbinger of doom: the Eagles had gotten those throughout. However, at a 1980 benefit show for Senator Alan Cranston, the tensions between band members that had been bubbling throughout the last three frustrating years finally boiled to a head. The on-mic Felder and Frey were spitting venom at each other, and barely avoided a fistfight afterward. Within days, the Eagles were finished.

Henley released one of the best singles of the eighties in the shape of "The Boys of Summer," Frey one of the worst in "Sexy Girl," but both men had successful solo careers. That latter fact only added to the air of the impossible surrounding notions that the Eagles would reunite: Henley famously said it would happen when "hell freezes over." The Eagles' 1994 reunion album was, naturally, given that title. It was a mixture of live tracks and four new studio recordings. Massively successful tours followed, but no new product emerged until *Long Road Out of Eden* (2007), their first double album. It topped the US charts despite initially only being available via selected retail outlets and the band's website. It also gave the Eagles their first UK No. 1. That the album didn't feature Felder, fired in 2001, didn't seem much of an issue for a band that had kept getting more successful regardless of lineup changes. However, few doubted that the death of Frey from multiple illnesses in 2016, at the age of sixty-seven, meant the end of any truly consequential Eagles activity.

As for *The Long Run*, whatever its shortcomings, it was perfectly appropriate that it put the Eagles atop the charts at the close of a decade in which, sales-wise, nobody could touch them.

From DIY to EMI: The Buzzcocks

The Great Rock 'n' Roll Swindle soundtrack might have demarcated 1979 as the year in which the Sex Pistols sold out, but the fact that punk's values had continuing resonance was illustrated by the belated entry of *Spiral Scratch* into the UK charts. The Buzzcocks' four-track EP was a totemic punk release, the epitome of the genre's do-it-yourself ethos. Its January 1977 release date was an arrestingly early point on the punk timeline, just three months after the first UK punk record, the Damned's "New Rose," and two months before the Clash's "White Riot." Not that it constituted the sum total of the Buzzcocks' achievements: 1979 also saw the release of their third album.

In February 1976, Howard Devoto (born Howard Andrew Trafford) and Pete Shelley (Peter McNeish) read an article about an intriguing new group called the Sex Pistols. The two traveled from their native Manchester to see the band perform in London, then arranged for the Pistols to come and play their home city in June. By July, the pair had mustered enough musicians to form the Buzzcocks and play their debut as support act on the Pistols' second Mancunian date.

That same we-can-do-it-too spirit motivated the Buzzcocks to record and press up their own record. "That was made out of a stroke of genius, but also a stroke of necessity," explains the Buzzcocks' Steve Diggle of *Spiral Scratch*. "[We thought,] 'This sounds the most uncommercial music possible at that moment. If we took that to a record company, they'd laugh us out of the place.' So we just didn't bother and made our own." Easier said than done, of course. Shelley explains, "My father took out a loan of £250, which took care of half of the thing, and then our manager Richard Boon and Howard [Devoto] had some friends who were at university in the days of student grants. That's where we got the other 250." The record contained the songs "Breakdown," "Time's Up," "Boredom," and "Friends of Mine." Though it was the first track on side two, not side one, "Boredom" was the keynote, and most celebrated, of the quartet, partly because of its remarkable keening guitar work, but mostly because of the fact that its lethargic disaffection was the quintessence of UK punk. A thousand copies were pressed up on the band's own New Hormones label and quickly sold out. Re-pressed, the record went on to sell approximately sixteen thousand, an astonishing amount in a pre-internet era, where artists were dependent for promotion on word-of-mouth and sympathetic elements of the mainstream media. "It was the beginning of it, really," says Shelley when it's suggested that the record epitomized punk DIY. "Even independent record companies were just offshoots of major companies."

Yet rather than continue down that DIY route, the Buzzcocks exploited the splash *Spiral Scratch* made to acquire a major-label deal. "That gives you a day job," says Shelley, of the possibility that the Buzzcocks might have remained self-publishers. "If you want to be in a band, you want to be making the music and then let somebody else take care of all of that." The Buzzcocks were signed to United Artists. Though their November 1977 debut single, "Orgasm Addict," was never going to garner the airplay necessary to become a hit, by early 1978 their second single, "What Do I Get?," had taken them into the UK Top 40, where they would henceforth feature regularly. Not even a band name that many erroneously thought a reference to vibrators could stop them getting broadcast now. (The derivation was actually the English Northernism–suffused headline to a TV review, "It's the

Buzz, Cock!") Their major-label success had an unexpected side effect on *Spiral Scratch*. "As the band became more popular, the price of the record became higher and higher," says Shelley. "Scarcity breeds value. So we thought, 'Well, it's a shame that people have to pay silly amounts of money to get hold of something which only cost a pound when it came out.' The worst thing with any self-published endeavor is for it to be out of print." The Buzzcocks put *Spiral Scratch* back into print with a 1979 re-release. Shelley notes, "We changed the cover slightly to say 'But with Howard Devoto,' to show it wasn't the Buzzcocks that people had been used to."

Indeed. It was in the glow of the triumph of the original release of *Spiral Scratch* that Devoto announced he was quitting the group. Diggle remembers the precise moment that Devoto dropped the bombshell. "Me and Pete were sat on the sofa in his house. He said, 'I've achieved what I wanted to and made a record. Now I'm leaving.' We were shocked. We'd done about ten shows pre–*Spiral Scratch*. It was beyond [our] control." While Devoto obtained a degree and laid the ground for a new band that would ultimately become Magazine, the Buzzcocks front line rearranged itself in front of drummer John Maher. Shelley assumed vocal duties, Diggle switched from bass to his preferred guitar role, and Steve Garvey became bassist, following a stint on that instrument by Garth Smith. "That enabled us to [become] Buzzcocks Mark II," notes Diggle. "Some people call it the classic lineup. It was a new audience as well. A lot more girls were getting into it. That's where you got the classic Buzzcock sound: me and Pete playing a lot of similar things on the rhythm, but in and out of phase. So we had this buzz-saw sound and became known for that. We'd moved into more tunefulness as well."

That combination of buzz-saw abrasiveness and pop euphonious-ness was evident on albums *Another Music in a Different Kitchen* and

Love Bites (both 1978), as well as a host of standalone singles. In the fall of 1978, the soaring, anthemic Shelley composition "Ever Fallen in Love (With Someone You Shouldn't've)" took the Buzzcocks to No. 12 in the UK. With follow-up "Promises" making the Top 20 later that year, the band entered 1979 on a high.

The group's first release of 1979 came in March, with Shelley's song "Everybody's Happy Nowadays." Diggle: "A bit bizarre, really. It's not like jazz, I don't know what it is." In July, Diggle got his first A-side with "Harmony in My Head," a ditty about alienation which juxtaposed a cooing title line with shouted verses. "'Ever Fallen in Love' was quite poppy, and I thought, 'Now the door's open at *Top of the Pops* and those places, we can probably steamroll a song,'" he says. "'Harmony in my Head' . . . was inspired a little bit by James Joyce's *Ulysses*. I tried to cram as many words as I could rather than a linear song."

"Harmony" only made No. 32, one place lower in fact than *Spiral Scratch* would shortly manage. Asked if their incrementally declining chart positions since "Fallen in Love" were something the Buzzcocks worried about, Shelley says, "Not personally. Chart positions are for people who follow those things and for marketing men at record companies. You really have no control over it."

A Different Kind of Tension, the Buzzcocks' third album, was released in September 1979. The process of assembling the album with producer Martin Rushent was very different to how previous Buzzcocks LPs were recorded, or, come to that, most albums. "With the other two albums, we'd set up all the equipment and the band would play the track," says Shelley. "With *A Different Kind of Tension*, we'd do a guide guitar and we'd record the bass and drums. Martin would cut out the sections on the two-inch tape and send those away to another place to get duplicated. We'd take the best verse and the bass and drums, then we'd copy that section of the multitrack tape. Then he'd splice together the master tape. We'd have loads of tape everywhere. Some of the interesting musical bits is because we stuck the wrong piece of tape in, but it sounded good so we kept it. Then me and Steve did the overdubs on guitars. It was a precursor to sequencers."

The first side of the album showed Diggle advancing as a composer and nabbing three tracks. Of his "You Can't Help It," he says, "That was kind of tongue-in-cheek, because of 'Ever Fallen in Love' and all that. People go, 'Oh, you're the guys that write love songs.' I thought, 'I'll do a piss-take of it.' But also, I was reading D. H. Lawrence. In the chorus it says, 'Sex is known as a screw / A bloody silly thing to do.' Which to me sends the whole thing up in a Joe Orton way. Even the greatest men in the world have been [brought] down by sexual deviancy and cravings."

While the Shelley material that filled out the remainder of side one was fairly standard Buzzcocks fare, the other side of the LP (all Shelley songs) was more experimental—almost as through the band were trying to wean their audience off their old sound. "The split of the album into side one and side two was intentional," says Shelley. He also describes side two as, "a bit like side two of *Abbey Road*, which is all basically one song which runs through different ideas." Says Diggle, "It was like, 'Let's try and take the audience to other places.' We was bringing out our Can influences." Shelley: "Right at the end is a track called 'Radio Nine.' You tune into the radio dial and you hear a bit of 'Everybody's Happy Nowadays' and [previous single] 'Why Can't I Touch It.' It was meant to show a bit of a journey."

Penultimate track "I Believe"—with its seven-minute playing time and vocal refrain "There is no love in this world anymore"—was the album's grand statement. "It's a bit like Bob Dylan's 'Hard Rain's A-Gonna Fall,'" avers Shelley. "Lots of lines put together in a sort of stream of consciousness. During '78 and '79, there was a lot of good acid around. I was exploring the nature of belief. The dissolution of ego is part of the theme." Diggle: "We'd gone a long way from 'Ever Fallen in Love.' The whole album was a lot darker and heavier and we was hoping the audience'd move on with us. Sometimes you've got to make the great statement and live or die by it. Even if it fails, when people look back they go, 'What a great album,' or, 'Great painting,' or whatever. I'm glad we made that, 'cause if we'd made another album like the first two then that would have been boring."

Although *Tension* was not as successful as the band's two previous long-players, it still made the UK Top 30. It also secured the band their first placing in the US album charts. There certainly seemed no reason to believe that, from this point, the Buzzcocks' career would slowly unravel. However, it was in 1979 that United Artists was gobbled up by EMI, which meant that the band who had kicked off the whole own-label boom were now signed to the biggest record company in the land. Though that had never done the Beatles much harm, the Buzzcocks found the experience disagreeable. Diggle recalls, "I remember meeting about three different A&R people, telling the story, and then they'd be gone and you have to tell it again."

In 1981, plans were underway for producer Martin Rushent to helm a fourth Buzzcocks album. The album was never made, as a consequence of Shelley using synthesizers on the demos on which he was working with Rushent. "I thought, 'Well this is more fun than actually being in a band,'" recalls Shelley. "And it was a bit hard to imagine how it would be improved by bringing in the band. So that was the reason I left." Shelly contacted his lawyer.

"That's when we got the letter saying he's no longer in the band," recalls Diggle. "Which pissed me off a little bit. 'Why didn't you just fucking phone me and tell me, "Steve, I've had enough"?' It just seemed a little bit cold."

Shrugs Shelley, "We had a partnership, so in order for me to get out we had to dissolve the partnership. I'm sure there's far worse things happened in bands." Tellingly, though, he also notes, "The good thing was that, by me leaving the band, I was out of the contract."

Come 1989, the Buzzcocks were back together. Their six albums between 1993 and 2014 tripled their LP legacy. Aside from their musical legacy, the Buzzcocks have of course left another mark in the form of their key part in the punk movement—and Shelley insists that it was a movement, as opposed to a genre.

"It was about people's involvement in a whole culture," he says. "A lot of people tried to dismiss punk as just being about the music, but if it was just about the music, it wouldn't have lasted that long."

10
OCTOBER

Chicago quintet Styx were another band in the faceless industrial-rock mold of Foreigner. They scored their biggest album yet with *Cornerstone*, their ninth long-player, which rose to No. 2 in the States. Its single, "Babe," was glitzy, over-earnest, and banal, but it was also pretty and catchy. It was a transatlantic hit, making the US top spot.

Tom Petty and the Heartbreakers' breakthrough record, *Damn the Torpedoes*, made a steady ascent up the album chart after its October release, spinning off two US hits as it did and peaking the following year at No. 2, where it sat for seven weeks, only held off the summit by Pink Floyd's *The Wall*. The Heartbreakers' third LP was, like all the music of this Floridian five-piece, joyously but never cleverly traditionalist. The success probably meant even more to the gleaming-haired, sparkling-toothed Petty at that point than it normally would: in the middle of '79, he'd filed for chapter-eleven bankruptcy, with debts of over half a million dollars.

In October 1979, two very different major black artists released albums that had the common characteristic of constituting an artistic dip. Bob Marley and the Wailers' *Survival* was a self-consciously weighty offering, following the criticisms the Jamaican reggae superstars had received for their previous album, *Kaya*, whose apolitical sunniness was characterized by the joyous "Is This Love." *Survival* was instantly recognized as the calculated affair it was, its protest-by-numbers exemplified by the almost comically scattershot "So Much Trouble in the World." Marley would find the right balance on the following year's *Uprising*, where the likes of the chugging, romantic "Could You Be Loved" sat cheek-by-jowl with stark social commentary such as "Redemption Song." The artistic salvage job was highly fortunate for his legacy: it was Marley's final album before his untimely death.

Technically, Stevie Wonder had been another recently dilatory musical titan, but—it being culturally problematic for white kids to level charges of decadence against blacks—he was never much denounced as such. Steeped in self-indulgence and pretension, his *Journey Through "The Secret Life of Plants"* had all the worst hallmarks of the rock aristocracy. It was the most bizarre of projects: a blind man's soundtrack to a documentary film he couldn't see. Even had Wonder not been relying on producer Michael Braun to describe the images to which he was providing musical accompaniment, it's unlikely that this double LP would have possessed much gravitas, and for the same reason that few soundtracks do: they're not meant to be heard in isolation. A handful of reasonably good "real" songs were swamped by synthesizer-dominated instrumentals. The album was successful—making the Top 10 in both the UK and Wonder's native US—but surely only because the world was glad to have the classy pop-soul merchant back after three years. As with Marley, Wonder would the next year prove what he could really do, in his case with the effervescent, hit-stuffed *Hotter Than July.*

Indulgence and Experimentation: Fleetwood Mac

Compared to Roxy Music's *Manifesto*, Led Zeppelin's *In Through the Out Door*, Pink Floyd's *The Wall*, and the Eagles' *The Long Run*, Fleetwood Mac's *Tusk* was turned around relatively briskly, appearing eighteen months after its predecessor, *Rumours*. The main issue with the product of this element of the quintet of long-absent behemoths was its disappointing sales.

That *Tusk* sold an initial four million copies indicates that the word "disappointing" is, in this context, relative. However, *Rumours* was a sales juggernaut. Having at the point of *Tusk*'s release already sold sixteen million copies, it remains to this day one of history's top-ten bestsellers. While nobody at Warner Bros Records was expecting that level of preternatural success, they were naturally hoping for *Tusk* to shift considerably more units than it did. That it sold so "few" was put down to the fact that *Tusk* was everything *Rumours* was not: experimental, bloated, and mired in time-consuming decadence. For some in a music industry that considered itself to be facing a life-threatening crisis, *Tusk* was an irresponsible squandering of momentum.

Fleetwood Mac was originally the pet project of hot young London guitarist Peter Green. When in 1967 he was looking for a name for his new ensemble, on a whim he decided to call it after its drummer Mick Fleetwood and its soon-to-be bassist John "Mac" McVie. Said titular oddity became highly useful when members, including Green, peeled away, because it justified Fleetwood and McVie continuing to use the brand name, even though, as non-writers, they were always the least talented components of any lineup.

Following Green's departure, John McVie's wife, Christine, came aboard as vocalist and keyboardist. Guitarist Bob Welch joined around the same time. His tenure constitutes the least remarked-upon stage of Fleetwood Mac's career, but he appeared on no fewer than five of their albums. The Welch period was largely washed from history because of the spectacular success of the lineup of Fleetwood Mac that came into being when he left at the end of 1974, replaced by a pair of unknown Americans named Lindsey Buckingham and Stevie Nicks. For Fleetwood, their enlistment created a magic combination of musicians. "When Stevie and Lindsey joined, it reminded me of the power and chemistry we had when we first started," he says. "Not musically, but just the feeling with the people and knowing something was look-ing really strong and good."

Christine McVie's recruitment had already made the band very unusual for the time in being "co-ed." Nicks's enrollment only deep-ened that revolutionary strain. However, with the mixture of genders came issues that didn't usually apply to single-sex bands. Buckingham and Nicks were lovers. In the calendar year preceding the release of *Rumours*, they split up. So did the McVies. The subsequent songs indi-vidually written by Buckingham, Christine McVie, and Nicks dripped with a heartbreak and recrimination that was made worse by the fact that their composers were all obliged to continue to work with their ex-partners—and indeed perform with them on songs that were postmor-tems on their relationships. This soap-opera aspect possibly contributed as much to *Rumours'* massive sales as did its high-class, burnished soft rock.

Following up a phenomenon like *Rumours* is always difficult. It was made more difficult by a determination to not replicate it, or even produce anything like it. "*Tusk*, from my point of view, was an attempt to derail the machine that kicked in after *Rumours*," Buckingham told *Classic Rock's* James Halbert in 2003. That the guitarist would cut off his mass of curly hair and remove his beard during the *Tusk* sessions would seem to be symbolic: he was inspired by the punk and new-wave revolution that had largely taken place during the year of *Rumours'* release. "Although I wasn't directly influenced by that music, it gave me a kick in the pants in terms of having the courage to try to shake things up a little bit," he told Nigel Williamson of *Uncut*. "I wanted something that had a little more depth." This might sound like the groan-making "punk-certainly-had-a-lot-of-energy" line trotted out by old-guarders who wanted to seem with-it but didn't really want to change, but there is no denying how different—how, in fact, punky—were the songs Buckingham began to write at this juncture.

Of course, that left him with the task of persuading colleagues who—having secured colossal validation of their art—would naturally be minded to think, "What's not to love?" Buckingham seems to have got his way by, intentionally or not, planting in their heads the idea that the band would be finished in its current form if he didn't get his way. In 1987, Christine McVie told J. Kordosh of *Creem*, "We 'allowed' him to experiment within the confines of Fleetwood Mac instead of saying, 'We don't want you doing stuff at your studio and putting it on the Fleetwood Mac album'—he might've said, 'I'm gonna leave, then.' We didn't want him to leave, for obvious reasons."

In fact, those reasons might not at that point have been obvious to an outsider. After all, Fleetwood Mac by now was a flag of convenience under which had sailed ten different lineups and a dozen different musicians. However, Buckingham's value to the group was greater than his immediately appreciable contributions to *Rumours* (three compositions, including the hit single "Go Your Own Way"; one co-write; and the most prominent vocal part on the Christine McVie–written hit "Don't Stop"). The album's sleeve had credited production to "Fleetwood Mac with Richard Dashut and Ken Caillat," but nobody seems to dispute that Buckingham was the record's *de facto* producer. His musical savvy enriched songs and even disguised their shortcomings, especially those of Nicks, who had a knack for evocative imagery but not for a multiplicity of melody lines. As Buckingham lamented to Alan di Perna of *Guitar World* in 1997, "I didn't ask for a production credit on *Rumours* and I didn't get it. Richard feels bad about that. There were band politics involved in that." Things would improve slightly on *Tusk*, but the band politics dictated that his directorial contribution only be acknowledged in the form of a parenthesized "Special thanks from the band to Lindsey Buckingham."

The new album had long been thought of as a two-LP set. "Having three frontline artists within a band means that they don't have a lot of song content, or not nearly as much as if they were on their own," Fleetwood pointed out to Steven Rosen in 1997. "So we made a double album." There was resistance to the idea from the band's label. Double albums are not favored by record companies for the logical reason that their higher retail price creates an impediment to purchase. Had it been a different point in Fleetwood Mac's career, they might have capitulated to this pressure, but at this juncture in their history the band's manager was Mick Fleetwood, and he was in concordance with the idea of a double.

While recording would take place at Los Angeles's Village Recorder, some of the work there, quite bizarrely, constituted overdubbing on material Buckingham had laid down at home. He explained to the *NME*'s Chris Salewicz in 1980, "The trappings and technology of the studio are so great that the blocks between the inception of an idea and the final thing you get on tape are so many that it just becomes very frustrating. . . . For a number of years it's been a process of having to sacrifice certain parts say, for example, to give to Stevie to contribute to her music." To di Perna, he admitted that telling all this to his colleagues did not make for a comfortable meeting. "I understand: in everybody else's eyes, I was being a troublemaker. I wasn't playing ball." However, that Buckingham was intoxicated by the work he proceeded to produce on the twenty-four-track machine he installed in his home was evident in his comments to *BAM*'s Blair Jackson the year after the album's release. "It becomes much more intimate," he veritably drooled. "It's more like a painter, because you can respond to your intuitions, take an idea and just go with it. Sometimes it's hard to stop. It gets very,

very exciting." Nonetheless, he did assert of *Tusk*, "In general, it wasn't *that* different than *Rumours*. We cut tracks, overdubbed some parts, put on the vocals."

One difference, though, was the recording's protracted and dissolute nature. While Buckingham's haircut, attitude, and yelping home tapes might have been broadly punkish, the fact that *Tusk* became the first album to rack up recording costs in excess of a million dollars was precisely the sort of extravagance that the new wave detested. Although Fleetwood Mac's wealth dated back further than most realize—the 1975 eponymous album on which Buckingham and Nicks made their debut was the one that enabled John McVie to fulfill his dream of buying a boat—it was still enough of a novelty for them to be gleefully indulging their every whim. "Recording *Tusk* was quite absurd," Christine McVie later caustically recalled to *Uncut*. "The studio contract rider for refreshments was like a telephone directory. Exotic food delivered to the studio, crates of champagne. And it had to be the best, with no thought of what it cost. Stupid. Really stupid."

Then there were the indulgences Christine McVie doesn't mention. "Everybody was so busy doing drugs that nobody was organized," Nicks told Sylvie Simmons of *Mojo* in 2007. "And you do things that you would think were just marvelous and the next day you'd come back in and it wasn't, so you'd have to do it again." As someone who eventually ingested so much cocaine that she blew a hole in her septum, Nicks was probably not excluding herself from this criticism.

Nicks had another grievance about the sessions: their interminability. "I had *very* little to do with that record," she told Jackson in a 1981 interview. As she composed fully a quarter of the album's twenty tracks, including the US Top 10 single "Sara," this might sound like an exaggeration. However, Nicks's contributions to Fleetwood Mac were writing, singing, harmonizing, and providing an ethereal stage presence:

she only played instruments to compose. "*Tusk* took us thirteen months to make, which is ridiculous," she lamented. "I was there in the studio every day—or almost every day—but I probably only *worked* for two months . . . most of the time I'd be looking at them through the window in the control room. After four or five hours, they'd forget I was even there, they'd be so wrapped in little details. It was very frustrating."

That it was a two-LP set was not the only reason people would compare *Tusk* to the "White Album." Like that eponymous 1968 Beatles work, *Tusk* showed the composers within the group going off on their own tangents rather than sublimating their writing characteristics within a group sound. The absence of the harmonies that had provided *Rumours* a sonic unity only accentuated the divergent approaches. Christine McVie contributed mainstream love songs of quivering vulnerability like "Brown Eyes" and "Never Make Me Cry." Nicks proffered compositions suffused with otherworldly poetry like "Sisters of the Moon," "Angel," and "Beautiful Child." Buckingham provided creations of a roughhewn and peculiarly belligerent, even adolescent, timbre, like "What Makes You Think You're the One" and "Not That Funny." A perfect example of the album's contradictory nature was the way McVie's oddly slow and soporific album opener, "Over and Over," was followed by Buckingham's raggedy, herky-jerky "The Ledge," wherein for two minutes the narrator taunted his lover that she would never walk out on him over a backing track that consisted of nothing more than a snare drum, a bass, and a distorted guitar.

In contrast again, the record's title track—also composed by Buckingham—could not have been more grandiose. "This came from a riff we used to jam on in soundchecks," Fleetwood told Johnny Black of *Mojo* in 1995. "When we started the album we worked on it but everybody lost interest in it. It went in the dustbin for about a year until I pulled it out again. I . . . had the idea of using a brass band and about forty-five drummers." To his colleagues' chagrin, Fleetwood elected to deploy the USC Marching Band and hire out L.A.'s Dodger Stadium. "They were sure I'd gone round the twist, so I paid for it myself." The track's throbbing drums and exotic guitar were augmented by dramatic brass and a lyric that had the flavor of walking in on an argument between two lovers. This mysterious concoction augured well for the album it preceded, making No. 8 and No. 6 in the US and UK singles charts, respectively.

That the tusk of the title song was a reference to a giant phallus was undermined—possibly deliberately—by the album's sleeve artwork, which featured in one corner of its otherwise featureless front cover a photograph of a small dog nipping at a man's ankle. It seemed slovenly and random compared to *Rumours'* considered cover photograph of Nicks twirling sensuously around an aloof Fleetwood, both of them exotically costumed. However, this was in turn upended by the luxurious design and packaging that was revealed when *Tusk* was opened up. Many, though, didn't get that far. That *Tusk* was afforded Warner Bros' largest-ever promotional campaign was to little avail. Of course, the point could be made—and repeatedly was, by Buckingham—that shifting four million copies of a double album was sort of the same as selling eight million copies of a single LP, but that still left it adrift of *Rumours'* sales figures by half. (The gap has widened since.)

In interviews over the following years, Buckingham complained of a backlash against him by his colleagues about what they came to perceive as Fleetwood Mac's grand folly. He told Jackson, "It's weird because everyone was very supportive at the time." He also publicly protested once again about band politics, in this instance ones dictating that, from that point on, experimentation was banned. "On *Mirage*, I was treading water, saying, 'Okay, whatever,' and taking a passive role," Buckingham told Williamson. Said 1982 effort was solid, and spun off more hits than *Tusk*, but few actually remember the album now. Buckingham was unable to be so submissive on *Tango in the Night* (1987). By common consensus, his production artistry is the main thing that prevented this record sounding like what it was: the product of a band disintegrating amidst inertia and drug issues. His success in fashioning a silk purse from a pig's ear made *Tango in the Night* a worldwide, hit-festooned bestseller. However, no sooner had he succeeded in remaking Fleetwood Mac for a new decade than he departed, the start of a new Fleetwood Mac personnel merry-go-round. Subsequently, Christine McVie departed, then returned; Buckingham returned, then departed again; and Nicks has been something of a dilettante. These upheavals were different to the changes pre-1975 in that they were always attended by a public assumption that no Fleetwood Mac activity would be truly authentic until the "*Rumours* Five" were back together again.

Curiously, *Tusk* has been rehabilitated, not so much among critics—a lot of whom liked it precisely because it made Fleetwood Mac a more interesting proposition than the quasi-MOR outfit they had become before it—but within the group. In 2001, Fleetwood told this writer of *Tusk*, "That's probably my favorite Fleetwood Mac album of all time. I think musically that album has influenced anyone from the Corrs to Aerosmith to a whole load of people. That album is a very important album to Fleetwood Mac. We were pushing some rather strange envelopes. We'd come off the *Rumours* album, and we made a very different album with *Tusk* . . . when you get a magical formula that works, it's very tempting just to repeat it. And we didn't. Lindsey was a big influence to really push and do something different and take the risk of it not being a huge success."

That sort of viewpoint was one thing, at least, that made the perennially brooding Buckingham happy. Back in '97, he noted to *Guitar*

World, "In retrospect, I've heard everyone in the band say, 'Gee, *Tusk* was a really cool album.' But it took a long time."

A New Sound: The Police

White reggae was everywhere in the UK in the year of 1979, whether it be the output of the 2 Tone roster, the Ruts' "Jah War," the Members' brilliant denunciation of tax evasion "Offshore Banking Business," or much of the new album by the Clash. The Police were even more than any of those artistes responsible for reggae becoming "crossover" music, yet theirs was a unique brand of the field. This was demonstrated by "Roxanne." It first appeared in April 1978 but didn't become a UK hit until a full year later. At first, its risqué subject denied it wide airplay, but everybody who did manage to hear this mysterious and unique record was talking about it. Its lyric was a demand that a woman give up her job as a prostitute. It was sung by a man with a strikingly plaintive voice. Its music was atmospheric but still soulful, and minimalist but still textured. Its genre, meanwhile, was uncategorizable. Although it possessed the ambience and some of the techniques of reggae, the guitar was on the downbeat, the drums weren't playing the three-beat, and the overall sensibility was rock. The artists in question had managed to achieve something that few ever do: create a sound never quite heard before.

The Police's prosaic name was rather a juxtaposition with their unique music, but it didn't hold them back. There are several ways to measure prominence, but many people who were UK pop consumers at the turn of the eighties will attest that they remember the Police as the biggest band in the country at the time. In 1979, they had four major hits, including two No. 1s, and a chart-topping album. Less empirically measurable is their cultural presence, but it was unquestionably pervasive. Across 1979–1980, the Police were genuine teen idols, inspiring fanaticism among adolescent girls and securing blanket coverage in pop magazines.

Drummer Stewart Copeland was born in 1952, in Virginia, and brought up in Cairo and Beirut. He was a member of prog-rockers Curved Air when he first clapped eyes on Gordon Sumner playing in his native Newcastle in jazz group Last Exit. Sumner, born in 1951, was already widely known as "Sting" due to his penchant for wearing a black-and-yellow-hooped jersey. He had film-star good looks, played nimble bass, and sang in a falsetto voice that should have been objectionable but was in fact hypnotizing. "I remember thinking, 'Jesus, that guy's really got it all,'" Copeland says. Before long, the two had ditched their respective groups and joined forces.

French guitarist Henri Padovani became the original third member of the Police (a name Copeland had devised before he even had a group). That Padovani's skills were limited was no problem: the new ensemble cold-bloodedly adopted a minimalist approach to fit in with the prevailing punk style. The band began rehearsing in January '77, played their first gig in March, and released their debut single, "Fall Out," on their own Illegal label that May. Most of the songs played at the first few Police gigs and on their early demos were Copeland's. "They're all rubbish," Copeland says easily. "The real Police stuff came later." Nonetheless, Copeland would beat the Police to the British charts with "Don't Care," a 1978 solo release under the guise of Klark Kent.

In July, the Police became a four-piece with the recruitment of guitarist Andy Summers, born in 1942 in Lancashire, England. Not only was Summers ten years older than the other members of the Police, but he had a rarified musical pedigree that involved stints in Zoot Money's Big Roll Band, Eric Burdon & the Animals, and Soft Machine, as well as much session work. The Police's sophisticated musical hinterland (Padovani excepted) always spelt doom for their hopes of acquiring street credibility in the UK. They were widely depicted by the British music press as old-fart musos hoping to con the musically naïve into thinking they were the genuine punk article. Tellingly, Copeland seems to choose his words carefully when asked if the Police liked the music of the Sex Pistols: "We had a great respect for what they had accomplished and recognized that they were at the front of the wave that we were riding."

In August, Padovani was deemed superfluous to requirements. "Henri left the band due to artistic differences," says Copeland. What were they? "He couldn't play guitar!" The remaining members elected to carry on as a trio. This is always a high-risk strategy, requiring each musician in the setup to work harder to compensate for the resultant holes in the sound. Or, as Copeland puts it, "All three points of the triangle need to be pretty sharp." Adding to the difficulties was the fact that, with the prevailing atmosphere being hostile to virtuosity, covering the cracks via soloing wasn't an option. "In the places where maybe ordinarily there would be a guitar solo, Andy would take a left, and we would go off into more of a group improvisation, where we're all in it together going off into a strange place." It was here that Copeland began to truly appreciate Summers's skills. "He would use massive technique to get around the strange places and provide really oblique harmonies to the weird rhythmic places that Sting and I would go." Copeland had to adapt as well. "I started very young, and I'm classically trained, but it wasn't until I started playing with Andy and Sting that I developed a musical personality."

It was to be a year before the public heard any further recordings from the Police. When they released "Roxanne" on A&M (a deal arranged by Miles Copeland, Stewart's brother, who became their long-term manager), it sounded like the product of a completely different band. It reflected the fact that Copeland had fallen in love with reggae while in college. "I got the Bob Marley stuff and immediately went nuts for it. I was a cult following of one in Berkeley, California, and in '77, when I got together with Sting, I had this record collection, and he immediately got it as well." Of "Roxanne," Copeland says, "It's actually, strictly speaking, not reggae. We drifted towards the real reggae eventually. 'Walking on the Moon'—that's absolutely a reggae beat. . . . We had a different take on it . . . we thought, 'Let's play a rock song that breaks the rhythmic rules the way reggae does.'"

Tellingly, "Roxanne" was written by Sting. The bassist's move into composition was what would ensure that the trio's career took off. "Sting actually wasn't really writing so much before then," recalls Copeland. "He was writing jazz compositions, but it was the punk [ethic]—the three-minute song—that focused his mind on verse-chorus-verse-chorus-bridge-verse-chorus." Once converted to succinct and tidy structures, it transpired that Sting had a quite astonishing facility with them. Copeland: "Getting an interesting idea that's emotionally engaging into a lyric that tells the story in three minutes and a piece of music that catches the ear—all that it takes to make a hit pop song—is a real knack. Sting just has it in spades." This, though, does not mean that the Police's hits were ever conventional. The latter is something for which Copeland gives credit to their guitarist. "Any strange directions that the band would take that you hear on a record, that's normally Andy Summers. He said, 'Come on guys, we've gotta push this somehow.'" Copeland doesn't mention that his own virtuoso, adventurous drumming contributed significantly to the exoticness of the soundscapes: at this point, he was arguably the best drummer in the world.

"Roxanne" emerged from the sessions that produced the Police's debut album, *Outlandos d'Amour* (1978), if "sessions" is the right word for such a piecemeal set of recordings. "The first album we recorded in bits and pieces, whenever we could find some studio time," Copeland remembers. The band will be forever grateful to Nigel Gray, who owned Surrey Sound Studio, where the recordings took place. "We made it without any money. Everybody eventually got paid, but it was all kind of on a song and a promise." The album boasted a cover picture in which the band were seen sporting the uniform blonde tresses they'd adopted the previous February when appearing in a chewing-gum commercial. Some of the material was triumphantly good. "Hole in My Life" was a long, atmospheric, endlessly absorbing reggae-jazz jam. That "So Lonely" was a number that alternated heartbroken slow verses with the sort of rousing, up-tempo choruses rarely heard in Jamaican music emphasized how the Police were bringing something of their own to the punky reggae party. Meanwhile, "Can't Stand Losing You" was an extended suicide note bristling with hooks and informed by a break-neck energy incongruous with the subject matter. However, not even the band's ingenuity and Sting's expressive vocals could save material like the hectoring "Peanuts," the boorish ode to a blowup doll "Be My Girl—Sally," or the aimless, space-filling "Masoko Tanga." The Police never really shook off this inconsistency, their inspiration often sagging on material they knew would never be more than an album track.

It was the US that first recognized the Police's talents. Their live work there saw "Roxanne" and *Outlandos d'Amour* climb by mid-1979 to No. 32 and No. 23, respectively. Clear Police UK chart momentum was finally achieved when the re-released "Roxanne" hit a peak of No. 12 in May 1979. Come July, "Can't Stand Losing You"—which had first charted the previous October—also made a belated ascent to the UK hit parade's upper reaches. Its self-harm theme would certainly have made for one of the most remarkable chart-toppers ever, but instead it had to nurse its grievances in the loser's saloon bar inhabited by "Oliver's Army," "Up the Junction," and other wooden-spooners. Nonetheless, hitherto neglected great records had finally got their due and a sense of vindication informed the Police's attitude to recording their second album, *Reggatta de Blanc* (which translates, sort of, as "white reggae"), released in October '79. "The second one was really exciting, 'cause by that time we could feel the buzz going," says Copeland. "The material wasn't the strongest material, but we'd just come back from America, and we'd been improvising a lot there and developing a sound, and we really [felt] that we'd hit the good foot. We whacked that album out, and it had a lot of energy. That's my favorite album."

The band's chart momentum reached a crescendo with the album's first single. "Message in a Bottle" was both a commercial milestone—when it made UK No. 1 in late September, it was the first Police chart-topper—and an artistic peak. It was yet another of Sting's brood-ing songs of heartbreak, a trait so noticeable that parody band the HeeBeeGeeBees were soon to draw attention to it with their Police-alike track "Too Depressed to Commit Suicide." However, it boasted so many attractions as to be almost ridiculous, from a tumbling guitar riff to a rippling chorus, to nifty bass-lines-cum-riffs, to captivating drum patterns, to a giddying number of key shifts. Although subse-quent Police fare would make for bigger worldwide hits, Copeland says, "We all still think that was really where it came together. 'Message in a Bottle' is definitely our signature tune." The record created such interest in the Police that it caused even "Fall Out" to finally be dragged into the UK Top 50.

Reggatta de Blanc followed it to the top of the charts two weeks later. While Copeland's admission that not all of the album's eleven tracks were up to par certainly applied to the likes of the tuneless "On Any Other Day" and the makeweight instrumental title track, what was good was sublime. "Bring on the Night" and "The Bed's Too Big Without You" were both exquisitely melancholic, the Police mining that self-pitying seam so skillfully that they continued to come up with gold. Moreover, in "Walking on the Moon" the album possessed a song that would once more bring dazzling imagination to humdrum radio airwaves. A languid, spacey offering with an unusually buoyant Sting lyric, it found the band, as Copeland puts it, "snapping off the echo and having a different echo come on and go out hard, and doing things sonically to the track that are unexpected and emphasize the fact that it's a recording rather than conceal the fact that it's a recording." In a nutshell, it was a record that cleverly sounded like a dub-wise mix without actually being one. "We were all deeply into dub, and, yes, we were nicking ideas off the dub mixers," says Copeland. "At the same time, we were contributing to the ideas of the dub mixers."

While, slightly disappointingly, *Reggatta de Blanc* went no higher than No. 25 on the *Billboard* 200, "Walking on the Moon" confirmed the Police's superstar status in Britain, perfectly rounding off a marvelous 1979 for them by topping the UK chart in December. Yet that elevated position had negative repercussions for the group's third album. *Zenyatta Mondatta* (1980) found artists who suddenly seemed self-conscious. The HeeBeeGeeBees might have been suspected of thinking up the LP's title or writing its formulaic taster single, "Don't Stand So Close to Me." The latter made No. 1 in the UK, but only because it was the archetypal keenly awaited new record by the hottest act around. Yet *Zenyatta* contained the single that would finally put the Police on the map in America. That it was "De Do Do Do, De Da Da Da" is a slight shame: Americans didn't go through the exhilarating experience the British had of a band redefining the notion of what constituted a hit single. Still, the record—a thumbed nose (written in appropriately infantile terms) to posturing politicians—did mark at least something of a development in Sting's writing. As he later observed, "The songs on *Outlandos* were all me, me, me. With *Zenyatta*, I've turned to what's happening outside."

Breaking America felt different. "They didn't know that we were 'fake,'" says Copeland. "They didn't know the [British music weeklies] *NME*, *Sounds*, and *Melody Maker* had written off [the band]: 'Ex-Curved Air, for God's sake!' In America, they were hearing an interesting story of a new wave. The Sex Pistols came over and fucked it all up—'Oh they suck' and everybody was laughing at them—but the idea of something new was still [in the air]. When the Police came over, we were able to be the thing that everyone was looking for."

There was only the industry-standard year between *Zenyatta Mondatta* and its follow-up, but when the Police re-emerged with *Ghost in the Machine*, they had reinvented themselves again. This was assisted by the fact that Nigel Gray was no longer the Police's producer, having been replaced by Hugh Padgham. Sting's yelping vocals and knack for a tune were present and correct, but the foreign-sounding portmanteau album titles, reggae strains, and trebly guitars were all gone (and, it turned out, gone forever). A maturing lyrical outlook, doomy synthesizer tones, and the fact that the politically flavored "Invisible Sun" was chosen as the record's harbinger helped the Police do what many pop idols had tried to and failed: make a transition into a heavyweight proposition. However, almost as if to stay the teenage girls and housewives who might have been tempted to abandon the group because of stern-browed fare like "Spirits in the Material World," *Ghost* boasted an effervescent slab of pop as catchy as anything the Police had ever produced: "Every Little Thing She Does Is Magic." Naturally, it went to No. 1 in Britain. It also fared well in the States, climbing to No. 3.

Synchronicity (1983) was in some ways an action replay of its predecessor: musical darkness, head-scratching concepts, and, of course, the token sure-fire smash single. The latter this time took the form of "Every Breath You Take," a song that was ostensibly a good-natured hymn of romantic adoration but which, on closer listen, transpired to be rather sinister. "If they're gonna play one Police song, that'll be the one," says Copeland. "But it's too bad, because it isn't the one that captured everything. My memory of the Police was something much more energetic, much more fired-up. The biggest hit happened to be a ballad."

"Every Breath You Take" was a transatlantic No. 1, as was its parent album. Setting the final seal on the Police's superstardom was a milestone August 1983 Shea Stadium gig in front of seventy thousand devotees. Yet at the peak of their success it was all falling apart. During the making of the Police's fifth long-player, relations between Copeland and Sting—two very strong-headed characters—had been so bad that it seemed obvious to everyone involved that it was all over. Though they managed to remain civil for the duration of a world tour, once it was over the Police members dispersed and moved onto solo ventures. Inevitably, Sting's solo career has been hugely successful, even if not so inevitably middle-of-the-road verging on soporific.

"Don't Stand So Close to Me '86'—recorded for a compilation—was a minor hit in that titular year, and the Police embarked on a triumphant, stadium-filling world tour in 2007–2008. (Padovani joined them onstage for two Paris shows.) However, there has never existed sufficient enthusiasm among the Police personnel to make a sixth album. Maybe this was par for the course, though. They had already done more than one thing few else achieve: created a new sound, and made the transition from pop stars to serious artists. By never properly restarting their recording career, the Police have sustained another uncommon feat: bowing out at the very top.

One Step Beyond Ska: Madness

"It was a pain when we used to go and do TV shows, especially in Europe. The TVs were like lion tamers: 'You be nutty! You be wacky!'

And it was like, 'Fuck off.' You'd just been up half the night, traveling or doing a gig or going on a bit of a binge."

Lee Thompson is discussing the downside of the "nutty-boy" image cultivated by Madness, the seven-piece ensemble for whom he played saxophone. The band never quite escaped their aura of lovable scamps, but, as their 1979 LP debut illustrated, behind it lay a formidable and even exotic musical talent.

Madness hailed from Camden, North London. Forming in 1976, their initial membership was revised on their journey to stardom along with their name: the Invaders became the North London Invaders before ending up as Madness. In addition to Thompson, their ultimate lineup would constitute Suggs (born Graham McPherson) on vocals, Mike Barson on keyboards, Chris Foreman on guitar, Mark Bedford on bass, Dan Woodgate on drums, and Chas Smash (born Cathal Smyth, known as Carl) on trumpet.

Not only were the group comprised of an unusual instrumental lineup, but their influences were uncommonly diverse. First and foremost, at least up to and including their first album, was ska—a taste they developed in complete isolation from the similarly inclined Jerry Dammers and co up in Coventry. Ska's progenitor is widely considered to be Prince Buster, born Cecil Campbell. So deeply did the early Madness venerate Prince Buster that they wrote a song about him, took their name from one of his compositions, and recorded two of his numbers.

Another influence was fifties rock 'n' roll and R&B. "Coasters, Fats Domino, and stuff," elucidates Thompson. Considering their insistence on singing in their own London accents, it's also significant that the group's other influences included the Kinks and Kilburn and the High Roads, who both pioneered spurning pseudo-Americanisms long before punk made it fashionable. It wasn't just the accent of the Kilburns' singer that Madness mimicked. Foreman told Ian Dury biographer

Richard Balls, "We had a sax player, a piano player, exactly the same lineup, and we used to do some of their songs."

It was Thompson who secured the accolade of writing Madness's first single when they obtained a one-off deal with the 2 Tone label. Their debut 45, "The Prince"—released in August 1979—was his bubbling tribute to Prince Buster. The B-side was a cover of said ska lodestar's "Madness," the song after which they had styled themselves on the not-entirely-serious suggestion of Foreman. Although Madness were an all-white band, their fusion of black and white musics would have made them a perfect fit for a label predicated on the sonic and social celebration of multiculturalism. However, the record—which made No. 16 in the UK chart—didn't auger a long association with 2 Tone. "They could only offer us a single deal," recalls Thompson. However, he adds, "The idea was to get away from that pigeonhole. Although most of the band liked ska reggae, we also had a wide range of other influences."

Madness attracted considerable and unwanted major-label interest. Thompson: "We had a meeting with Chrysalis, A&M, Virgin, EMI, Magnet. It was a free lunch, really. What we wanted was artistic freedom. If we hadn't gone with Stiff, we would have definitely gone with an independent."

"I had been told by several people that this band was something I would like," recalls Stiff supremo Robinson. "I wanted to see them live, inevitably, and they just didn't have any gigs at the time." Robinson's wedding was scheduled for August 17, 1979. Naturally, the nuptials of a music-industry figure were going to feature musical entertainment. "So I tied the two of them together. My wife has never entirely forgiven me, although Madness turned out to be a success. I paid them to play at the wedding."

While Thompson avers that the artistic freedom offered by Stiff was the label's chief attraction, Robinson himself suspects that

Stiff's capacity for quick decision-making was the decider. "I was told Chrysalis were looking at them. Chrysalis in those days were very slow. They had to see a band eight or ten times to make a decision about them, so I thought I'd better speed this up a bit. I invited the group around to have a chat. They came to the pub next door to the office. I said, 'What do you want to do? What's your plan?' They said, 'We just want to record.' Within an hour of meeting and a couple of pints, we had booked the studio, booked the producers, and the band were going in ten days later. They couldn't believe that a record company would do that kind of direct carry-on."

Madness records would be produced by Clive Langer (who'd helmed "The Prince") and Alan Winstanley. The team purveyed a bright sound that some might find too sharp-edged and unsupple, but, in alignment with them, Madness proceeded to storm the ramparts of success and public affection. The cockneyfied "blue beat" of their debut might have seemed a little niche (even if unique), but Thompson indicates that the band were brimming with confidence about their potential. "We knew we had other tricks up our sleeve," he notes. "Stuff was now being written by Mike. . . . He realized, 'Hold on, that's where the publishing is.' It was mainly Chris, Suggs, Mike, and meself on the first couple of albums, maybe even three albums. Mark hardly done anything. Woody, I normally wrote flipsides with him. But it was Mike that generally wrote a catchy tune." Robinson certainly saw Barson as the musical lynchpin, even on tracks that didn't bear his compositional credit. "Everything went through Barson," he says. "It was his band, to a degree."

The songs Madness wrote explored their North London, working-class culture. "I believe in folk music," says Robinson. "It's music made by the group in the social environment that they find themselves. Madness were one of the greatest folk bands around. They epitomized the entire society that they grew up in."

Despite their proletarian vignettes, Madness—unlike many of the punk and 2 Tone groups—were not much interested in political songwriting. "Partly 'cause we didn't know enough about it," says Thompson. "Suggs and Chris were pretty politically aware but we wasn't really into politics, didn't want to mix that with music. We were more into fun lyrics." Barson, in fact, later told Dave Simpson of the *Guardian* that it was Thompson who was responsible for the band's semi-comedic bent: "He came in one day with 'That nutty sound' sprayed on his jacket and talked about our music being a mixture of pop and circus."

Of course, writing North London vignettes made singing in anything other than Estuary English (commonly but inaccurately known as "cockney") out of the question. Due to the influence of Kilburn and the High Roads and the subsequent career of their lead singer, Suggs even exaggerated his accent and slang. He told Radio 2 in 1999, "I can tell you, there was a lot more cockney on the early albums than there actually was in real life as a consequence of listening to Ian Dury." Meanwhile, Thompson laughingly proffers an anecdote that puts Robinson's lauding of the band's folk orientation into context: "Dave Robinson did say to us once, 'Look, if you want to crack it in America, you've got to play more guitar solos, and, Suggs, you've got to try and sing with an American accent.' There wasn't a hope in hell of that happening." Madness's vocals, though, never conflated London inflections with studied uncouthness. Their singing styles (especially that of Suggs) were instead somehow polite and lovable, and if that sometimes tipped over into something uncomfortably resembling cap-doffing servility, there were plenty who would have been prepared to say—especially in that particular era—that it constituted a blessed relief from the posturing and yowling of British punk and rebel rock.

The song that had served to really get Robinson interested in Madness was the one that gave their debut album its name and opening cut. "They had this instrumental track with this announcement at the beginning: 'Don't watch that, watch this.' I hadn't heard it before. I immediately thought, 'What a great album title: *One Step Beyond . . .*' I could see it on a T-shirt. . . . I wasn't aware of the fact that it was a Prince Buster song. I thought, 'That could be a single which would really take them away from the 2 Tone thing.' I saw the music hall."

There was one small problem with Robinson's grand, multiplatform plans for the song/single/T-shirt: "They didn't record it. They had heard that I was a really pushy kind of geezer, and so the deal which we negotiated was that I would not go to the studio while they were recording. So I got there and they played me the album. I thought it was really good. It only took them three weeks. But there was no 'One Step Beyond.' . . . I said, 'Where the fuck is "One Step Beyond"? That's the album title.' They said, 'No, we're not doing that.' . . . I had ranted on about 'One Step Beyond' being something I considered would be a great single. They had obviously made the decision that it wasn't going to be a single. Afterwards, they told me they thought that people would think they were just a Prince Buster cover band."

There followed a five-hour debate, at the end of which Madness finally capitulated and agreed to lay down a version. Yet this still didn't entirely resolve matters. "When they played it to me, it was one minute and twenty-five seconds long. They were still trying to stitch me up. So I went into the studio after them and did a lot of editing and harmonizing, and made it into the single that it is. They weren't aware of that process at all—they didn't know that could happen—so they were gobsmacked. But they went along with it." The track did indeed become the hit Robinson perceived it as, making No. 7 upon its October '79 release. "When it was then a hit, they—to their credit—allowed me to pick all the singles thereafter."

The echo-drenched, spoken-word imprecation by Smash to watch the "heavy, heavy monster sound" made for an arresting start to the album. Thompson's smoky, snaking sax dominated the track, which was taken at a faster clip than Prince Buster's 1964 original. Even with Robinson's artificial lengthening, though, it was still half a minute shorter than said original (although, on the plus side, you couldn't see the join).

By the LP's second track, the band were demonstrating that they were in no way reliant on covers. Mike Barson's composition "My Girl" was a gem, remarkable for being a love song that featured no posturing, boasting, or bitterness but instead temperately explored the nuances of a relationship in which a man's partner was mildly aggrieved with him because he sometimes preferred to "stay in and watch TV on my own every now and then." Also then quite novel was that its pathos was not dented by it being rendered by Suggs in his natural inflections: class-bound Britain was only just learning that a London accent could be used in love songs for purposes other than comedy. Released as a single in December 1979, "My Girl" took Madness into the UK Top 3 for the first time.

Completing a remarkable opening triumvirate was "Night Boat to Cairo," written by Barson and Suggs. The skanking rhythm guitar was authentically Jamaican, but the lead guitar, sax work, and classical strings were lovingly suffused with the faux-Eastern exoticism of old black-and-white movies. Meanwhile, "Norf Lahndan" irreverence was represented by lines like "It's just gone noon, half past monsoon."

As it would have been difficult, even impossible, to sustain the quality of those three tracks across the course of an album, it's perhaps not surprising that the remainder of the record didn't live up to them. Some of it came fairly close. The herky-jerky "Believe Me"—a collaboration between Barson and Hasler—was a love song of less nuance than "My Girl," but touching nonetheless. Thompson's Borstal (juvenile prison) memoir "Land of Hope and Glory" hinted at the fact that, for all their good cheer, some of Madness hailed from tough backgrounds. The Suggs/Foreman "In the Middle of the Night," which opened side two, was a cheerful ditty about a "knicker thief underwear-taker." ("The nearest [we] got to politics," chortles Thompson.) Barson's "Bed & Breakfast Man" employed a yearning melody to accompany a character portrait of a couch surfer. Thompson's mildly jazzy "Razor Blade Alley" related the nature of the pain of an STD, as recounted in the movie *Boys in Company C*. Bedford's "Mummy's Boy" mocked a man who "lived with mother for forty years." Re-recordings of "The Prince" and "Madness" also featured.

On the debit side, the instrumental "Tarzan's Nuts" might possibly have been fun if it weren't so clearly a rip-off of the theme tune to the sixties Ron Ely *Tarzan* TV series, inexplicably credited to Smash and Barson. "Swan Lake" was at least public domain (as PiL also well knew). No law against a rocked-up, skank-inflected rendition of a classic, but it seemed cheap to subject majestic music to such treatment in order to pad out an album. 'Rockin' in A♭' was a cover of a song by Barson's brother's band, Bazooka Joe, and seemed to owe a debt to "Beatnick Fly," an instrumental by Johnny and the Hurricanes. As for the sub-minute album closer, "Chipmunks Are Go!," a pseudo-military chant credited to Smash and his brother Brendan, even Thompson admits, "It's a filler."

Though he had briefly been the band's bassist, at this point Smash was not formally a member, even if his onstage role as compere and dancer was an integral part of the whole Madness experience. Even so, the Madness personnel was still too large to comfortably fit onto an LP sleeve design. The problem was solved by depicting a Madness visual signature inspired by a sketch on comedy show *The Two Ronnies* that posited employees at a sardine factory arriving en masse at their workplace, jammed together like the product they packed. At a photo session, they transformed the line into what became known as the Nutty Train by pumping their arms. As for the auxiliary man, Robinson's enthusiasm about his stage presence, as well as advice from lawyers, saw Smash shortly become a full-blown member, on the proviso that he pay his way by taking up trumpet.

Released in October 1979, *One Step Beyond . . .* debuted at No. 16, and, over the next three months, climbed slowly to a peak of No. 2. It eventually racked up seventy-eight weeks on the UK album chart and went platinum. This elongated success was partly due to the fact that "Night Boat to Cairo" (against Madness's wishes) ultimately brought its number of hit singles—counting "The Prince"—to four. "We just thought, 'Hold on, we've rinsed it now,'" Thompson recalls. However, Robinson was convinced of the commercial potential of "Night Boat to Cairo." A compromise was reached, involving more studio time. Thompson: "The EP had three tracks on it not on the album. That was the way of giving them VFM." No doubt the new songs played their part in the success of *Work, Rest & Play*—as the EP was titled, when it was released in March 1980—but it was "Night Boat to Cairo's" delightful mix of the faux-exotic and the studiedly commonplace that saw it rise to No. 6 in the singles chart. ("Extended Play" charts had been discontinued back in the sixties.) The promo for "Night Boat to Cairo"—the nutty train being enacted in pith helmet and fez, against a line of patently blue-screened pyramids—helped set the slapstick template for Madness videos.

As indicated by Thompson's previous comment, some didn't understand that the collective nutty-boy persona that said promo epitomized couldn't be turned on like a light switch. A comment by Suggs to Jim

Green of *Trouser Press* in 1983 suggested the group felt that assiduously cultivated image to be backfiring on them: "The image of the band is itself almost as strong as the music, if not more memorable, to the average person. I don't know if it's right or not, but musically we've been looked on as something instant, not really worthy of analysis." In retrospect, however, the public never stood in the way of the band's accelerating musical and lyrical sophistication. *One Step Beyond* . . . made a sufficient impact to kick-start a career that would ultimately span— excluding reissues—twenty-seven Top 40 UK hits, sixteen of them Top 10s. In fact, also in retrospect, the album was more a beachhead than a definitive artistic statement. "For naivety, being green, and just going for it like a gang of schoolkids, definitely *One Step Beyond* . . . ," says Thompson of Madness' album hierarchy. He personally gravitates toward its 1980 follow-up, *Absolutely*, as the group's masterpiece. It happened to feature "Embarrassment," a Barson/Thompson co-write about the familial rejection suffered by Thompson's sister when she became pregnant with a black man's child. That when released on single it climbed only one place lower than the album's preceding, much jollier 45—the schooldays memoir "Baggy Trousers"—was, for Thompson, a "turning point." He reflects, "'Embarrassment' definitely pricked up the public's ears. They realized, 'Oh, this isn't just the 'My Girl'/'Baggy Trousers' stuff, it's got a serious tone to it."

For the most part, Madness's success was restricted to the "Rest of the World," the dismissive music-industry terminology for all the territories outside the United States. Says Thompson of the US, where the group's wares were initially purveyed by Sire, "It just wasn't their cup of tea." Because of the parochial lyrics, or the music? "I think both, really. It appealed to a very, very small minority." The exception to American imperviousness was "Our House," written by Foreman and Smash. Not even the US could remain resistant in the face of this joyous celebration of home, hearth, and house-proud mum. It made No. 7 on *Billboard*, a success that also dragged into the US Top 40 Madness' sweet 1981 cover of Labi Siffre's "It Must Be Love." How ironic that Chas Smash—the man credited on the back of that first Madness album only with "backing vocals, various shouts and fancy footwork," and whom the other members weren't exactly ecstatic about granting official membership—should end up reaping such a bonanza.

Fifth Madness album *Keep Moving* (1984) was Barson's farewell before emigrating to Holland. After the loss of such a pivotal member, the group was understandably never the same. They shed members and added a definite article to their name before finally splitting toward the end of the eighties. For a period, they were consigned to what was in those days a quite frightening territory: has-been land.

Said land no longer exists, conquered by the nostalgia industry, and the Madness story since the early nineties has been one of commercials licensing, hit reissues, chart-topping compilations, musicals based on the band's career, and—of course—a reunion. "We write new stuff as well, 'cause it keeps the interest up rather than going round that same old treadmill," notes Thompson. Of course, few among the crowds Madness continue to effortlessly draw would be able to name any of their "second act" albums. Thompson is sanguine about this. "We've had a charmed life. It seems the public don't want to let us go."

The icing on the cake may be that that the bugbear Madness couldn't lose by will has retreated naturally: time and tide have eroded the nutty-boy image that once irked them. "We're sixty, mate," Thompson points out. "I'm not walking about in me school uniform like AC/DC."

The CBGBs Runts Come Good: Blondie

Within any given year, an artist's success, no matter how massive, tends to be restricted to one part of the calendar. Not with Blondie in 1979. The New York band were highly visible from the start of the year to the very end. Their keenly awaited new album, *Eat to the Beat*, was released in October and bequeathed a clutch of hit singles that bled into the following year. However, preceding that, Blondie and their record company were still busily exploiting their previous long-player. In Britain—where their popularity was always the most intense—their September 1978 album *Parallel Lines* had only recently left the Top 10 when *Eat to the Beat* heaved into view. One of its constituent parts, "Heart of Glass," released on single in early 1979, transformed them from the runts of the litter of the New York club colloquially known as CBGBs into international superstars, and lead singer Debbie Harry into a global sex symbol.

Located on New York's Bowery Street, the Country, BlueGrass, and Blues club had by the mid-seventies bred an almost ridiculously fecund scene, even if no element of said scene conformed to the musical genres in the establishment's name. The scene included, among others, Television, the Patti Smith Group, the Dead Boys, the Dictators, the Voidoids, Talking Heads, and the Ramones. This was the original punk movement, predating the less varied, more abrasive British variety by easily a year. American punk was so lacking a generic sound that it also encompassed Blondie, formed out of a desire to combine the sassy style of the Shangri-Las with the vocal punch of an R&B group.

The idea was laughable, though, that Blondie would ever be perceived as fit to mention in the same breath as those aforesaid CBGBs acts. Their melodies were too conventionally pop and their lyrics too lacking in edge or abstraction. Additionally, though their singer was undeniably beautiful and able to carry a tune, she also resembled a mother gatecrashing a teenager's party: Harry had been knocking around since the late-sixties, when she sang in folkie band Wind in the Willows. Blondie were also a terrible live spectacle, the musicians prone to fumbling and Harry to gaucheness. The only record company interested in signing them was the independent Private Stock, and its US Blondie releases were flops.

Foreign climes initially proved more hospitable to Blondie. In 1977, the soaringly melodic "In the Flesh" made them stars in Australia, while Britain was receptive to their charms from their agile 1978 cover job "Denis" onward. Following their fun first album, *Blondie* (1976), their contract was bought by Chrysalis Records, which major label issued *Plastic Letters* (February 1978). While not as good as the debut LP, it made the Top 10 in the UK. Chrysalis heads Terry Ellis and Chris Wright then decided to replace Blondie's producer, Richard Gottehrer, with Mike Chapman.

The latter was given the specific brief of breaking the band in the States. At this point, Chapman's American track record was actually no better than Blondie's. In the UK, however, he was a pop legend, via his songwriting with Nicky Chinn on an endless stream of seventies hits for Sweet, Mud, Suzi Quatro, Smokie, and others, most of which he also produced. Chapman's role with Blondie would be far more hands-on than Gottehrer's, as can be gleaned from his response when asked if he found producing as fulfilling as he had songwriting: "With the Blondies it was, because I was so instrumental in creating the songs . . . songs like 'Heart of Glass' were a million miles from where it ended up." Moreover, "I'd made it clear that one of the uses they could put me to is my song selection. I've got a pretty good ear."

"At that point we were crap," Harry told Lucy O'Brien of *Mojo* in 2007. "Disorganized, hectic and not very well focused. Mike . . . said, 'You gotta stop foolin' around. You got some songs here. . . . You got different styles of playing that are gonna be a unique blend.' He was very visionary in that respect."

Helping craft songs and assisting in song selection was one thing. What some of the band didn't respect so much were the occasions when Chapman dictated what they should play. "Clem and I had a very bumpy relationship," Chapman says of the group's drummer. "It was from him thinking that he was one of the best drummers in the world. I had to try and convince him one way or another that he wasn't." It's now one of the most famous anecdotes surrounding Blondie that Chapman and Clem Burke took an entire day to lay down the "Heart of Glass" drum track. With the recording's slinky rhythm deemed so essential, it's not surprising that there were also issues with Nigel Harrison, who had recently replaced Gary Valentine on bass. Though the only Englishman among a bunch of "outer-borough" New Yorkers, Harrison was far from temperate in his reaction to Chapman's instructions. "We had a stand-up argument right out in the studio, with him telling me to go fuck myself," the producer recalls.

"Heart of Glass," written by Harry with Chris Stein (the band's guitarist and her romantic partner) was—like so many disco releases by established rock and pop acts of the time—not quite disco, whether it be because the group were too stubborn to completely let go of their usual methods or because they lacked the requisite skills. It was, though, a great record—one in which Harry glacially denounced the glacial nature of an ex-partner while the band (assisted by a Roland drum machine) percolated, pulsed, and preened behind her.

"We planned to release 'Heart of Glass' as a single, but we wanted to hold it back, because we knew we were gonna get tagged with the disco thing," Stein noted to Jim Green. "The album was out six months before it came out." In the meantime, Chrysalis had released two of the LP's covers as American singles—Buddy Holly's "I'm Gonna Love

You Too" and the Nerves' "Hanging on the Telephone"—and both had tanked. "Hanging on the Telephone" had at least been a British No. 5. "Heart of Glass," however, made all of that mere preamble. It reached No. 1 in the UK in February '79, and the top spot in the States in April. Although they had considerable success still ahead of them, Blondie had already outpaced all their old CBGBs rivals and detractors. Chapman also supervised a twelve-inch mix that artificially extended the song from four minutes to six. That this gained it valuable exposure under glitter balls—there were by now over a thousand discos in New York alone—was not surprising. Perplexingly, though, this mix replaced the original version on re-pressings of the album, thus ensuring that the now-standard version is not the one that most of the public remember.

Whatever the musical excellence of "Heart of Glass," it can't be denied that its success was assisted by a Harry makeover. She dispensed with a hairdo that had always been something of a rat's nest (blonde at the front, dark at the back, but tangled everywhere) for an elegant and consistently golden bob. (She grew it out but continued to invest in combs.) In photographs, she posed with glossed lips in front of shimmering lights. Harry always defended her sex-bomb image by citing irony or subversion. It's not quite clear whether that irony or subversion filtered through to the millions of people who, before long, were adorning bedroom walls with Debbie Harry magazine pinups and store-bought posters.

Although Blondie's next two US singles only made the lower reaches of the Top 30, *Parallel Lines* reached No. 6 on *Billboard*. Britain, meanwhile, gorged itself on the group. When the UK branch of the label pulled from the LP "Sunday Girl"—a solo Stein composition as sweet as "Telephone" was scorching—it too scaled the summit.

When it came to the follow-up album, the preparation period Chapman organized prior to going into the studio was a much shorter one than that for their first collaboration. "On *Eat to the Beat*, it couldn't have been more than a couple of weeks of rehearsal," he reflects. "There were so many ideas that were just floating around that nobody knew how to assemble. I'd just say, 'Well, look, we've got the basis there.'" Whereas *Parallel Lines* was recorded in New York's Record Plant, this time Chapman opted for the same city's Power Station studio, with forays also made to Media Sound and Electric Lady. The record was laid down in three weeks, most of it done live, with the band sharper not only due to Chapman's previous boot-camp approach but also because they'd just come off the road. All of this streamlined productivity happened despite Blondie simultaneously having to conduct job interviews. "We were looking for new management," Harry told O'Brien. "That was very distracting."

Despite their recent successes, Blondie were not interested in resting on their laurels. Chapman: "We knew what we'd just done with *Parallel Lines*, and we all made a collective decision, 'Let's make this sound different from the last one.'" Variety was to some extent inbuilt in Blondie, because all except Burke were composers. "I was blessed," reflects Chapman. "Debbie and Chris were the people that I went to for the hits and for the main songs, but at the same time Nigel and Debbie had already written 'One Way or Another' and a few other things, and Jimmy [Destri, keyboardist] and Debbie were very productive together, so it was fascinating. There was productivity coming from all different sides." As for Harry, despite her guileless interview persona, Chapman points out, "Debbie would come along with these wonderful, deep, intensive, left-field lyrics. Debbie's a cacophony of different styles and attitudes. She's a very deep human being, a tough nut to crack."

That Chapman had to practice considerable psychology when assembling Blondie albums is demonstrated by "Dreaming," one of the first tracks he heard during the *Eat to the Beat* rehearsal period.

Although a Harry/Stein co-write, Burke was determined to put his stamp on this keening tribute to the pleasures of fantasy. "He came in very adamant that he wanted that to have a big, Spector-esque attitude, big drums," recalls Chapman. "I let him do it because, if I didn't get that album off the ground, I knew I was in for a rough ride on the album."

"Dreaming" ended up opening the finished LP. Of second track "The Hardest Part" (Harry/Stein), Chapman recollects, "That was Debbie telling me, 'This is about a bank heist and I want it to be aggressive and loud and raucous.'" Chapman complied, to stomping but strange effect. "I don't even know what you'd call that kind of music." The overarching feeling of space on "Union City Blue"—a collaboration between Harry and Harrison—was helped by a yearning tune and a reverberating guitar riff, the latter from Frank Infante, also a sort of new boy: he'd played on the second album, but his membership had only recently become official.

"Shayla" was a psychedelic Stein composition. As with several other cuts, Chapman enhanced the sublime musicianship with some mysterious background effects, in this case a noise like a train sliding along tracks in a tunnel. However, it was Stein's multiple guitar parts that detained the producer the most. "Took me days to do those things with him. His inspiration way exceeded his abilities on the guitar, so I had to sit there and punch him in, line after line after line. . . . There was always this attitude that Chris didn't want Frankie overshadowing him, but he knew that Frankie could play his ass off. I pushed him to the point where he came to tears many times." At times like this, the rest of the group were unneeded, and would be happy to take a day off. "We were all going to bed at four or five in the morning," says Chapman. "We were at Studio 54 every night." Despite this, Chapman insisted on what were uncommonly early starts for the sessions. "I would start working anywhere from ten to twelve in the morning. I know to a normal person that's fairly late, but . . . Chris smoked a lot of weed. By four or five in the afternoon, he was so stoned he just fell asleep."

"Eat to the Beat" (Harry/Harrison) was really only notable for Burke's characteristically blurred drum patterns. Chapman admits it's an improvised throwaway. "Debbie said, 'I want to call the album *Eat to the Beat*, so we need a song called that.' We put it together in the studio." Side-one closer "Accidents Never Happen" was a double-time piece of lust-inspired Destri philosophizing.

The Harry/Stein reggae "Die Young Stay Pretty" kicked off side two in infectious style, its sunniness not even undermined by a fatalistic lyric that might offend those who don't aspire to leave behind a beautiful corpse. One of the most delightful aspects of the track was the fact that Harry artfully pronounced the final word of the title phrase as "pritt-ayy," the sort of vocal quirkiness Chapman encouraged. The upbeat, soulful "Slow Motion" was a collaboration between Destri and his session-drummer girlfriend, Laura Davis. On "Atomic," the keyboardist worked with Harry on a song that was a complete contrast to that: a surreal, futuristic epic with a larger-than-life guitar riff. A lengthy respite featuring fine throbbing bass work illustrated how eccentric was the track's architecture.

Ethereal insomniac's lament "Sound-A-Sleep" was written by Harry and Stein. Chapman was mightily impressed by the "dark and reverb-y" performance of a woman he'd often found to lack vocal application. "The two of us were always very diplomatic with each other and got along like a house on fire, but we had our issues," he reveals. "With Richard, the previous two albums, there was one pass and she just wouldn't sing anymore. But I'd say, 'That was a great vocal, let's make another one that's better' . . . I think on tracks like 'Sound-A-Sleep,' she was showing off, almost. She wanted to show me that she could do it on her own."

That the previous album had featured three cover versions (another Nerves song, "Will Anything Happen," was the other) worked to disguise the fact that, while Blondie had an unusual breadth of songwriting ability, they lacked depth of productivity. This was illustrated by the new album's two closing tracks. The Harry/Infante collaboration "Victor" was the LP's oddest song, a collage of Native American–like chanting, Far Eastern melody lines, choppy guitars, and shrieked Harry protestations ("I'm not a whore!"), the latter something of a shock after "Sound-A-Sleep's" lullaby cooing. Of Destri's frantic, untuneful "Living in the Real World," Chapman says, "I never thought it would make the album." (Any assumption from that last comment that the producer didn't have influence on final contents would be incorrect. Chapman: "They left sequencing and mixing entirely to me.")

On the *Parallel Lines* cover, the uniformly dark-suited Blondie men stood smiling behind a white-dress-wearing, grim-faced Harry. It couldn't help but foster an image the male band members resented—a queen bee surrounded by subservient drones—but it was, at the same time, striking and memorable. The headshots design of the *Eat to the Beat* jacket was, in contrast, rather pedestrian. This could almost be read symbolically, for the majority opinion was that *Eat to the Beat* was not as good as its predecessor. Yet the producer considers *Eat to the Beat* the superior work. "There's a more cohesive feel, not just to the playing but to the songs themselves," he insists. Not that Chapman thinks comparisons are easy. "Those albums are chalk and cheese."

In the US, *Eat to the Beat* made No. 17 and generated a pair of minor hits. Britain's love affair with Blondie, though, continued at the passionate pitch at which it had started. "Dreaming" got to No. 2 and

"Union City Blue" No. 13. That "Atomic" then sailed to the top spot is made remarkable by the fact of the UK being a VFM-oriented country that frowned on third singles from albums. Blondie ended the year as the UK's biggest-selling act in both 45 and 33 1/3 rpm formats.

The success of "Atomic" was assisted by a promotional film in which Harry could be seen wearing what looked like a plastic refuse sack. The surreal ambience already created by the sonics was enhanced with X-Ray washes. The next year, said clip formed part of a VHS release that billed itself as "the world's first video album," wherein all twelve of the album's tracks were presented either in dramatized promos like "Atomic" or in pseudo-live performance.

From this vantage point, Blondie had by now probably peaked artistically. However, they certainly hadn't gone off the boil commercially. With *Autoamerican* (1980), the group's compatriots were now finally favoring them more than their British fans: the album gave Blondie back-to-back US No. 1s, in the shape of lovely reggae cover "The Tide Is High" and pioneering hip-hop track "Rapture." From there, though, things went very awry very quickly.

Harry's 1981 debut solo album, *KooKoo*, produced by Chic's Nile Rodgers and Bernard Edwards, was a moderate success. When Blondie reconvened to make the 1982 album *The Hunter*, Harry and Stein were on heroin, Stein was struggling with the early stages of the debilitating skin disease *pemphigus vulgaris*, Harry had banned Infante from the studio, and Destri was so "fucked up," Chapman says, that at one point he "threw his Synclavier at me." The producer recalls "a fractured band completely disintegrating before my eyes. I just had to make the best album I could under the circumstances."

In the US, *The Hunter* could struggle only to No. 33. It dropped from that peak to No. 70 in the space of one week—"with a bullet," it was being cracked. Other derisory comments revolved around Harry's new green hair coloring: it was as though the blonde dye alone had sustained her career. Blondie had gone in the blink of an eye from chart gods to a joke. Not so funny was that, when the group dissolved six months later, they had nothing to show financially for their stupendous successes—a consequence, they claimed, of mismanagement by third parties. "I'd seen a band that had imploded in four and a half years," recalls Chapman. "There were some wonderful hits that were never written."

Since 1999, there have been five post-reunion Blondie albums, sometimes of surprisingly high quality, even if not featuring many personnel familiar to long-term Blondie fans. Perhaps it's not sufficient compensation for one of the most shocking and precipitous acts of self-destruction in music history. However, something that might be is the enduring chart stats, pinups, and audio recordings, which show that, in 1979 at least, Blondie could do no wrong.

11
NOVEMBER

The Damned had been as important in the UK punk moment as the Sex Pistols or the Clash, but by 1979 they had fallen on hard times. Brian James, the guitarist who had written most of the contents of their first two albums, had departed because he felt the band's potential exhausted. The other three members casually dispersed to other ensembles but—chastened by their respective lack of pulling power—quickly got back together. It seemed bad enough that they were going against punk's anti-corporatist ethos by seeking the commercial security of the Damned brand name, but actively pathetic that legal obstacles obliged them to use the moniker the Doomed. Eventually, they obtained the right to use the Damned name and secured a record deal with Chiswick. Algy Ward joined on bass, while Captain Sensible switched from bass to guitar. Dusky-toned vocalist Dave Vanian and rapid-fire drummer Rat Scabies remained familiar elements. The recalibrated group's 1979 effort was *Machine Gun Etiquette*. It boasted, in "Love Song," a romance number as brusquely heartfelt as their famous debut, "New Rose," and, in the unhinged form of "Smash It Up," a quintessential nihilistic punk anthem. However, there was also some material that was more sophisticated than had been heard in the James days. Mildly psychedelic production tricks were sprinkled on songs that often featured slower tempos and flourishes of keyboard. Although not a great album, *Machine Gun Etiquette* rescued the Damned from the status of a laughing stock.

The Advantages of Self-Education: The Jam

Up until late 1979, whatever success the Jam had enjoyed was shot through with ambiguity.

The three-piece from London suburb Woking had, like many young UK bands of the era, obtained a recording contract by riding the coat-tails of the Sex Pistols. However, they escaped the type of opprobrium directed at, say, the Vibrators because there was sincerity behind their conversion to punk, as demonstrated by the heartfelt social commentaries of front man, guitarist, and main songwriter Paul Weller. The fact of their excellent musicianship also helped. Their 1977 debut album, *In the City*, demonstrated that Weller and his colleagues—Bruce Foxton (bass) and Rick Buckler (drums)—were the archetypal trio who thrillingly compensated for their lack of a second guitarist with hyperactive virtuosity. Despite that record's high quality, though, their detractors were numerous. They inspired disdain because of their uncool out-of-town roots, refusal to feign contempt for all pre-punk music, spurning of confrontational punk fashions for throwback mod suits, and—most grievously—Weller's provocative press statements about admiring the Queen and intending to vote for the Conservative Party at the next general election. Those detractors were given some ammunition by *This Is the Modern World*, the band's substandard second album. Released only six months after their entrée, it found Weller—still only nineteen—trying to take his lyrics into more mature territory and revealing himself woefully out of his depth. It confirmed the suspicions of those who considered the Jam the runts of the punk litter.

Things improved slightly with *All Mod Cons* (1978), on which the Jam revealed that they were ahead of the pack in finding a way to maintain punk integrity while dispensing with its now overstressed studied primitivism, in their case by framing punk sensibilities within power-pop structures. The delicate acoustic ballad "English Rose," meanwhile, was not just beautiful but innovative in the simple fact of being sung in an English working-class accent. Moreover, the vituperative "Mr. Clean" saw Weller taking sides in the class war in such a way as to implicitly repudiate his conservative past. For all that, though, *All Mod Cons* was derivative, and Weller's lyrics often cringe-worthy in their unworldliness.

"Quantum leap" is an overused phrase, but little else seems appropriate to describe the progress made by the Jam over the next twelve months. With November 1979's *Setting Sons*, they suddenly assumed greatness. Originally, *Setting Sons* was to have been a concept album depicting three once-idealistic friends who met up after a civil war to find that their political philosophies had diverged—an idea that reflected the way the country's political opinions were being polarized by Thatcherism. However, the idea was abandoned. "I think after a while I just thought, 'Oh fuck this, let's make a record,'" says Weller. "I just lost interest in it. It got too complicated in my mind." In a comment that reveals that, though he declined to embrace its year-zero attitudes, he was simpatico with punk's suspicion of pretension, he adds, "I'm not really sure about concept records."

While the narrative idea was jettisoned, the album was in no way devoid of intellect. Indeed, the most noteworthy aspects of *Setting Sons* were Weller's sharpened intelligence and the commensurately enhanced sophistication of his lyrics. As someone who had left school at what was then the minimum leaving age of sixteen, armed with only two CSEs (second-tier high-school qualifications), his song words had hitherto rarely been as clever as they were earnest. However, his subsequent self-education—during the Jam's short lifespan he tackled works by, among others, Geoffrey Ashe, Adrian Henri, Roger McGough, Colin

MacInnes, George Orwell, Brian Patten, Erich Maria Remarque, Percy Bysshe Shelley, Alan Sillitoe, and Robert Tressell—now began showing in his compositions.

Possibly connected to that development of intellect was a greater degree of empathy. The epistolary *Setting Sons* track "Burning Sky" saw an arriviste stiffly decline to attend a reunion of old friends on the grounds that business called, explicating that the values that he and his friends held once upon a time now seemed stupid because the rent must be paid "and some bonds severed and others made." The conformist tenor was as perfectly sustained as the letter conceit. Even more impressive an act of inhabiting a completely different persona was "Private Hell," a brilliantly observed depiction of an empty-nester housewife. Weller—not only conventionally masculine but unusually self-absorbed even for a twenty-one-year-old—somehow managed to get inside the head of a middle-aged woman enduring quiet, Valium-fuzzed agony over the fact that her looks were fading, her interest in her husband's sexual attentions waning, and her relevance to her grown children's lives diminishing. When Weller referred to the subject's son still being at college, and then triumphantly finished the couplet with "You send him letters which he doesn't acknowledge," it was the perfect summation of how, in the space of just twelve months, he had turned from an embarrassingly inept lyricist into a superbly assured wordsmith. As if that weren't enough, Weller reveals that "Private Hell" was dashed off. "We needed some more songs for *Setting Sons*, so I was put in a room in our old rehearsal rooms with a typewriter or notepad and acoustic guitar, and I bashed it out," he says. "Knocked out that, and the same day I did 'Girl on the Phone' as well. It was kind of, 'Get in there, son, and get some more tunes together' . . . they were just songs I had to get done to fulfill a quota, but luckily they come out sounding all right."

That necessity to meet an oncoming deadline also informed the creation of the music. Foxton's most vivid memories of the *Setting Sons* sessions are nocturnal hours and a quick turnaround from composition to finished track, both of which he attributes to "pressure of the label and pressure on Paul." Recording the album at Townhouse Studios in London's Shepherd's Bush from August to October '79, the Jam faced the novel situation of extemporizing. "They weren't all completely finished," says Foxton of Weller's latest batch of songs. "And it was quite experimental, a lot of it. We were playing cello on certain parts—I don't think you can write for that. . . . Paul was finishing off songs in the studio. Normally you'd do preproduction before you go into the studio, because studios are so expensive . . . this was kind of writing to order." He further says, "Paul was finishing off songs during the day in the studio, and Rick and myself would work through the night a lot of the time, working out parts to record the next day, or record in the early hours of the morning. It was very hard work. It's amazing that we came out with a great album, actually. It was the first time and last time we ever worked like that."

"Thick as Thieves" was a song lamenting the loss of a boyhood allegiance that managed to be both poignant and rousing. The anthemic "Saturday's Kids" explored the mundanity and predictability of the lives of the unskilled but did so humorously and even joyously. "Smithers-Jones" was a wholesale recalibration of a Foxton-written B-side. The story it told of the devastating redundancy of an office drone was—unlike the straightforward original—now set to the backing of a twenty-piece orchestra. The latter was the pinnacle of the layering conferred by Vic Coppersmith-Heaven. The Jam's producer since day one, he was increasingly influential in the studio, especially now that original co-producer Chris Parry had departed. All three Jam members are effusive in their praise for him. "He had some great ideas," says Foxton. "I would say in the studio he was the fourth person."

The centerpiece of the album was an extended version of "The Eton Rifles," the record's leadoff single. The song concerned a failed insurrection in which beer-swilling, cigarette-puffing, working-class malcontents left the security of their local pub to take on representatives of the ruling class and came off humiliatingly worse against people who were better educated, better connected, better equipped, and better fed. The composition had a comedic tinge: the narrator, lamenting that his comrade-in-arms turned out to be a poor catalyst for change, observed, "Loaded the guns then you run off 'ome for yer tea!" The song, however, sprang from deadly serious events. Weller was motivated to write it after hearing about Eton schoolboys jeering at people participating in a "Right to Work" march organized to protest about rising unemployment. Also deadly serious was the soundscape. Following an urgent, doom-laden introduction, Foxton's bass provided a broiling bottom end as Weller's multitracked guitar parts stuttered and crashed. Slivers of organ were the only glints of light in the all-encompassing gloom. Yet "The Eton Rifles" was also very easy on the ear, courtesy of dramatic shifts in key and a chorus that—appropriately for a military-related song—had the flavor of parade-ground call-and-response. This paradoxical concoction shot the Jam to dizzying heights in the UK singles chart, where it ultimately climbed to No. 3. "Can you imagine that being on the radio or [a] Top 3 record now?" marvels Weller. "Wouldn't happen, would it?"

Even *Setting Sons'* weak tracks had considerable qualities. Anti-war anthem "Little Boy Soldiers" was a widescreen affair punctuated with sound effects. It also had a stunning kiss-off line where, to the accompaniment of a spiraling piano part, the narrator imagined his mother receiving his coffin with an attached letter reading, "Find enclosed one son, one medal, and a note to say he won." "Wasteland" featured unconvincingly florid phraseology but struck a chord in its evocation of the aching misery of underprivileged teenagers idly traversing their litter-bedecked concrete jungle and wondering, with the quiet terror of youthful inexperience, if life was ever going to get better. Opener "Girl on the Phone" was a glorified jingle with no sociological import, but it was also perfectly enjoyable. On the surface, the inclusion of Holland-Dozier-Holland classic "Heat Wave" as a closing song bordered on the absurd. However, though it was blatant filler possessing absolutely nothing to do, musically or thematically, with what preceded it, its joyousness cleansed the palate after all the preceding grimness.

Against a background of critical hosannas, *Setting Sons*—housed in a sleeve depicting a dramatic statue of first-aid workers—climbed to a UK No. 4. Both the position and the record's nineteen-week occupancy of the album chart were Jam milestones. *Setting Sons* even secured the first-time Jam feat of cracking the US Top 200, reaching No. 137.

It wasn't only their rapidly improving art that brought the Jam a whole new slew of fans that year. The steady, organic growth in Britain since the previous year of a mod revival was given a sudden outside boost in the very month of the appearance of *Setting Sons* by the release of the movie adaptation of the Who's *Quadrophenia* album. While the whole new mod cult might have been nebulous (a never quite convincing or accurate avowal of adherence to sixties mods' musical and fashion interests) and contradictory (nostalgia for the values of "modernism"), it nonetheless existed. Although the Jam had dispensed with their mohair suits the previous year, this mini Parka-clad army naturally gravitated toward a band considered to have an association with mod.

The Jam's new success, however, was predicated on something more substantial than serendipitously chiming with the latest trend. *Setting Sons* transpired to be a stepping-stone to even greater achievements.

Early the next year, "Going Underground," the group's scorching hard-rock denunciation of nuclear militarism, sailed to the top of the UK singles chart, making for an even more unlikely chart smash than "The Eton Rifles." *Sound Affects* (1980) was less ambitious than *Setting Sons* but once again rock-solid in quality. It contained the band's second No. 1 single in "Start!" By this point, the Sex Pistols had splintered, the Damned and Sham 69 were floundering, and the Clash were beginning a descent into self-parody. What this meant was that the unthinkable had effectively happened—the punk paupers were now kings. If ever there could be said to be a formal anointing, it took the shape of the success of the Jam's early 1982 double-A-side single "Town Called Malice" / "Precious." Not only did it sail to the No. 1 spot but it saw the group granted the symbolic accolade of being the first act to perform two tracks back-to-back on *Top of the Pops* for more than a decade-and-a-half.

In turning themselves into consistent chart-toppers, the Jam had brought social commentary to the masses, thus fulfilling a key aspiration of punk. They also fulfilled another one: refusing to get old and irrelevant. The fact that the long, slow decline of the Rolling Stones, the Who, the Kinks, *et al.* had been an impetus for the punk movement was something not forgotten by Weller. In July 1982, four months after the release of sixth album *The Gift*, he made the decision to leave the group, thus effectively bringing down the curtain on the Jam's career. They played their farewell gig in December. It was a dissolution that permanently preserved the Jam in amber as young, vital, and happening.

12
DECEMBER

David Sylvian, the pancaked and elaborately coiffured vocalist of London quintet Japan, was touted as the "most beautiful man in the world." There was musical substance beyond that managerial hype. The eight songs on *Quiet Life*, the band's third album, melded krautrock with strains that betrayed the members' teenage glam-rock hinterland. It was an elegant and singular sound, if shot through with ridiculously affected depressiveness, and was their first album to chart. Ultimately, enough people were susceptible to their iridescent dejection to leave Japan with nine UK Top 40 singles.

The Clash and a Belatedly Acknowledged Classic

In its review of *Setting Sons*, *Record Mirror* adjudged the Jam LP "the last great album of the seventies." Not quite. It being so close to year's and decade's end, the UK music weekly's precipitousness was understandable, but December 14 brought *London Calling* by the Clash. (The album was released in the States in January 1980, enabling it to later be voted by *Rolling Stone* the best album of the eighties. The American 1979 Clash album was, slightly bizarrely, a tweaked version of their 1977 debut, whose rough-hewn production had seen it denied a US release—a decision only reversed when it racked up an estimated hundred thousand sales on import.)

There again, some critics didn't consider the Clash's third long-player a classic or anything like it. Absurd as it may now seem, *London*

Calling was detested by many upon release. The reason was summed up by the Jam's Paul Weller himself, when he told US journalist Dave Schulps, "*London Calling*'s a cop-out. It is for British people anyway. It's alright for Americans. . . . I used to be a fan of theirs, but ever since they started getting it together in America every picture of them you see is this quasi-American gangster sort of stuff and there are all the Americanisms in their music." That Weller's reaction was by no means uncommon was reflected in the fact that the Clash's Joe Strummer was still complaining about the album's reception more than two years later, when he insisted to the *New Musical Express* of its genesis, "I never thought about beef burgers once, or Mickey Mouse, or the Statue of Liberty."

Such was the climate of the times that, for some, neither *London Calling*'s patent excellence nor its value for money (quite remarkably, the double album was, at the Clash's insistence, retailing for the price of one) cut any ice. This will be bewildering to young people today, or quite possibly anybody domiciled outside of the United Kingdom at the time. However, in the afterburn of punk, continued studied Britishness on the part of those artists who had cut their teeth on the movement very much mattered. The Clash were felt to have a particular duty to avoid Americanisms because of their first album's broadside against cultural imperialism, "I'm So Bored with the U.S.A."

Even more bewildering will be the fact that *London Calling* in no way found the Clash abandoning their Englishness. Indeed, closing track "Train in Vain" was revolutionary in being a soul number sung in pure London, hitherto an absurd concept. Nor had they ceased to write songs about indigenous injustice and deprivation. Rather, the accusations of having "gone all American" (with the implicit assumption that it was to acquire Stateside success) were based around somewhat more nebulous transgressions. Their music was suddenly glossy, melodic, and even life-affirming. No one expected them to still be purveying the primitivism of their first album—it was by now fully understood that, by dint of practice, punks would learn how to play—but horn charts, keyboards, sunny melodies, cheerful lyrics, and immaculate, wides-creen production just somehow seemed wrong for a band of the Clash's vaunted guttersnipe mentality. The fact that the album contained a cover of Vince Taylor's "Brand New Cadillac"—a song drenched in Americana—was another black mark. Additionally, all this came wrapped in a sleeve featuring rock-dinosaur iconography: bassist Paul Simonon was shown smashing his instrument onstage à *la* the Who's Pete Townshend, adjacent to lettering deliberately redolent of the first Elvis Presley album. Thus did the fact that the Clash had delivered one of the greatest albums in the history of popular music go, for the first few years after its release, to some extent unrecognized.

London Calling was forged in the fires of desperation. Second album *Give 'Em Enough Rope* (1978) had attracted its own sellout accusations due to its mainstream production by Sandy Pearlman (an American, to boot). Moreover, powerful though much of it was, it was an aesthetic step down after their already classic debut. The band had also rancor-ously split with Bernard Rhodes, who had been their mentor as much as their manager. Moreover, they were broke. Strummer, for instance, was living with his girlfriend's family in one of London's most notori-ous housing projects.

There was also the issue of a lack of new material. The group's *Cost of Living* EP of May 1979 was very enjoyable, but was topped by a cover of "I Fought the Law" and tailed by a re-recording of early Clash number "Capital Radio." Said tracks sandwiched "Groovy Times" and "Gates of the West," fine songs but ones that—unbeknown to their fans—recycled unused Clash melodies. Things, therefore, did not auger well for the next album.

Clash drummer Nick "Topper" Headon attributes the quality of *London Calling* to something most bands three albums into their career don't have the luxury of: practice. "We spent a lot of time in rehearsals with that album," he says. The four to six months (estimates vary) the Clash spent working up and honing songs behind a garage in Pimlico, south-west London, meant that, when they took them into Wessex Sound Studios in North London, the material was in optimum form. Guy Stevens, legendary ex-manager of Mott the Hoople, was nominally the album's producer, but his role seems in reality to have been more that of cheerleader. That the finished work's glistening, panoramic production was indeed very reminiscent of Mott the Hoople's 1973 masterpiece *Mott* is down to the fact that Bill Price engineered both records.

With the exception of the cover versions and Simonon's smoldering "The Guns of Brixton," the songs were—as usual—the handiwork of rhythm guitarist/vocalist Strummer and lead guitarist/vocalist Mick Jones. The widespread assumption that Strummer was always responsible for lyrics and Jones melody wasn't always correct—for instance, Strummer had written the first album's "London's Burning" on his own, while Jones was solely responsible for their acclaimed 1977 single "Complete Control"—but in this case it pretty much held true: only on "Train in Vain" did Jones provide words. This role-demarcation was disguised a little by the fact that Jones handled lead vocal duties on four of the album's nineteen tracks—usually numbers like "The Card Cheat" and "I'm Not Down" whose vulnerability suited his tremulous delivery.

The first album had famously included "White Riot," an exhortation to disaffected Caucasian youth to follow the lead of their Caribbean counterparts and burn the town down. While exciting, it was hardly adult or responsible. Aside from a tweak of the lyric of reggae cover "Revolution Rock" that incited listeners to smash up their seats (a reference to Clash fans' behavior at a gig at London's Rainbow Theatre), there was nothing like that here. *London Calling* evinced a new maturity that seemed to be due to Strummer feeling his age. "I'm now twenty-seven and it's something you gotta learn by the time that you're twenty-five, that before then your body doesn't keep a record of what you do to it," he told *Melody Maker*'s Chris Bohn. "After that you get real sick, sort of burning the candle at both ends. . . . I wrote 'Rudie Can't Fail' about some mates who were drinking brew [lager] for breakfast. They think nothing of it. Me, I'm past the stage where I can." Simonon explained to Ben Myers of 3ammagazine.com, "Having traveled, we had become more worldly and our thoughts more international, as opposed to being eighteen, nineteen, and getting the group to sing about 'Career Opportunities' or 'Garageland.'"

The philosophical maturation was matched by musical growth. "There was a point where punk was getting narrower and narrower in terms of what it could achieve and where it could go," Jones reasoned to Mal Peachey. "It was like painting itself into a corner, and we wanted to do anything and everything. We thought you could make any kind of music."

Headon was exhilarated because the Clash's evolution was something he hadn't previously envisaged. A soul-oriented muso, he had considered the band a temporary berth when he replaced their original drummer, Terry Chimes, in April 1977. "When I went to the audition, I thought, 'Yeah, it's good, but it's not going to go much further,'" he says. "And, as you know, most of the punk bands didn't . . . you couldn't deny the charisma of the three of them and you couldn't deny the power of the music and they looked absolutely amazing together, but it was very one-dimensional."

A transformation in his attitude began during the recording of *Give 'Em Enough Rope*. "It was starting to change, and I was starting to have a little bit of influence. For example, the beginning of 'Tommy Gun,' I was putting drum fills in. 'Julie's Been Working for the Drug Squad,' put some stuff in that. By the time we came to record *London Calling*, the music was progressing. We were recording jazz and bits of funk and bits of soul. It just grew, a natural thing."

Unfortunately, the exhilaration had to come to an end because of the band's live commitments. Headon: "We couldn't finish *London Calling*. We were always in the studio or on the road. We left the end of *London Calling* in the hands of Bill Price, who started to mix it and was then sending us out tapes in the States to listen to. I remember us all sitting on the bus one night in New York, having had the latest tapes sent to us, and we just sat there and we thought, 'Wow. This is good. All that hard work has paid off.'"

The album's title track became a hit single even though both its apocalyptical nature and the Clash's ideals—always as important as their music—would seem to very much militate against that possibility. *Top of the Pops* might have been the single most important promotional tool in the UK music industry, but the Clash were disgusted by its cheesy aura and requirement to lip-synch to a backing track, which (because of trade-union rules) wasn't even the original record but a perfunctory re-recording. As such, they refused to either appear or allow their promos to be screened on the show. Consequently, their singles tended to be only minor hits. This time round, their low media visibility proved less important than their record's grim infectiousness, and it climbed all the way to No. 11. It could conceivably have gone much higher, as testified to by the even grimmer record that closed out the year at the top of the UK singles chart.

When the album followed a week later, it proved a quite startling and sumptuous smorgasbord. "Rudie Can't Fail," "The Guns of Brixton," "Wrong 'Em Boyo," and "Revolution Rock" saw the Clash finally master the "riddims" they had previously only been able to deploy as part of a reggae-rock hybrid. "Spanish Bombs," "Lost in the Supermarket," and "Lover's Rock" were gliding soft rock with serious messages. The strutting "Jimmy Jazz" finger-poppingly lived up to its title. The towering "The Card Cheat" was worthy of its Phil Spector Wall of Sound aspirations. Only its Estuary English prevented "Train in Vain" seeming like a bona fide product of the Stax studios. The Clash's evolution was evident even when they were found purveying their trademark anthemic rock: unnoticed by many, "Death or Glory" appeared for all the world to contain a self-lacerating admission that the band's no-compromise ideals were absurd and impossible to live up to.

The album's real triumph was its home stretch. Side four of its vinyl configuration was a rollercoaster ride (something accentuated by segues that meant that listeners could barely catch their breath) taking in the sweet but saucy "Lover's Rock"; the latest in a line of self-aggrandizing Clash anthems, "Four Horsemen"; the galloping and moving assertion of perseverance in the face of setbacks "I'm Not Down"; the tear-jerking condemnation of Jamaican gangster culture "Revolution Rock"; and finally "Train in Vain," whose heart-wracked but mellow strains acted as a comforting balm following the emotional tumult of the preceding four tracks.

Today, the sociopolitical and cultural imperatives that led to, for instance, Barney Hoskyns of the *New Musical Express* claiming that the album had only one good track, have disappeared into the cracks of history. Removed from the climate of the times, aesthetic quality is the sole criteria on which *London Calling* is now judged. It regularly appears in critics' polls of greatest-ever albums. It should also be pointed out that it was hardly a commercial flop. As if to emphasize that music critics are not representative of the populace, the album went Top 10 in the UK and Top 30 in the States.

It was the band's artistic pinnacle. *Sandinista!* (1980) contained some excellent material, especially "The Magnificent Seven," which was not only ahead of the curve in purveying rap but brought to the form a social relevance that is now its defining characteristic. However, this time out the Clash managed to contaminate a value-for-money approach with hubris: despite its low price, many would have preferred a double album—or even a single disc—to this bloated three-LP set. *Combat Rock*—a single LP released in 1982—sounded surprisingly uncertain, with the harrowing "Straight to Hell" and the jocular "Rock the Casbah" the only tracks truly worthy of "Clash Classic" status. Nevertheless, assiduous promotion orchestrated by a returned Rhodes saw it lucratively climb into the US Top 10. Shortly after its release, Headon was sacked over his heroin addiction. Jones followed him out of the door in late 1983, his offence his prima-donna airs. Strummer and Simonon pushed a new five-man Clash who released *Cut the Crap* (1985), the Americanism of whose title was as shameless as the record's music was self-parodically awful. A remorseful Strummer was rebuffed by Jones when he asked him to return to the fold, following which the band sputtered into nonexistence.

"There's a lot of reasons," Headon says of the Clash's unraveling. "By the time we came to record *Combat Rock*, we'd lost interest in each other. When we recorded *London Calling*, it was when we loved being together as friends, and the music was getting better and better. Recording *Sandinista!*, cracks began to appear. By the time we came to record *Combat Rock*, we'd been on the road and living in each other's pockets for five years, and we'd just lost that fun spirit." There was another problem, one that probably wouldn't apply to any other ensemble: "Joe felt very uncomfortable because he was in a band that was getting more and more successful all the time." Although they repeatedly came close, the Clash never reunited—something for which Headon is glad. "I wouldn't change it for all the tea in China, because that's why we're talking now about thirty years down the line—because we imploded at the top."

For Headon, no Clash memory gleams brighter than the period around *London Calling.* "It was like a dream come true . . . it just became a magical album, really."

Spitting in the Face of Success: Pink Floyd

The music scene in 1970s America was characterized on several levels by lack of change. One example was the album charts. In contrast to the way that Led Zeppelin and the Eagles monopolized the acme of the *Billboard* Top 200 from September 15 onward (almost a third of the year), eight different discs reached the summit of the UK LPs table in the same period. In one way, though, the British album chart was more conservative than its Stateside counterpart. Britain loved compilations, that buying preference of the "casual" music consumer—a breed distinct in some people's eyes from the genuine music lover. Whereas *Barbra Streisand's Greatest Hits Volume 2* was the sole compilation to make the top in the States in '79 (a three-week tenure), the UK summit played host to no fewer than seven. As well as the Streisand record, it was at various points occupied by three various-artist disco collections, plus greatest-hits packages by ABBA, Leo Sayer, and Rod Stewart. All told, compilations sat atop the British chart for just under half the year. In the crucial Christmas period, it was Rod Stewart's *Greatest Hits* that picked up the most sales, occupying the LP top spot from December 8 through to the end of the year and eleven days beyond.

Stewart, though, might well have preferred to have the No. 1 Christmas single. In Britain, securing the top spot in the singles chart over the Yuletide period is of profound importance, partly because for many years it was inextricably linked to the cultural milestone of the

Christmas Day broadcast of *Top of the Pops*, which—like everything on the BBC at Christmas—enjoyed sky-high viewing figures. "It's like being crowned," observed music journalist Sian Pattenden of achieving the UK No. 1. "It's like winning the year." As might be expected of songs swept to the top spot by the goodwill-to-all-men spirit steeping the public as they set about their present-buying, Christmas UK chart-toppers are usually of the feel-good variety. Some are specifically Christmas-themed, like Slade's "Merry Xmas Everybody" and Mud's "Lonely This Christmas." Others are simply the latest release by artists thought fondly of by huge swathes of the nation, especially if their release is generous of spirit (it's no coincidence that the Beatles—the ultimate life-affirming artists—racked up four). When "Bohemian Rhapsody" was the top-seller over the 1975 Yuletide season, its tragic storyline might have made the achievement incongruous, but its overall ambience counteracted that: its epic, outlandish timbre was the sonic equivalent of tinsel and ribbons. Nothing really prepared the British public, then, for the fact that that the 1979 UK Christmas No. 1 was "Another Brick in the Wall (Part II)" by Pink Floyd.

That the Cambridge quartet even secured a hit single at all was a shock in itself: their days as hit-makers had seemed over in April 1968, when their onetime guiding light, Syd Barrett, departed the band after having become an LSD casualty. Floyd's subsequent journey from psychedelic ensemble to prog-rock outfit (and hence albums band) seemed to preclude not just potential for, but even interest in, singles success. They'd allowed the likes of "Money" to come out on 45 abroad, but "Brick" was the first single in Floyd's native UK for more than a decade. It was the subject matter, though, that made "Another Brick in the Wall (Part II)" surely the most bizarre Christmas chart-topper up until the anti–Simon Cowell protest No. 1s of the twenty-first century.

Like many of his vintage, Floyd bassist and chief composer Roger Waters received a brutally authoritarian education. This fact clearly informed a tormented creation in which education was likened to thought control, and which ended with the hysterical, spoken-word rantings of a schoolteacher. The song was additionally un-hit-like in the fact that it constituted merely a chorus, sung twice. For all its unusualness, though, the track had a definite sing-along-ability. Workplaces and school playgrounds were soon resounding to its refrain, "We don't need no education!" (sometimes humorously adjusted to "We ain't 'ad no edu-cay-shun!").

It was also funky. The song's pumping bass line and regulated drumbeat were the final proof of the fact that no area of popular music that year was immune to the influence/infection (delete according to taste) of disco. Guitarist David Gilmour credited/blamed producer Bob Ezrin. He later told Sylvie Simmons of *Mojo*, "He said to me, 'Go to a couple of clubs' . . . so I forced myself out and listened to loud, four-to-the-bar bass drums and stuff and thought, 'Gawd awful!' Then we went back and tried to turn one of the 'Another Brick in the Wall' parts into one of those so it would be catchy." Ezrin had worked on Alice Cooper's "School's Out" and now copied that record's gimmick of a defiant school-kid chorus. He also took the unilateral decision to artificially lengthen a song too short for single release in its present state. Floyd's new pop stardom, perhaps purposely, didn't grant recognizability to a group so faceless that they were able to breeze unnoticed past paparazzi at airports. The band members didn't appear in the song's widely seen video, which instead featured surreal Gerald Scarfe animation and film of shadowed, chanting schoolchildren. The record's ascent was assisted by them being more permissive with the dissemination of their promos than were the Clash, who could have conceivably have had the Christmas No. 1 if their policy hadn't been so absolute. However, Floyd's video did not appear on the Christmas Day *Top of the Pops*, which as ever was oriented around live—i.e., mimed—performance, something out of the question for artists of such standing-cum-hauteur.

In Ezrin, the band were employing an outside producer for the first time in a decade. Waters had engaged his services because he felt he needed something approaching a collaborator to help make sonic sense of the complicated concept to be found on the single's parent album, *The Wall*. The group's eleventh studio LP, it marked the point where Pink Floyd became Waters's band. In contrast to the compositional collaboration that marked previous Floyd wares, he wrote 85 percent of *The Wall* on his own.

Ten years on from Floyd being the darlings of London's LSD-drenched underground movement, the Sex Pistols' Johnny Rotten had walked around the very same capital in a customized T-shirt reading "I HATE PINK FLOYD," a sentiment informed by resentment of Floyd's musical self-indulgence, in-concert pretension, and rarified lifestyles. However, it wasn't this that had triggered the crisis of confidence that motivated Waters to write a magnum opus double-LP—as with all "dinosaur" groups (except perhaps Emerson, Lake, and Palmer, and Crosby, Stills, and Nash), Floyd's sales (as opposed to cachet) were completely unaffected by punk. Rather, it was the very trappings of Floyd's success that bothered Waters. On Floyd's world tour in the first half of 1977, he found the new experience of playing in the stadia necessary to accommodate their now vast fan base to be extremely unsettling. His resentment of audiences unwilling to quietly concentrate on the music culminated in an incident that left him feeling dirty but inspired. "One night at the end of the *Animals* tour in Canada, there was a fan clawing his way up the storm netting to try and get to us and yes, I just snapped and spat at him," he told *Mojo*'s Johnny Black in 2003. Although he said he was immediately disgusted with himself, he also observed, "After I'd thought about it, the idea of actually building a wall between us and the audience, it had wonderful theatrical possibilities." His relationship with his audience wasn't the only subject Waters proceeded to explore through the life of a character called Pink. He also addressed his cruel education, the early death of his father, his difficult relationship with his mother, and war. Pink—despite acquiring the privilege of being a rock star—desired to psychologically wall himself in as protection against such traumas.

Not only did Waters hijack the songwriting process but he changed the nature of Floyd's sound. A band whose trademark was long songs with extended instrumental passages were now purveying short, lyric-heavy tracks. Gilmour lost his role as lead vocalist, and the few compositions he got onto the album were at Ezrin's insistence. The latter fact is what ensured that some of the old Floyd tranquility was present in the chorus and timbre of "Comfortably Numb."

The album was demoed in Britannia Row Studios in London, recorded in Super Bear in France, and finished up in New York's CBS 30th Street Studio and L.A.'s Producers Workshop. The length of time involved was technically around a year, but the gaps in recording meant that the actual work amounted to five months. Not long into the process, the band discovered they were in deep financial trouble as a consequence of accountancy incompetence—something that must surely have contributed to the cheerlessness of the material. The album's lyrics were relentlessly depressing, even sometimes whining, exemplified by the line, "How can you treat me this way?" from "Don't Leave Me Now."

The Wall was released on November 30, 1979, with a sleeve bearing a white brick design. The album may have been a world removed from the spaced-out grooves of their 1973 mega-seller *Dark Side of the Moon*, or indeed any previous Floyd music, but their fans had no problem with that. Although it didn't sell quite as many copies as *Moon*, it proceeded to join it in the ranks of history's all-time bestselling albums. In fact, its success rather put paid to the ah-but-it's-a-double excuses offered by Fleetwood Mac for the underperformance of *Tusk*. *The Wall* made No. 3 in the UK, where it was in the Top 20 for three and a half months. This, though, was as nothing compared to its American success. It entered the *Billboard* 200 unspectacularly at No. 51, but by January 19, 1980, it was in the top spot, where it remained for fifteen weeks. "Another Brick in the Wall (Part II)" also hit the top Stateside, enjoying a four-week stay. By 1982, *The Wall* was multimedia. Alan Parker directed the movie adaptation, with Bob Geldof taking the role of Pink.

There was only one further "proper" Floyd album (i.e., featuring Waters). *The Final Cut* (1983) saw Waters take further control. Keyboardist Rick Wright (a dilettante presence on *The Wall*, according to both Waters and Gilmour) had long been fired. All of the album's twelve tracks were written by Waters, and all but one exclusively sung by him. The subject matter, unfortunately and tediously, seemed like a second stab at exorcising the hang-ups Waters had explored at length in *The Wall*.

It would have been logical to tour *The Wall*, but even Waters—a character who doesn't convey a capacity for self-awareness—realized that performing it in the kind of venues that had created the psychoses that led to its creation would be peculiar bordering on hypocritical. *The Wall* was played only twenty-nine times by Floyd. During its staging each night, a wall would literally be built onstage to signify the distance between the artists and audience. The audience, of course, loved it.

That a colossus like Floyd sat atop the charts at the end of 1979 with a work bearing all the hallmarks of the rock aristocracy suggested that—whatever the inroads made that year by punks, post-punks, new-wavers, and synth-pop merchants—it was back to business as usual. Of course, it never would be. The coming decade would see changes to popular music that would have been unimaginable a few years before, many of them relating to the digital revolution, whether it be the decreasing frequency with which guitars were sighted or the rise of the click track, which gave a mechanical feel to even traditionally untidy, emotion-charged rock.

Those changes could, at least theoretically, have been predicted from the events of '79. Other developments would have been laughed at if anybody had posited them. September '79 had seen the release of a record that was puzzlingly similar to Chic's "Good Times" and, just as puzzlingly, wasn't so much sung as spoken, albeit in a rhyming, syncopated style. "Rapper's Delight" by the Sugarhill Gang crept into the *Billboard* Top 40 the following year. That it climbed to No. 3 in the UK in December '79 seemed consistent with nothing more significant than the country's historical love of novelty records. "Rapper's Delight," however, was not the flash in the pan associated with gimmicks but, rather, heralded the future. Whatever the limitations suggested by the practice of lifting portions of other people's records, or of the very notion of spoken word, this first significant rap record and first significant release to feature something resembling sampling would ultimately prove to have established a genre that would—unthinkable at the time—overtake the sales of rock within little more than twenty years.

Nineteen seventy-nine had seen incredible and unexpected changes in music. If "Rapper's Delight" tells us anything, it's that there will always be more ahead.

ACKNOWLEDGMENTS

I would like to offer my grateful thanks to the following people who consented to be interviewed for this book:

Berton Averre, Mike Chapman, Steve Diggle, Richard Jobson, John O'Neill, Dave Parsons, Dave Robinson, Jon Savage, Pete Shelley, Bruce Thomas, and Lee Thompson.

Note: I spoke to Pete Shelley in July 2018, five months before his death. I have kept his quotes in the present tense for reasons of stylistic uniformity.

In addition to the above new interviews, I have drawn upon material—both published and unpublished—from interviews I previously conducted with the following people:

Jake Burns, Stewart Copeland, Simon Crowe, Chris Difford, Mick Fleetwood, Bruce Foxton, Topper Headon, John Paul Jones, Graham Lewis, John Lydon, Graham Parker, Garry Roberts, Glenn Tilbrook, and Paul Weller.

SELECTED BIBLIOGRAPHY

Books

Balls, Richard. *England's Glory: The Life of Ian Dury*. Omnibus Press, 2001.

Blake, Mark. *Pigs Might Fly: The Inside Story of Pink Floyd*. Aurum Press, 2007.

Difford, Chris, Jim Drury, and Glenn Tilbrook. *Squeeze: Song by Song*. Sanctuary Publishing, 2004.

Egan, Sean. *Love with a Passion Called Hate: The Inside Story of the Jam*. Askill Publishing, 2018.

Egan, Sean. *Our Music Is Red—With Purple Flashes: The Story of the Creation*. Cherry Red Books, 2004.

Glen, Allan. *Stuart Adamson: In a Big Country*. Polygon, 2011.

Gross, Michael, and Maxim Jakubowski. *The Rock Year Book 1981*. Virgin Books, 1981.

Grundy, Stuart, and John Tobler. *The Record Producers*. BBC Books, 1982.

Lewis, Dave. *Led Zeppelin: The Complete Guide to Their Music*. Omnibus Press, 2004.

McCain, Gillian, and Legs McNeil. *Please Kill Me*. Abacus, 1997.

Palm, Carl Magnus. *ABBA: The Complete Guide to Their Music*. Omnibus Press, 2005.

Savage, Jon. *England's Dreaming: The Sex Pistols and Punk Rock*. Faber, 1991.

Savage, Jon. *This Searing Light, The Sun, and Everything Else—Joy Division: The Oral History*. Faber, 2019.

Thomas, Bruce. *Rough Notes . . . and Grainy Images*. Rough Notes Press, 2017.

Williamson, Nigel. *The Rough Guide to Led Zeppelin*. Rough Guides, 2007.

Websites

http://2 Tone.info

www.americanradiohistory.com

www.elviscostello.info

www.everyhit.com

www.officialcharts.com

www.rockunited.com/hitchings.htm

https://en.wikipedia.org

www.billboard.com

www.discogs.com

www.officialcharts.com

www.robertchristgau.com

www.rocksbackpages.com

Articles

Pesca, Mike. "When 'I Hate Mondays' Means Murder." NPR, January 29, 2009

Tschmuck, Peter. "The Recession in the Music Industry—A Cause Analysis." https://musicbusinessresearch.wordpress.com, March 29, 2010.

Weinraub, Bernard. "Here's to Disco, It Never Could Say Goodbye." *New York Times*, December 10, 2002.

Index

ABBA, viii, 3–4, 74–77, 164, 245
Abbey Road, 186
The Absolute Game, 47
Absolutely, 216
"Accidents Never Happen," 224
AC/DC, 145, 217
Ace, 73
Adamson, Stuart, 40, 43–44, 47
The Adventures of the Hersham Boys, 122–27
the Adverts, 57, 95
Aerosmith, 198
"African Night Flight," 104
Aladdin Sane, 103
"Albatross," 38
Aletti, Vince, 152
Alive!, 171
All Mod Cons, 230–31
"All My Love," 165, 167
"All Night Long," 145
Alomar, Carlos, 104–5
Alpert, Herb, 67
"Alternative Ulster," 12–13
A&M, 70, 72, 201, 209
Ambler, Mark, 50
"American Squirm," 108
Andersson, Benny, 75
Andrews, Bob, 53
"Angel," 196
"Angel Eyes," 76
"Angels with Dirty Faces," 122
Animals, 248
Anka, Paul, 30
"Another Brick in the Wall (Part II),"
68, 246, 247, 250
Another Music in a Different Kitchen,
184–85

"Another World," 57
Appice, Carmine, 149
"Are 'Friends' Electric?," 72, 77, 78–79
Argy Bargy, 73
Arista Records, 55, 62, 98
Armed Forces, viii, 1–8
Armed Funk American tour, 5–6
Armoury Show, 47
"Arrow Through Me," 111
"As Good As New," 75
Ashe, Geoffrey, 231
"Atmosphere," 134
"Atomic," 226
the Attractions. *See* Costello, Elvis
Autoamerican, 226
Averre, Berton, 113–19, 127–28

B-52's, 145–46
"Babe," 189
"Babylon's Burning," 171
"Baby Talks Dirty," 127–28
"Back Door Man," 127
Back in Black, 145
"Back to Schooldays," 54
Back to the Egg, 110–11
Bad Girls, 51, 148
"Bad Girls," 148
"Baggy Trousers," 216
Baillie, Mike, 47
Baker, Roy Thomas, 109
"Ballad of Kitty Ricketts," 153
Ballard, J. G., 132
Ballard, Russ, 145
Ballion, Susan. *See* Siouxsie Sioux
Balls, Richard, 97, 209
BAM, 194–95
the Band, 71–72

Band Aid, 143
"Bang Bang," 64
"Barbed Wire Love," 14–15, 17
Barbra Streisand's Greatest Hits Volume 2, 245
Barrett, Marcia, 65
Barrett, Syd, 246
Barson, Mike, 208, 210, 213–14, 216
Barthe, John, 115
Barton, Geoff, 168
Basement Jaxx, 81
"Basement Tapes," 156
Batchelor, David, 43
Batt, Mike, 62
Bazooka Joe, 214
BBC Sessions, 169
the Beach Boys, 3
the Beat, 86–87
the Beatles, xii, 4, 83–84, 108, 111, 154, 163, 187, 196, 246
"Beatnick Fly," 214
"Beat the Clock," 52
"Beautiful Child," 196
"Be-Bop-A-Lula," 42
Be-Bop Deluxe, 44
Bechirian, Roger, 22, 23
Beckett, Barry, 156, 158
"Bed & Breakfast Man," 214
Bedford, Mark, 208
"The Bed's Too Big Without You," 204
the Bee Gees, viii, 4, 146–47
Beggars Banquet, 78, 81
Belew, Adrian, 104
"Believe Me," 213–14
Bellotte, Pete, 148
The Bells, 62
Belmont, Martin, 53
"Belsen Was a Gas," 32, 33
"Be My Girl—Sally," 203
Bentley, John, 73
"Berlin Trilogy," ix, 79, 101, 103
"Best of My Love," 176

Beverley, John. *See* Vicious, Sid
Big Country, 44, 47, 48
Big Roll Band, 200
"Billericay Dickie," 94
Birch, Will, 92
Bizarro World, 51
Black, Johnny, 196, 248–49
Black, Pauline, 86
"The Black Arabs," 33
Blackhill Enterprises, 93–94, 101
"Blackmail Man," 99
Blackmore, Ritchie, 145
Black Rose: A Rock Legend, 61
Black Sabbath, 161
Blair, Gordon, 9
Blair, Tony, 129
"Blockheads," 99
the Blockheads, 93–94, 98–100, 147
Blonde on Blonde, 154
Blondes Have More Fun, 149
Blondie, viii, 114–15, 147, 218–27
Blondie, 219
Blood on the Tracks, 155
"Blowin' in the Wind," 156
"Blue Monday," 137
"Blue Murder," 51
Bob Marley and the Wailers, 189–90
Bodnar, Andrew, 53
The Bodyguard, 108
Bodysnatchers, 87
"Bohemian Rhapsody," 140, 177, 246
Bohn, Chris, 241
Boney M., 65–67
Bonham, John, 161–70
the Boomtown Rats, viii, 39, 137–44
Boon, Richard, 183
"Boredom," 183
"Borstal Breakout," 121, 128
Bovell, Dennis, 173
Bowie, David, ix, 45, 79, 101–6, 153
"The Boys Are Back in Town," 61
Boys in Company C, 214

"Boys Keep Swinging," 105
"The Boys of Summer," 181
Bradbury, John, 85
Bradley, Lloyd, 178
Bradley, Michael "Mickey," 18, 22, 23, 25
Bramlett, Bonnie, 5–7
"Brand New Cadillac," 239
Braun, Eva, 140
Braun, Michael, 190
"Breakdown," 183
Breakfast in America, 52–53
"Breakout," 14, 17
Bremner, Billy, 107
"Bright Eyes," 62
Bringing It All Back Home, 154
"Bring on the Night," 204
Briquette, Pete, 138
Britannia Row Studios, 249
Britbop, viii
Britten, Terry, 64
"Bromley Contingent," 173
Brown, Hugh, 117
Brown, James, 6, 7, 162
Brown, Mick, 168
Browne, David, 177, 180
"Brown Eyes," 196
Bruce, Jack, 113
Brunkert, Ola, 75
Buckingham, Lindsey, 191–99
Buckler, Rick, 230, 233
Buell, Bebe, 3
Buffalo Springfield, 55
Buggles, 65
"Bully for You," 51
Burke, Clem, 220, 222
"Burning Sky," 232
Burns, Jake, 9–18
Burroughs, William, 45, 132
Bushell, Garry, 40, 126
Buster, Prince (Cecil Campbell), 88, 208, 209, 212, 213

"Busy Bodies," 3
. . . But the Little Girls Understand, 127, 128–29
the Buzzcocks, viii, 20, 40, 49, 182–88
Byers, Roddy, 85, 88
Bygraves, Max, 32
Byrne, David, 150

Caillat, Ken, 193
Cain, Mark "Dodie," 121, 123
Cale, John, 70
Callaghan, James, vii
Campbell, Cecil. *See* Prince Buster
Candy-O, 109
"Can't Put a Price on Love," 128
"Can't Stand Losing You," 203
"Capital Radio," 239
Capitol Records, 111, 114, 118
Captain Sensible, 229
"The Card Cheat," 240, 243
"Careering," 38
"Career Opportunities," 241
"Carouselambra," 167
Carrack, Paul, 73
"Carrie," 64
"Cars," 80–81
the Cars, 109, 143–44
"Casbah Rock," 25
Castle, Geoff, 93
CBS, 86, 118
CBS 30th Street Studio, 249
"The Celestial Omnibus" (Forster), 23
Chairs Missing, 174, 175
Chapman, Mike, 114, 115, 117–19, 127–30, 219–27
"Charade," 45
Charles, Charlie, 93
Charles, Ray, 6, 7, 156
Charlesworth, Chris, 177
Cheap Trick, 115, 171
Cheap Trick at Budokan, 171
"(I Don't Want to Go to) Chelsea," 2

"Chemistry Class," 3
Chic, 149, 251
Chimes, Terry, 241
Chinn, Nicky, 219
"Chipmunks Are Go!," 214
"Chiquitita," 76
"Chirpy Chirpy Cheep Cheep," 42
"Chorus," 175
Christgau, Robert, 56, 58
Christmas, 245–48
Chrysalis Records, 16, 86, 209, 210,
     219, 220–21
"City Lights," 62
the Clash, viii, 10, 17, 36, 85, 88, 172,
     182, 199, 229, 237–45, 247–48
The Clash, 17
Classic Rock, 192
Clay, Otis, 178
Cliff, Jimmy, 60
"Closed Groove," 13, 15
Closer, 136
Clover, 2
Cluney, Henry, 9, 14
Cluthell, Dick, 87
"C'mon Everybody," 32, 33
Cobain, Kurt, 136
Cochran, Eddie, 32, 53
Coda, 170
"Cold Blue in the Night," 123
Columbia Records, 111, 141
Combat Rock, 244
"Comfortably Numb," 249
the Commodores, 68, 151
"Common People," 4
Communiqué, 108–9
"Complete Control," 17, 240
"Complex," 80–81
"Concrete Jungle," 88
"Confusion," 84
Control, 136
Cook, Paul, 31, 32, 35, 126
Cool for Cats, viii, 70–73

"Cool for Cats," 71
Coon, Caroline, 120
Cooper, Alice, 247
Copeland, Miles, 71, 201
Copeland, Stewart, 200–207
Coppersmith-Heaven, Vic, 233–34
Cornerstone, 189
the Corrs, 198
Costello, Elvis (Declan MacManus),
     viii, 1–8, 2, 22, 38, 41, 88, 95,
     108, 138
Cost of Living, 239
Cott, Gerry, 138
"Could You Be Loved," 190
Coulter, Phil, 25
the Coventry Automatics, 85–86
"Coward of the County," 172
Cowell, Simon, 246
The Crack, 171
Cranston, Alan, 181
Creem, 119, 144, 193
Crépuscule, 135
Crosby, Stills, and Nash, 248
"Crossing Over the Road," 51
Crowe, Cameron, 101
Crowe, Simon, 138, 140, 141, 143
"Cruel to Be Kind," 107
Curtis, Ian, 130–37
Curved Air, 200
Cut, 173
Cut the Crap, 244

Dahl, Steve, 150, 151
Daltrey, Roger, 109, 110, 116
Dammers, Jerry, 84–91, 208
the Damned, 57, 95, 164, 182, 229, 236
Damn the Torpedoes, 189
"Dance Away," 50
"Dancing Barefoot," 83
"Dancing Queen," 74
Dark Side of the Moon, 249–50
Dashut, Richard, 193

Davies, Neol, 86
Davies, Ray, 70
Davies, Rick, 52
Davis, Clive, 98
Davis, Laura, 224
"Da Ya Think I'm Sexy?," 149
Days in Europa, viii, 40, 45–46
"Days of Rage," 51
"Dazed and Confused," 163
the Dead Boys, 218
"Death Disco," 37
"Death or Glory," 243
Deep Cut to Nowhere, 58
Deep Purple, 16, 145, 161
Delaney and Bonnie, 5
"Denis," 219
"Deny," 17
Depeche Mode, 81
Desire, 155, 156
Desperado, On the Border, 176
Destri, Jimmy, 222, 224, 225, 226
DeVito, Hank, 107
de Vorzon, Barry, 179
Devoto, Howard (Howard Andrew
    Trafford), 49, 182, 183, 184
Dexys Midnight Runners, 87
"Diamond Smiles," 142
the Dictators, 218
"Die Young Stay Pretty," 224
A Different Kind of Tension, viii, 185–87
Difford, Chris, 69–74
Difford & Tilbrook, 74
Diggle, Steve, 182, 184–87
DiMartino, Dave, 144
Dinosaur, 150
di Perna, Alan, 193
Dire Straits, 108–9
disco, viii–ix, 23, 37, 52, 63, 146–52,
    220, 221; of ABBA, 74–77
Disco Demolition Night, 150–52
"The Disco Strangler," 178, 179
"Discovering Japan," 56

Discovery, 84
Dixon, Willie, 127
"DJ," 104–5
"Do Anything You Want To," 61
Dodd, Coxsone, 88
"Doesn't Make It Alright," 88
"Does Your Mother Know," 76
Doherty, Billy, 18, 19
Do It Yourself, 91, 97–101
"Do Nothing," 89
"Don't Ask Me Questions," 54
"Don't Bring Me Down," 84
"Don't Care," 200
"Don't Leave Me Now," 249
"Don't Stand So Close to Me," 205, 207
"Don't Stop," 193
"Don't Stop 'Til You Get Enough," 148
Don't Tell Columbus, 58
"Don't Worry Baby," 3
the Doobie Brothers, 68
"Do Right to Me Baby (Do Unto
    Others)," 156
"Do the Dog," 88
Downes, Geoff, 65
"Down in the Park," 78
Down to Earth, 145
Doyle, John, 47
"Dreaming," 222–23, 225–26
Dream Police, 171
Dr. Feelgood, 139
Dr. Hook, 68
"Drive," 143–44
Drummond, Tim, 156
Drums and Wires, 153–254
Du Cann, John, 81
Dudanski, Richard, 37
Dury, Ian, 91–101, 146, 208–9
"D'yer Mak'er," 166
Dylan, Bob, ix, 1, 71–72, 108, 154–59,
    186
Dylan—What Happened? (Williams,
    P.), 155

the Eagles, ix, 49, 170, 175–82, 190, 245
Easlea, Daryl, 98
Easter, 83
East Side Story, 73
the Easybeats, 141
Eat to the Beat, 218, 222–23, 224, 225–26
"Eat to the Beat," 224
Eddie and the Hot Rods, 126
Eden, 22
Edmunds, Dave, 5, 107
Edwards, Bernard, 149, 226
Egan, Rusty, 45
Electric Lady, 222
Electric Light Orchestra, 83–84
Elektra/Asylum, 177
Ellis, Terry, 219
Elvis Costello and the Attractions. *See* Costello, Elvis
Ely, Ron, 214
"Embarrassment," 216
"The Embezzler," 34
"Emergency Cases," 20
Emerson, Lake, and Palmer, 248
EMI, 86, 174, 187, 209
Empire Burlesque, 159
"Endless Grey Ribbon," 108
England's Dreaming, 30
"English Rose," 231
Eno, Brian, 102, 104
Ensign Records, 139
Entertainment!, 173–74
Eric Burdon & the Animals, 200
"Escape (the Piña Colada Song)," 68–69
"The Eton Rifles," 234, 236
"Ever Fallen in Love (With Someone You Shouldn't've)," 185, 186, 187
"Everybody's Happy Nowadays," 185
"Every Breath You Take," 206–7
"Every Day Hurts," 174
"Every Grain of Sand," 159

"Every Little Thing She Does Is Magic," 206
"Everything Rocks and Nothing Ever Dies," 58
Exile, 114
Ezrin, Bob, 247, 248, 249

Facades, 174
Factory, 132–33
A Factory Sample, 132–33
Fairbairn, Bruce, 45–46
"Fall Out," 200, 204
Faloon, Brian, 9, 17
"Family Life," 121
"Fantastic Voyage," 104
Farian, Frank, 65, 66–67
Father Ted, 25
Fätskog, Agnetha, 75
Fear of Music, 153
Felder, Don, 176, 177–81
Ferguson, Andy, 26
Fieger, Doug, 113, 115, 116, 118, 130
52nd Street, 170
The Final Cut, 250
The Fine Art of Surfacing, viii, 141–42
"Fingerprint File," 178
Fingers, Johnnie (John Moylett), 138, 140
First Issue, 37
Fleetwood, Mick, 191–92, 194, 196–97
Fleetwood Mac, ix, 49, 190–99, 250
Flesh + Blood, 50
Flogging a Dead Horse, 33
"Fly Dark Angel," 123–24
the Flying Burrito Brothers, 176
Foo Fighters, 81
"Fool in the Rain," 166
Foreigner, 172
Foreman, Chris, 208, 210–17
Forster, E. M., 22–23
"Four Horsemen," 243
Foxton, Bruce, 18, 230, 233, 234

Frampton, Peter, 171
Frampton Comes Alive!, 171
Franklin, Aretha, 156
"Le Freak," 149
"Frederick," 83
"Free Nelson Mandela," 91
Frey, Glenn, 175, 177, 178–82
Fricke, David, 8
"Friday on My Mind," 141
"Friends of Mine," 183
"Friggin' in the Riggin'," 32
the Fun Boy Three, 91

Gabriel, Peter, 51
Gallagher, Mick, 99
The Game, 128
Gang of Four, 173–74
"Gangsters," 84, 86, 89
"Garageland," 241
Garfunkel, Art, 62
Garvey, Steve, 184
Gary, Bruce, 113, 114, 130
Gaye, Marvin, 95
Gaynor, Gloria, viii, 4, 146
Geldof, Bob, 137–44, 250
"Get Over You," 22, 26
Get the Knack, 114–18, 127
"Getting Closer," 111
Ghost in the Machine, 206
Ghostown, 153
"Ghost Town," 89, 90–91
The Gift, 236
Gilbert, Gillian, 137
Gilder, Nick, 114
Gilmour, David, 247, 249, 250
"Gimme Gimme Gimme," 76
"Girl on the Phone," 232, 235
"Girls Don't Like It," 23
"Girls Talk," 5, 107
Give 'Em Enough Rope, 239, 241–42
"Glad to Be Gay," 50
Glitterbest, 31

Glossop, Mick, 45
Goddard, Simon, 4
"God Save the Queen," 4, 29–30, 33
"Going Underground," 236
Golding, Lynval, 85, 91
Goldstein, Rick, 123, 126
Gomm, Ian, 107
"Goodbye Girl," 73
"Good Girls Don't," 119
"Goodnight Tonight," 110
"Good Times," 149, 251
Good Vibrations, 20, 22
"Gorblimey," 72
"Gotta Go Home," 66
"Gotta Serve Somebody," 158
Gottehrer, Richard, 219
Goulding, Stephen, 53
"Go Your Own Way," 193
Graves, Robert, 41
Gray, Nigel, 203, 206
Greatest Hits (Rod Stewart), 245
"The Great Rock 'n' Roll Swindle," 32
The Great Rock 'n' Roll Swindle, 30–35,
    182
"The Greeks Don't Want No Freaks,"
    180
Green, Jim, 215–16, 220
Green, Peter, 191
"Groovy Times," 239
Grundy, Stuart, 104, 178
Guardian, 144, 211
Guitar World, 193, 198–99
Gunnarsson, Rutger, 75
"The Guns of Brixton," 240, 242
Guthrie, Woody, 139
"Gypsy Blood," 54

Halbert, James, 192
Hall, Terry, 85, 91
Handsome, 93
"Hanging on the Telephone," 221
Hannett, Martin, 132, 133

Hansa Studio, 101
"The Harder They Come," 60
The Harder They Come, 66
"The Hardest Part," 223
"Hard Rain's A-Gonna Fall," 186
"Harmony in My Head," 185
Harrison, George, 163
Harrison, Nigel, 220, 222, 223, 224
Harry, Debbie, 218–27
Harvest, 174
Hasted, Nick, 91
"Having My Picture Taken," 141
Head Games, 172
Headon, Nick "Topper," 240, 244–45
"(Sexual) Healing," 95
"Heartache Tonight," 179, 181
"Heartbeat," 115
"Heart of Glass," 115, 146, 218, 219,
    220–21
Heat Treatment, 54
"Heat Wave," 235
the HeeBeeGeeBees, 204
Helliwell, John, 52
Hell,Richard, 57
Hendrix, Jimi, 40
Henley, Don, 175, 177, 178–81
Henri, Adrian, 231
"Here Comes the Summer," 25, 26
"Here We Are Nowhere," 14
"Heroes", 103
"Hersham Boys," 125–26, 127
Hewitt, Paolo, 89
Heyman, Preston, 51
Hibbert, Tom, 78
Highway 61 Revisited, 154
Highway Star, 9
Highway to Hell, 145
Hipgnosis, 168
Hitchings, Duane, 149
Hitler, Adolf, 140
"Hit Me with Your Rhythm Stick," 97,
    100, 146

Hodgson, Roger, 52
"Hold Out," 51
"Hole in My Life," 203
Holland, Jools, 70
Holley, Steve, 110
the Hollies, 116
Holly, Buddy, 220–21
Holmes, Rupert, 68–69
"Hong Kong Garden," 173
Honoré, Annik, 135
Hook, Peter, 131
Hooley, Terri, 20
Horizon Studio, 88
Horn, Trevor, 65
"Horray Horray It's a Holi-Holiday," 66
Horses, 83
Hoskyns, Barney, 164, 243
"Hot Child in the City," 114
"Hot Dog," 166–67
Hotel California, 175, 176–77, 178, 180,
    181
the Hot Rods, 19
"Hot Stuff," 148
Hotter Than July, 190
House of Dolls, 132
Houses of the Holy, 162
Howlin' Wind, 53–54
"How Long," 73
Humble Pie, 115
Hunky Dory, 103
The Hunter, 226–27
"Hurry Up Harry," 122, 125
Hypnotised, 27

"I Am the Walrus," 84
"I Believe," 186
"I Can Only Give You Everything," 25
"I Can't Explain," 23
"I Can't Tell You Why," 179, 181
An Ideal for Living, 132–33
"I Don't Like Mondays," 138, 140, 141,
    143–44

"I Don't Wanna," 121
"I Fought the Law," 239
"If the Kids Are United," 88, 122, 128
"I Gotta Getta," 23
"I Know a Girl," 25
"I'm Born Again," 66
"I'm Gonna Crawl," 167
"I'm Gonna Love You Too," 115,
    220–21
"I'm Not Down," 240, 243
"I'm So Bored with the U.S.A.," 238
I'm the Man, viii, 58–60
Infante, Frank, 223, 225, 226
Infidels, 159
Inflammable Material, viii, 13–17, 18
In the City, 230
"In the City," 179
"In the Evening," 166
"In the Flesh," 219
In the Long Grass, 142
"In the Middle of the Night," 214
In the Studio, 91
In Through the Out Door, 165–70, 180,
    190
Into the Music, 154
"Into the Valley," 41–43
the Invaders, 208
Island Records, 15, 86
"Is She Really Going Out with Him?,"
    59, 60
"Is This Love," 189
"It Must Be Love," 217
"It's Different for Girls," 59, 60
"It's Going to Happen," 27
"It's So Dirty," 72
"I Want You Back," 55
"I Will Survive," 4, 146

Jabsco, Walt, 87
Jackson, Blair, 194–95
Jackson, Joe, viii, 44, 58–60
Jackson, Michael, 148–49, 170

Jackson 5, 55
Jagger, Mick, 149, 163
"Jah War," 171, 199
the Jam, viii, 39, 90, 121, 230–36, 238
James, Brian, 229
Jankel, Chaz, 93, 97, 98, 100
Japan, 237
Jenkins, Chris, 43
Jenner, Peter, 93
"Jimmy Jazz," 243
"Jimmy Jimmy," 22, 23
Jobson, Richard, 39–48, 135–36
Joel, Billy, 170
"Joey's on the Street," 123, 124
John, Elton, 51
John, Robert, 68
"John, I'm Only Dancing (Again)," 105
Johnny and the Hurricanes, 214
"Johnny Was," 14
Johns, Glyn, 176
Johnson, Brian, 145
John Wesley Harding, 156
Join Hands, 173
Jones, Francis, 13
Jones, John Paul, 161–70
Jones, Kenney, 110
Jones, Mick, 172, 240, 244
Jones, Steve, 31, 32, 34, 35, 126
*Journey Through "The Secret Life of
    Plants"*, 190
Joy, 47
Joyce, James, 185
Joy Division, viii, 130–37
Juber, Laurence, 110
"Julie's Been Working for the Drug
    Squad," 242
"Jump Boys," 23

Kakoulli, Harry, 70
"Kashmir," 167
Kaya, 189
Kaye, Lenny, 83

Keep Moving, 217
Kellichan, Thomas, 45
Kenny, 172
Kent, Klark, 200
The Kids Are Alright, 109–10
Kilburn and the High Roads, 93, 208, 211
King, Andrew, 93
King Crimson, 161
"King of Hollywood," 179
the Kinks, 70, 208, 236
Kiss, 171
"Kiss Me Again," 150
"Kiss You All Over," 114
the Knack, viii–ix, 62, 112–20, 127–30, 150, 180
Knebworth Festival, 167–68
"Knocked It Off," 64
"Knock on Wood," 148
Knopfler, Mark, 109, 156
KooKoo, 226
Kordosh, J., 193
Kral, Ivan, 83
Kristofferson, Kris, 67
Kustow, Danny, 50

"Labelled With Love," 73, 74
Labour of Lust, viii, 107
Lange, Mutt, 139
Langer, Clive, 210
Last Exit, 200
"Last Gang in Town," 88
"Last Train to London," 84
Latham, Laurie, 98
Laughter, 100
Lavis, Gilson, 70
"Law and Order" (the Troubles), 15
"Law and Order" (TRB), 51
Lawrence, D. H., 186
Leadon, Bernie, 175, 176
"The Ledge," 196

Led Zeppelin, ix, 16, 49, 159–70, 190, 245
Led Zeppelin II, 162
Led Zeppelin III, 162
Led Zeppelin IV, 162
Lennon, John, 6, 7, 69, 73, 112, 163. *See also* the Beatles
"Less Than Zero," 1
"Let Me Out," 115
"Let My People Be," 51
Levan, Larry, 146
Levene, Keith, 36, 37
Lewis, Dave, 165
Liddle Towers, 51
"Life's Been Good," 64, 179
Lillywhite, Steve, 153
Little Boots, 81
"Little Boy Soldiers," 234–35
Little Feat, 19
Live Aid, 143
Live Rust, 110
"Living in the Real World," 225
Livingstone, Dandy, 87
Lodger, 103–6, 153
Lofgren, Nils, 62
London Calling, viii, 237–45
Londoners Madness, 86
"London's Burning," 240
London Town, 111
"Lonely Boys," 32
"Lonely This Christmas," 246
"The Long Run," 181
The Long Run, 170, 175–82, 190
"Look Back in Anger," 104–5
"Looking After No. 1," 139
Look Sharp!, viii, 58–59
"The Lord's Prayer," 173
"Lost on Highway 46," 124
"Louie Louie," 25
Love Bites, 185
"Love Gets You Twisted," 56

"Lovers (Live a Little Longer)," 76
"Lover's Rock," 243
"Love Song," 229
"Love Will Tear Us Apart," 137
Lovich, Lene, 23, 64–65
Low, 102
Lowe, Nick, viii, 2, 5, 94, 107–8
"Lucinda," 116
"Lucky Number," 23, 64–65
"Lullaby for Francies," 99
"El Lute," 66
Lydon, John. *See* Rotten, Johnny
"Lyin' Eyes," 176
Lyngstad, Anni-Frid "Frida," 75
Lynn, Jeff, 83–84
Lynott, Phil, 61

Machine Gun Etiquette, 229
MacInnes, Colin, 231–32
MacKinnon, Angus, 104
MacManus, Declan. *See* Costello, Elvis
Madness, viii, 87, 207–17
"Madness," 209
Magazine, 47, 49, 184
Magnet, 209
Maher, John, 184
Main Course, 147
"Making Plans for Nigel," 153–54
"Male Model," 23
Mallet, David, 141
Mancuso, David, 146
Manifesto, 50, 190
Manson, Marilyn, 81
"Mantovani," 89
The Man Who Fell to Earth, 102–3
Manzarek, Ray, 114
"Map Ref. 41°N 93°W," 174
Marcus, Greil, 7
Marley, Bob, 14, 189–90, 202
"Mars Bars," 23
Martell, Lena, 67

Martin, Gavin, 13
"Mary of the 4th Form," 139
"Mary's Boy Child / Oh My Lord," 66
"Masoko Tanga," 203
Mason, Terry, 132
"Masquerade," 44–45, 46
Masters, Barrie, 126
Matlock, Glen, 29, 30
McCartney, Linda, 110
McCartney, Paul, 69, 73, 110, 163. *See also* the Beatles; Wings
McGeoch, John, 47
McGough, Roger, 231
McGregor, Craig, 154, 155
McLaren, Malcolm, 30, 32, 33–35
McLoone, Paul, 28
McMordie, Ali, 9, 18
McNeish, Peter. *See* Shelley, Pete
McPherson, Graham. *See* Suggs
McVicar, 109
McVie, Christine, 191, 192, 193, 195, 196, 198
McVie, John "Mac," 191, 195
Media Sound, 222
Meisner, Randy, 175, 177
"Melancholy Soldiers," 41
Melody Maker, 89, 177, 206, 241
the Members, 199
"Memories," 38
"Mercury Poisoning," 53, 55, 56
Mercury Records, 54–55
"Merry Xmas Everybody," 246
"Message in a Bottle," 204
"A Message to You Rudy," 87
Metal Box, viii, 35–39
"Milk and Alcohol," 108
Mingus, ix, 108
Mingus, Charles, 108
Mink Deville, 57
Minute by Minute, 68
Mirage, 197–98

Mitchell, Joni, ix, 108
Mitchell, Liz, 65
"Moby Dick," 163–64
Mojo, 195, 196, 219–20, 247, 248–49
Mondo Bongo, 142
Money, Eddie, 114
Money, Zoot, 200
"Money," 123, 124, 246
the Monkees, 17
Moon, Keith, 110
Moorcock, Michael, 132
"More Songs About Chocolate and
    Girls," 23
More Specials, 89
"More Than a Woman," 148
Morley, Paul, 16, 78
Moroder, Giorgio, 51–52, 148
Morris, Stephen, 131, 133
Morrison, Van, 154
"Moss Garden," 103
Mott, 240
Mott the Hoople, 240
Moulding, Colin, 153
Mountain Studios, 103
"Move On," 104
Moylett, John. *See* Fingers, Johnnie
"Mr. Clean," 231
MTV, 65
Mud, 219, 246
Murray, Charles Shaar, 59–60
Murray, George, 105
the Muscle Shoals Horns, 156
*Music from the Soundtrack of the Who
    Film Quadrophenia*, 110
My Aim Is True, 2
Myers, Ben, 241
My Generation, 26
"My Generation," 116
"My Girl," 213
"My My, Hey Hey (Out of the Blue),"
    110
"My Oh My," 174

"My Old Man," 94
"My Perfect Cousin," 22, 23, 27
"My Sharona," 62, 116–17, 119, 128,
    130, 150
"My Way," 30, 31–32

Nelson, Bill, 44–45, 46
the Nerves, 221, 225
Neu!, 104
"Never Gonna Fall in Love (Again)," 51
"Never in a Million Years," 142
"Never Make Me Cry," 196
New Boots and Panties!!, 92, 95–97, 99,
    100, 101
"New Dawn Fades," 134
New Hormones, 183
New Musical Express, 16, 238, 243
New Order, 137
New Romantic movement, 28
"New Rose," 13, 57, 182, 229
A New World Record, 84
Nicks, Stevie, 191–98
Nieve, Steve, 2, 3
"Night Boat to Cairo," 213, 215
"Night Disco Died," 150
the Nightlife Thugs, 139
Niles, Prescott, 113, 116
Nine Inch Nails, 81
"96 Tears," 180
Nirvana, 136
Nitzsche, Jack, 55–57
NME, 12, 59, 78, 104, 194, 206
No. 1 in Heaven, 52
No Bad, 40
Nobody's Heroes, 17–18
"No More of That," 14
"No One Is Innocent," 32
"Norf Lahndan," 213
Norman, Chris, 114
"Norn Iron," 19
North London Invaders, 208
"Nothing Happened Today," 141–42

"Not That Funny," 196
Nugent, Steve, 93
Nuggets, 23
Numan, Gary (Gary Webb), viii, 44, 72, 77–82, 105–6
"The Number One Song in Heaven," 52
the Nutty Train, 215

Oblique Strategies, 102
O'Brien, Lucy, 219–20
Oceans of Fantasy, 66
"Offshore Banking Business," 199
Off the Wall, 148, 170
Ogilvie, Gordon, 10, 13, 17
"Oh Sister," 156
"Oh Tara," 115–16
Oldfield, Mike, 96
"Old Siam, Sir," 111
"Oliver's Army," 3–4, 38, 138, 203
"On Any Other Day," 204
the 101'ers, 37
154, 174–75
"One Chord Wonders," 57
"One Day at a Time," 67
O'Neill, Damian, 18, 23, 25, 27
O'Neill, John, 16, 18–29
One of These Nights, 176
One Step Beyond . . ., viii, 212, 215–16
"One Step Beyond," 212
"One Way or Another," 222
"On My Radio," 86
"Orgasm Addict," 183
Orton, Joe, 186
Orwell, George, 232
"Our House," 216–17
Outlandos d'Amour, 202–3, 205
"Over and Over," 196
Owen, Malcolm, 171
Owen, Wilfred, 41

Padgham, Hugh, 206
Padovani, Henri, 200–201, 207

Page, Jimmy, 161–70
"Painter Man," 66–67
Panter, Horace, 85
Parallel Lines, 218, 221, 222, 225
Parker, Alan, 250
Parker, Graham, viii, 53–58
Parker, Ian, 51
Parry, Chris, 233
Parsons, Dave, 120–29
Partridge, Andy, 153
Patten, Brian, 232
Pattenden, Sian, 246
Patti Smith Group, 83, 218
Payne, Davey, 93
"(What's So Funny 'Bout) Peace, Love, and Understanding," 5, 108
"Peaceful Times," 46
Peaches and Herb, 68, 151
Peachey, Mal, 241
"Peanuts," 203
Pearlman, Sandy, 239
Pearson, Deanne, 85
Peel, John, 9–10, 12–13, 28, 40
"Penny Lane," 4
Perry, Mark, 120
Peter Gunn, 38
"A Petition," 115
Petty, Tom, 114, 189
Phillips, Eddie, 66–67
Phonogram, 54
Physical Graffiti, 163
Pickett, Kenny, 66–67
Pickett, Wilson, 156
PiL. *See* Public Image Ltd.
Pink Flag, 174, 175
Pink Floyd, viii, ix, 16, 49, 68, 189, 190, 245–51
"Plaistow Patricia," 96, 99
Plant, Robert, 161–70
Plastic Letters, 219
The Pleasure Principle, viii, 80–81
poet, j., 79

Polar, 75
Polar Studios, 164
the Police, viii, 143, 199–207
"Police and Thieves," 17
Polydor Records, 121, 124
Pop, Iggy, 105
the Pop Group, 61–62
"Pop Muzik," 67
"Positively Fourth Street," 71–72
Positive Touch, 27
Power in the Darkness, 50
"Precious," 236
"Precious Angel," 156
Presence, 164, 170
Presley, Elvis, 1, 163, 239
"Pressing On," 158–59
"Pretty Vacant," 13
Price, Bill, 242
"The Prince," 86, 209, 210, 214, 215
"Private Hell," 232
"Problem Child," 54
Producers Workshop, 249
the Professionals, 36
"Promises," 185
"Pros and Cons," 46
"Public Image," 36, 37
Public Image Ltd. (PiL), viii, 35–39,
    214
Pulp, 4
"Pump It Up," 2
Pursey, Jimmy, 120–29

Q, 4, 78, 152, 165
Quadrophenia, 109, 123, 235
Quatro, Suzi, 114, 219
Queen, 52, 109, 140
"Queen of Hearts," 107
? and the Mysterians, 180
"Questions and Answers," 122–23, 124
Quiet Life, 237
"Quinn the Eskimo (The Mighty
    Quinn)," 156

Radio 2, 211
"Radio 4," 38
Radio Ethiopia, 83
"Radio Nine," 186
Rainbow, 145
the Ramones, 19, 218
"Rapper's Delight," 251
"Rapture," 226
"Rat Race," 89
Rat Scabies, 229
"Rat Trap," 139, 142
RCA, 103
Real Life, 49
"Reasons to Be Cheerful (Part 3)," 97
Record Mirror, 43, 237
Record Plant, 103, 222
The Record Producers, 104, 178
Redding, Otis, 53
"Redemption Song," 190
"Red Money," 105
"Red Sails," 104
Reed, Lou, 62, 98
Regatta de Blanc, viii, 204–5
Reid, Jaime, 30
Reilly, Jim, 17
Remarque, Erich Maria, 232
Repeat When Necessary, 107
"Repetition," 105
Replicas, viii, 78–80
"Rest of the World," 216
"Reunited," 68
"Revolution Rock," 240–41, 242, 243
Rhodes, Bernard, 85
Richard, Cliff, 64
Riefenstahl, Leni, 46
Riegel, Richard, 119
"Right to Work," 234
Rigid Digits, 11
"Ring My Bell," 148
"Rise," 67
*The Rise and Fall of Ziggy Stardust and
    the Spiders from Mars*, 102

Rising Free, 50
"Rivers of Babylon," 66
Riviera, Jake, 94–95, 96
Roberts, Garry, 138, 140
Robertson, B. A., 64
Robinson, Dave, 53–57, 92, 94–100, 209–12, 215
Robinson, John, 104
Robinson, Tom, 50–52
the Roches, 61
Rock Against Racism, 7
"Rock and Roll," 166
Rock and Roll Heart, 62
"Rock Around the Clock," 32
"Rockin' in A♭," 214
"Rock Lobster," 146
Rock 'n' Roll Juvenile, 64
Rockpile, 107
Rock's Backpages, 164
"Rock the Casbah," 244
"Rock with You," 149
Rodgers, Nile, 149, 152, 226
Rodriguez, Rico, 87
Roeg, Nicolas, 102
Rogers, Kenny, 172
Rogers, Rick, 84
Rolling Stone, 6, 7, 8, 101, 162, 168, 177, 245
the Rolling Stones, 49, 53, 55, 108, 169, 178, 236
Ronstadt, Linda, 2, 175
Rosen, Steven, 194
Rotten, Johnny (John Lydon), 30, 31, 34–35, 36–37, 41, 93, 248
Rough Trade, 13, 15–16, 86
"Rough Trade," 15, 17
"Roxanne," 199, 202, 203
Roxy Music, ix, 49, 50, 102, 190
Roy, David, 143
"Rude Boys," 87
"Rudie Can't Fail," 241, 242
"Rudy, a Message to You," 87

the Rumour, viii, 53–54, 56, 58
Rumours, 191–98
Rundgren, Todd, 50–51, 83
Rushent, Martin, 185, 187
Russell, Arthur, 150
Rust Never Sleeps, 110
the Ruts, 171, 199

Sad Café, 174
"The Sad Café," 180
"Sad Eyes," 68
Saint Dominic's Preview, 154
"The Saints Are Coming," 41
Salewicz, Chris, 194
Sanborn, David, 180
Sandinista!, 244
"Sara," 195
"Sarah," 61
Sassoon, Siegfried, 41
Saturday Night Fever, 148
"Saturday's Kids," 233
Savage, 81
Savage, Jon, 30–31, 32–33, 35, 131–36, 146, 151
Saved, 158
"Saving Grace," 159
Sayer, Leo, 245
Scared to Dance, viii, 43–44
"Scared to Dance," 43
Scarfe, Gerald, 247
"Scenes from an Italian Restaurant," 177
Schmit, Timothy B., 177, 179
"School's Out," 247
Schulps, Dave, 238
Schwarz, Brinsley, 53, 107, 108
Sclafani, Tony, 152
Scott, Bon, 145
Scott, Robin, 67
The Scream, 173
Second Edition, 38–39
Secondhand Daylight, 49

Seconds of Pleasure, 107
Seger, Bob, 178
"The Selector," 86
the Selector, 86, 87
"(She's So) Selfish," 119
Sellars, Marilyn, 67
"Sense of Doubt," 103
Setting Sons, viii, 231–36, 245
"Sex & Drugs & Rock & Roll," 95
the Sex Pistols, 4, 29–37, 85, 131,
          172–73, 182, 201, 206, 229, 236,
          248
"Sexy Girl," 181
"Shadowplay," 134
"Shakin' All Over," 38
Sham 69, 88, 90, 120–30, 236
the Sham Pistols, 126
the Shangri-Las, 23, 218
Shannon, Davy, 20, 22
Sharkey, Feargal, 19, 22, 27–28, 29
"Shayla," 223
Shelley, Percy Bysshe, 232
Shelley, Pete (Peter McNeish), 49,
          182–88
Shepherd's Bush, 233
"She's Lost Control," 133–34
"She's Out of My Life," 149
Short Circuit: Live at the Electric Circus,
          132
"Shot by Both Sides," 49
Shot of Love, 159
"Siamese Twins (The Monkey and Me),"
          115
Siano, Nicky, 150
Sid Sings, 33
Siffre, Labi, 217
Sillitoe, Alan, 232
"Silly Thing," 32
Silverton, Peter, 10, 12
Simmons, Sylvie, 195, 247
Simonon, Paul, 239–41, 244

Simpson, Bill, 47
Simpson, Dave, 144, 211
"Since You Been Gone," 145
"Sink My Boats," 99
The Sin of Pride, 27
Siouxsie and the Banshees, 172–73
Siouxsie Sioux (Ballion, Susan), 173
Sire, 216
"Sister Midnight," 105
"Sisters of the Moon," 196
ska, 85, 208
the Skids, viii, 39–48, 90, 135
Slade, 246
SLF. *See* Stiff Little Fingers
Slider, Albie, 121
the Slits, 172–73
"Slow Motion," 224
Slow Train Coming, ix, 155–59
"S&M," 61
"Smarter than U," 20
Smash, Chas (Cathal Smyth), 208, 213,
          215, 217
Smash Hits, 45
Smith, Garth, 184
Smith, Joe, 177
Smith, Patti, 83, 218
"Smithers-Jones," 233
Smokie, 219
Smyth, Cathal "Carl." *See* Smash, Chas
Sniffin' Glue, 120
Snow, Mat, 165
Soft Cell, 81
Soft Machine, 161, 200
"So It Goes," 94
"Solid Gold, Easy Action," 25
"So Lonely," 203
Some Girls, 169
"Someone's Gotta Help Me," 123
"Someone's Looking at You," 142
Some Product, 33
"Something Else," 32, 33

"Something's Burning, Baby," 159
"So Much Trouble in the World,"
    189–90
"Song of the Streets," 121, 125
The Song Remains the Same, 163–64
"Soul Shoes," 54
Sound Affects, 236
"Sound and Vision," 102
"Sound-A-Sleep," 224–25
Sounds, 10, 12, 40, 126, 168, 206
"South Bound Suarez," 165, 166
Souther, J. D., 178, 179
"Spanish Bombs," 243
"Spanish Stroll," 57
Sparks, 51–52
"Spasticus Autisticus," 92–93
Specials, viii, 89
the Specials, viii, 84–91
Spector, Phil, 55, 243
Speight, Edward, 93
Spencer, Brenda, 138
Spinal Tap, 162
Spiral Scratch, 20, 182–85
Spirits Having Flown, 147–48
Springsteen, Bruce, 6–7, 54–55, 114
Spungen, Nancy, 31
Squeeze, viii, 4, 69–74
Squeezing Out Sparks, viii, 53, 55–58
Stage, 103
"Stairway to Heaven," 162, 177
Stand, Mike, 97
Staple, Neville, 85, 91
Starr, Ringo, 163
"Start!," 236
"State of Emergency," 14
Station to Station, 103
Steely Dan, 98
Stein, Chris, 220, 223, 224, 226
"Stereotype," 89
Stevens, Guy, 240
Stewart, Amii, 148

Stewart, Rod, 149, 245
Stick to Me, 54
Stiff Little Fingers (SLF), viii, 9–19
Stiff Records, 1, 54, 57, 94–97, 209–10
Stigers, Curtis, 108
"Still," 68
Stills, Stephen, 5–7, 114
Sting (Gordon Sumner), 200–207
"Straight to Hell," 244
"Strange Little Girl," 174
the Stranglers, 39
"Strawberry Fields Forever," 4
Street Hassle, 62
Street-Legal, 155
Streisand, Barbra, 148, 245
Strength Through Joy, 46
Struck By Lightning, 58
Strummer, Joe, 37, 238, 240–41, 244
"Stumblin' In," 114
"Stupid Man," 62
Styx, 189
"Substitute," 33
the Sugarhill Gang, 251
Suggs (Graham McPherson), 208, 210,
    211, 213–16
"Sultans of Swing," 109
Summer, Donna, viii, 23, 51–52, 148,
    150
Summers, Andy, 200, 202
Sumner, Bernard, 131, 134
Sumner, Gordon. *See* Sting
"Sunday Girl," 221
"Sunday's Best," 4–5
Super Bear, 249
Supertramp, 52–53
"Surrender," 115
Surrey Sound Studio, 203
Survival, 189
"Susie," 123
"Suspect Device," 11–13
Sutcliffe, Phil, 12

"Swan Lake," 37, 214
Sweet, 219
"Sweet Black Angel," 51
"Sweet Gene Vincent," 94, 96
Sweets from a Stranger, 74
"Sweet Suburbia," 40–41
the Swinging Cats, 89
Sylvian, David, 237
Synchronicity, 206–7
Szymczyk, Bill, 176, 177

"Take It to the Limit," 176
"Take Me I'm Yours," 70
"Take on Me," 140–41
Talking Heads, 150, 153, 218
Tango in the Night, 198
Tarney, Alan, 64
Tarzan, 214
"Tarzan Nuts," 214
Taylor, Dolphin, 50
Taylor, Vince, 239
Tears for Fears, 37
Teenage Kicks, 20–22
"Teenage Kicks," 25
"Tell the Children," 128
Tell Us the Truth, 121–22
Temple, Julien, 33–34
"Tempted," 73
Thatcher, Margaret, vii, 89–91, 142, 231
That Petrol Emotion, 28
That's Life, 121–22
"That's What They All Say," 54
Their Greatest Hits (1971–1975) (the
    Eagles), 176, 177
Them, 25
"Thick as Thieves," 233
Thin Lizzy, 61
This Is the Modern World, 230
"This Is What We Find," 99
"This Town Ain't Big Enough for Both
    of Us," 51
This Year's Model, 2

Thomas, Bruce, 1–8
Thomas, Pete, 2
Thomas, Rufus, 88
Thompson, Lee, 208–17
Thompson, Mayo, 15–16
Thomson, Graeme, 4
"Those Shoes," 179
3D, 51–52
Three Degrees, 51–52
"Thunder and Rain," 54
"The Tide Is High," 226
Tight but Loose, 165
Tilbrook, Glenn, 69–74
Time Out of Mind, 159
"Time's Up," 183
"Tin Soldiers," 18
Tobler, John, 104, 178
"Tommy Gun," 242
Tom Petty and the Heartbreakers, 189
Tom Robinson Band (TRB), 50–52
Tonic for the Troops, 139–41
"Too Depressed to Commit Suicide,"
    204
"Too Hot," 88
"Too Much Too Young," 88, 89
Top of the Pops, 42–43, 87, 121, 142,
    185, 236, 242, 246, 248
"Top Twenty," 25
"Touching Me Touching You," 72
"Touch Too Much," 145
Tour Over Europe, 169
"Town Called Malice," 236
Townshend, Pete, 239
Trafford, Howard Andrew. See Devoto,
    Howard
"Tragedy," 4, 147
"Train in Vain," 238, 240, 243
"Transmission," 134
Travis, Geoff, 15–16
TRB. See Tom Robinson Band
TRB Two, 50–51
Treganna, Dave "Kermit," 121

Tressell, Robert, 232
T. Rex, 25
the Troggs, 25
the Troubles, 14–15, 29, 41
Trouser Press, 216
"True Confessions," 20, 23
"Trying to Live My Life Without You,"
  178
Tubeway Army, viii, 72, 77–82
Tubular Bells, 96
Tudor-Pole, Edward, 32
Tusk, 190–99, 250
"12XU," 174
"2-4-6-8 Motorway," 50
2 Tone, vii–viii, 84–89, 199, 211, 212
2 Tone Tour, 87
The Two Ronnies, 215
"Typical Girls," 173

Ultravox, 4
Ulvaeus, Björn, 74, 75
Ulysses (Joyce), 185
Uncut, 192, 195
the Undertones, viii, 9, 16, 18–29
The Undertones, viii, 26
Unfaithful Music and Disappearing Ink
  (Costello), 8
"Union City Blue," 223, 226
"Unite and Win," 128
United Artists, 183
Unknown Pleasures, viii, 133–37
The Up Escalator, 57–58
Uprising, 190
"Up the Junction," 4, 71–73, 74, 203
Uriah Heep, 161

Valentine, Gary, 220
Vanian, Dave, 229
V Deep, 142
Velvet Underground, 23, 70
Vertigo, 54
the Vibrators, 230

Vicious, Sid (John Beverley), 30–35
"Victor," 225
"Video Killed the Radio Star," 65
"Vienna," 4
Village People, viii, 50, 146
Village Recorder, 194
Virgin Records, 33, 40, 46, 86, 209
Visconti, Tony, 102, 104
"Voices," 123
the Voice Squad, 51
the Voidoids, 218
Voulez-Vous, 75, 76
"Voulez-Vous," 76

the Wailers. *See* Bob Marley and the
  Wailers
"Wait and See," 17
"Waiting for an Alibi," 61
"Wake Up and Make Love with Me," 94
"Walking on the Moon," 202, 205
Walkman, 160
The Wall, 189, 190, 248–50
Wall of Sound, 243
Walsh, Joe, 64, 176–77, 179
Walters, Barry, 152
"Walt Jabsco," 86
Ward, Algy, 229
Ward, Anita, 148
Wardle, John. *See* Wobble, Jah
Warner Bros Records, 114, 118, 191, 197
The Warriors, 179
Warsaw, 131–32
Warsaw Pakt, 132
"Wasted Life," 14
"Wasteland," 235
Waters, Roger, 247–50
Watership Down, 62
Watt-Roy, Norman, 93
Wave, 83
WEA, 81
Webb, Gary. *See* Numan, Gary
Webb, Russell, 47

"Wednesday Week," 27
"We Don't Talk Anymore," 64
Weegan, Steven, 138
Weinraub, Bernard, 152
Welch, Bob, 191
Weller, Paul, 121, 230–38
Wenner, Jann, 6–7
Wessex Sound Studios, 240
Westwood, Vivienne, 32
Wexler, Jerry, 156, 158
"What About the Lonely?," 121
"What a Fool Believes," 68
"What a Waste," 96–97
"What Can I Do for You?," 158
"What Do I Get?," 183
"What Have We Got," 125
"What Makes You Think You're the
    One," 196
"When the Night Comes," 142
"When You're in Love with a Beautiful
    Woman," 68
"Where Are You Tonight? (Journey
    Through Dark Heat)," 155
"Whiskey in the Jar," 61
"White Album," 111, 196
"White Honey," 53–54
"White Noise," 15, 17
"White Riot," 13, 17, 182, 240
the Who, 23, 26, 49, 93, 109–10, 123,
    235, 236, 239
"Who Killed Bambi?," 32
"Whole Lotta Love," 161
"Why Can't I Touch It," 186
Wide Open, 41
Wild Life, 111, 112
Wilkin, Marijohn, 67
"Will Anything Happen," 225
Williams, Maizie, 65
Williams, Paul, 155
Williams, Terry, 107
Williamson, Nigel, 192, 197–98
Wilson, Pete, 124

Wilson, Tony, 131–33
"Wind Chill Factor (Minus Zero)," 141
Wings, 110–12, 113
Winstanley, Alan, 210
"Winter Rose / Love Awake," 111
Wire, 174–75
Withers, Pick, 156
"With God on Our Side," 156
Wobble, Jah (John Wardle), 36
Woffinden, Bob, 80
Womack, Bobby, 149
"Woman Is the Nigger of the World," 6
Wonder, Stevie, 190
"Won't Get Fooled Again," 177
Wood, John, 70
Woodgate, Dan, 208
Woolley, Bruce, 65
Work, Rest & Play, 215
"Working for the Yankee Dollar," 45
Wright, Chris, 219
Wright, Rick, 250
Wright, Tony, 158
"Wrong 'Em Boyo," 242

XTC, 153–254

the Yardbirds, 124, 161
"Yassassin," 104
Yazoo, 81
"Y.M.C.A.," 50, 146
"You Can't Be Too Strong," 56
"You Can't Help It," 186
"You'll Never Walk Alone," 168
"You Need Hands," 32
Young, Neil, 56, 110
"You're a Better Man Than I," 124, 127,
    128
"You're Wondering Now," 88
"Your Number or Your Name," 116
"You've Got My Number," 27

Zenyatta Mondatta, 205–6